Roy Boy

Copyright © Christopher Bennett 2023
First published 2023

Published by
Roy Boy Publications
PO Box 112 Olinda
Melbourne, Victoria, Australia 3788
www.christopher-bennett.com

All rights reserved. Without limiting the rights under copyright reserved above, no part of this publication may be reproduced, stored in or introduced into a database and retrieval system or transmitted in any form or any means (electronic, mechanical, photocopying, recording or otherwise) without the prior written permission of both the owner of copyright and the above publishers.

Copy editing: Lu Sexton
Layout and cover design: Lorna Hendry

Cover photo: The author as a ten-year-old child in 1962, in front of his parents' fish shop in Brunswick Street, Fitzroy.

Printed by IngramSpark

ISBN: 978-0-6457129-0-2

ROY BOY

Christopher Bennett

About the author

Christopher Bennett was born and raised in the working-class suburb of Fitzroy in the 1950s and 1960s. A cheeky and boisterous kid of migrant parents, he roamed the streets and nearby haunts for fun and adventure and found much more than he bargained for.

Roy Boy took eleven years to write because life kept getting in the way. Other than writing, Chris has been a Tai Chi practitioner and teacher for more than 35 years and loves spending time photographing the world around him.

Though life has taken him out of Fitzroy to live among the gum trees and kookaburras of the Dandenong Ranges, he still considers himself a Roy Boy. Wherever he goes, Fitzroy will always be with him – it's part of his DNA.

Dedicated to Menka, Kosta and Lorna

Contents

Preface	1
Dead End	3
Old Country, New Country	7
The Centre of My Universe	39
More Early Memories	61
My Family	93
In Exile	111
Back Home Again	123
Up to Mischief	133
Mucking About with Mates	145
The Yabby Adventure	159
Roy Boy Antenna	170
Characters	178
Still and Moving Pictures	189
George Street Primary School	199
The Big School	225
Good Blokes, Ratbags and Toughs	237
The Choir, Band and Cadets	244
Organised Sport	253
Relentless	259
Girls	263

Contents

Feeling Unsafe	271
Hobbies	277
Favourite Hangouts	285
Farewell Mate	298
Duelling Identities	312
A Final Reflection	324
Acknowledgements	332
Aussie Slang	335
Family Trees	342
Bibliography	346

Preface

Roy Boy is my story of a knockabout kid of migrant working-class parents growing up in Fitzroy during the 1950s and 1960s.

The stories my mother told me about her experiences growing up in Greece and settling in Australia helped inspire me to write this memoir. But perhaps the genesis went back to the early 1980s when I decided to write a family history. I remember I bought a dark-blue, two-ring A4 folder and a bundle of typing paper. I sat down at my table, rolled a sheet of paper into my old typewriter and typed the heading, 'Family History'. That folder and sheet of paper with just a two-word heading stayed in my closet for several years. Occasionally I'd rediscover it and think, 'One day I'll finish this.' I never did. Not continuing that project is something I now regret, because I lost the opportunity to have in-depth discussions with my father about his early life in Greece and Australia. He passed away well before I decided to write my story.

The eleven-year journey of writing this memoir began with regular weekday early-morning sessions, usually before breakfast for up to an hour, or bits of time after a workday, during weekends and holidays. Eventually I wrote a huge collection of vignettes that needed to be edited and turned into what I hoped would be an interesting narrative.

I've used names of people and places, as I knew them, growing up in Fitzroy. Some names are:
- Original names dating back to the early 20th century
- Hellenised names of original names
- Unofficial Australian versions of Hellenic and/or original names
- Hellenic or Macedonian names officially changed to Anglo Saxon names in Australia

The word Maco, pronounced mass-oh, is an abbreviation for Macedonia or Macedonian. It's used to refer to the Macedonian region of Northern Greece, as well as to the language spoken by my family and relatives. In terms of language, Maco has also been described by some as 'po narshi' (local dialect) and/or of South Slavic origin. Maco and Greek are completely different languages. The Maco words I have used are phonetically spelled and are as close to the correct pronunciation as I can remember.

I've used the Imperial system to describe weights and measurements and the Fahrenheit scale, rather than Celsius, to describe temperature, because that's what I learned and used in the 1950s and 1960s.

Writing this story about my migrant background and the adventures and misadventures I experienced as a kid has been an interesting journey.

I hope you enjoy reading it.

Christopher Bennett, February 2023

Dead End

One small section of the Victoria Police Statement condemned me.

'Likely to lapse into a life of vice & crime, school attendance irregular, environment outside the house appears to be bad, associates are bad. Contributing factors to delinquency appears to be lack of parental control, bad company, suggestibility ... shows a defined criminal (tendency).'[1]

Jeez, I was well and truly stuffed!

---

1 Victoria Police Statement – Form No. 276 – Children's Court Prosecutions – 9 May 1960 – P1.
   When I first read this document in 2011, I was stunned to see a summary of my life categorised into two parts. Part 1 contained my name, address, age, religion and, in a few words, a prediction of my future life. Part 2 contained the following sections: Occupation – Education – Parentage – Home Conditions – Environment – Contributing Factors. Every time I read this and other documents about my encounters with the authorities I feel instantly catapulted back in time when I was a kid. The facts are clear and mostly accurate but the typed and written words are 'cold' and it doesn't feel like I'm the kid they are describing. There was more to me than just text.

Two policemen in plain clothes had questioned me and three of my mates in Bourke Street, Melbourne on a chilly Tuesday, at 6:30 pm. We were then taken to the office of the Special Uniform Squad at police headquarters in Russell Street, a few blocks away, and formally interviewed. I was alone in a room with a copper who pointed to a small torch, a large torch in new condition, two pocketknives, one purse, one padlock, and a key. He said, 'Where did you get these things?'

'We found them in the garden.'

'Did you find them all in the garden?'

'Yes, and also two cameras.'

'I think you stole these things?'

'No, we found them.'

The copper left the room, spoke to my mates, returned, and said, 'Are you sure that you didn't take these things?'

'Yes, we pinched them out of cars.'

I had just dobbed myself in. I wasn't good at lying and I always ended up telling the truth; it was obvious I was never going to become a master criminal.

'How did you get into the cars?'

'We kept trying the doors until we found some that were open.'

'Why weren't you at school today?'

'We went to school this morning, but we came to the cars after lunch.'

I also admitted that we had wagged school the previous Tuesday and Wednesday afternoons, when we nicked some books and a pound note.

I remember very little of our 'crime wave'. But I do remember hanging out with a mate outside the several storey high Commonwealth Centre, known as the 'Green Latrine' because of its green facade. This building was across the road from the Exhibition Gardens[2], near Spring Street and Victoria Parade. We'd been having a great old time laughing and waving our stolen cameras around while office workers came in and out.

After the interview I was taken home in a police car and the copper told my parents about the 'seriousness of these offences' and that we would have to go to court. He added that if it continued, I would be placed in a boys' home. I learned later one of my mates had also been taken home and he'd admitted we'd been knocking things off from cars for two or three months.

Six days after our interview at police headquarters, we were all sprung again by coppers in the city at 8.30pm and interviewed in the manager's office of the Lyceum Theatre. I told the truth again and admitted to taking things from cars near the Exhibition Gardens. 'Yes, we took some cups, which we sold for three shillings, and a big pocketknife, which we sold for two shillings, and I've got a key in my pocket.'

Telling the truth certainly got me into a lot of trouble.

After this second interview we were taken to the policewomen's office in Russell Street before being transported to Turana boys' home in nearby Parkville. Later that evening my parents were informed by a police officer about what had happened.

---

2 The official name was the Carlton Gardens but I always knew it – and still refer to it – as the Exhibition Gardens.

Three days later I was taken to the Children's Court and sentenced to be placed in the care of the Children's Welfare Department after which I was returned to Turana.[3]

I remember sitting on a carpeted floor inside an office at Turana, stripped to my underpants, cross-legged and slightly hunched over – as was another boy next to me. In front of us was a man sitting behind a desk and asking questions while filling out a form.

I could feel the heater behind me warm the room, a welcome relief from the cold May night. But I still trembled – with fear. All I could do was answer the questions and think of my family who were far away. I was alone. I'd had my chances, but I'd stuffed up big time and no one was going to rescue me now.

When the interview was over, we were given a shirt, jumper and pants to put on. I dressed myself in these new, ill-fitting clothes and walked past my old ones; a tartan shirt, singlet, cardigan, black jeans, all stacked in a bundle nearby.[4] I now felt completely lost.

It was early May 1960. I was almost seven and half years old.

---

3   Victoria Police Statement – Form No. 288 – 12 May 1960
4   Children's Welfare Department – Turana Reception Centre – Document No. 4217 – 9 May 1960

Old Country, New Country

So how did I end up in Turana?
I guess there were several reasons but I should tell my story from the very beginning – even before I came along.

My father was born Kosta Gulefsi[5] on the 24th of December 1915, in the north-western part of Macedonia, Greece, in a village called Bitusha, about nine miles from the town of Lerin. Bitusha was a poor farming village, like many villages in the area, and had a population at the time of about 500 – though that has now dwindled to only a handful of residents.

He was raised in a large family with three brothers (Yon, Pandili, and Vasili) and four sisters (Vena[6], Santa, Fania, and

---

5 Gulefsi was my father's original family name before it was compulsorily Hellenised to Goulopoulos by the Greek government in the early 20th century. We used Goulopoulos as our family surname here in Australia.

6 I met Vena for the first time in 1996 when my mother, sister and I visited Greece. When I returned to Greece in 2014 to research this memoir, I planned to visit Vena again. I arrived in Lerin and rested for three days in the hotel where I was staying, before driving to her place where I was met by her son who told me she had passed away three days earlier.

A skinny, nervous looking young fella, my dad, aged about 19. Photo taken here in Australia soon after his arrival from Greece in about 1934.

Karafilka). Borsher, his father, emigrated to Australia in 1927 when my father was 12 years old. They did not see each other again for seven years when he, his brother Yon, sister Santa and their mother, Zogia, eventually joined Borsher in Australia. His other sisters, Fania and Karafilka, emigrated to Canada and saw my father only once more in the 1950s when they visited here in Melbourne. Pandili, Vasili and Vena remained in Greece. My father never saw them again.

Emigration and separation were common for many families in Greece due to the harsh economic conditions, internal conflicts, and wars. For many it would take years to be reunited with loved ones and, in some cases, people would never see their families and/or friends again.

Men would emigrate first, work at any job available – usually a labouring job – and send money home to support their families. They'd also try to save enough to bring out family members who wanted to emigrate to Australia. This happened in my family and with most of my relatives between the 1920s and 1950s.[7]

George and Pavlos Goulopoulos from Proti, two of my father's cousins, were in the first major wave of Greeks to arrive in Australia from the Lerin area (eventually about one third of the mountain villagers around Lerin would emigrate to Australia). They were the first Macedonian Greeks to settle on a farm in Werribee South. Soon after, between 1925 and 1929, the Australian government allowed only a hundred Greeks per month to immigrate here. Most of the immigrants

---

7   The impact on the remaining villagers must have been severe. Try to imagine one third of the population including your family members, emigrating overseas from the suburb or town where you live.

Roy Boy

My cane cutting dad, second from the left during the late 1930s or mid-1940s. Photo taken somewhere in Queensland.

who came to Australia in the 1920s and 1930s worked in the countryside or in the bush. Other Goulopoulos farms were established later in the Shepparton area.

My father arrived in Australia on the 10th of May 1934, at the age of eighteen and a half, after a six-week journey on board a ship called *San Remo*. For the next six years he worked as a labourer in the Queensland cane fields and as a market gardener in Little River, Victoria. In 1940 he became a naturalised Australian citizen and on the 3rd of January 1943 he was conscripted, as a private, into the Citizens Military Force, 22nd Australian Infantry Battalion. He served a total of 1040 days – 336 of them in Australia and 553 in New Guinea fighting the Japanese during World War Two. The 22nd Battalion, part of the 4th Brigade, was deployed to New Guinea in early 1943 and 'saw extensive service'. Sixteen months later it returned to Australia for 'rest and re-organisation' before returning to New Guinea for a second tour of duty.

However, my father didn't go back with the battalion for that second tour and his Certificate of Discharge[8] is stamped in red with the following words, – DISCHARGED IN ABSENTIA FOR MISCONDUCT (BECAUSE OF ILLEGAL ABSENCE). The words appear inside a red rectangle stamped twice on the front page and once on the back page.

But there's more to my father's story than just three red stamps on a document.

---

8   I was fortunate to find the original document among my family paperwork, which allowed me to get details of his army record.

Another of my favourite photos of my dad in his Australian army uniform. Photo taken in the early 1940s.

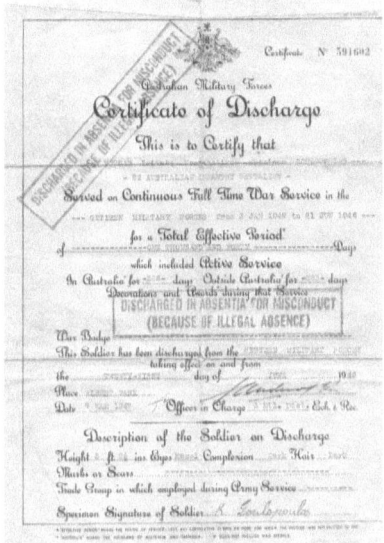

My dad's Certificate of Discharge from the Australian Military Forces. He officially served 1040 days from 3rd January 1942 to 21 June 1946. Of those days, 553 were spent in New Guinea fighting Japanese soldiers during World War Two. The text in both rectangular boxes reads 'Discharged in absentia for misconduct (because of illegal absence)'.

He didn't talk much about his wartime experiences, as was typical of his generation of men, but he did tell two stories about his combat experiences. When I was a kid, he showed me a scar on his ankle saying, 'That's where a Jap shot me.' He also told me how he had saved an officer's life while on patrol. My father had spotted a Japanese sniper in a tree and warned the officer, who ducked for cover. Years later, after the war, that same officer was a character witness for my father who had to front court for a minor misdemeanour. That's all he ever told me about the war, but I always wondered why he deserted the army after serving sixteen months of active duty.

Many years later, after his death, I was surprised and shocked to learn more about his wartime experiences from relatives in whom he'd confided at the time. It gave me a deeper understanding and appreciation of his character as a man.

My dad in his army uniform, sitting in a park. He looks like a bloke who could look after himself. Photo taken in the early 1940s.

In one traumatic incident he was confronted by a Japanese soldier who had jumped out of a concealed area, aimed his rifle at my father and was about to kill him. For two or three seconds they looked each other in the eyes, but my father managed to shoot to kill first. He leaned over the prone body, searched the pockets, and discovered a photograph of the soldier's family. He also experienced the terror of Japanese snipers picking off Australian soldiers on patrol. He'd walk along a path, hear rifle fire in the distance, and soldiers in front of him and behind him would fall dead. The humid climate was also debilitating, adding to the nightmare of war. A relative told me that when my father had come home on leave, his complexion was green and he looked very unhealthy.

He told another relative, 'I don't want to be in a war and kill people, they are human beings just like me.'

All these experiences profoundly affected him, and he decided not to return for the second tour of duty near the end of the war.

I believe his combat experiences, the ones I heard about and no doubt more, led to his decision at that point. He deserted – and that word sticks in my throat because it doesn't explain the character of the man and his experiences, though it does describe what he did.

When he failed to report for duty, the army searched my relatives' farm in Werribee South, but by that time he had left for Sydney where a Macedonian family took him in. In 1946 the army caught up with him and he received a dishonourable discharge. I think he avoided more serious consequences because of his war record, and possibly also because he told army officials his fiancée (not my mother) had left him and married someone else while he was overseas.

I think he was too sensitive and perhaps too traumatised to cope with any more combat, having experienced the safety and sanity of Australia while he was on leave. Though other soldiers in his battalion probably had similar if not worse wartime experiences than my father but did go back for a second tour of duty. I suppose I share a similar sensitivity and wonder what I would have done in his circumstances. I don't know; nobody can really know how they will act or react until they are faced with a similar situation.

After the war my father again worked in the tough environment of the Queensland cane fields. Anywhere up to twelve men worked in a gang, with days starting at 6:00 am

One of my favourite photos of my dad, on the left, dressed in his neat sporty outfit, looking like a movie star. Photo taken in Australia in the late 1930s or mid-1940s.

Always well dressed, my dad on a Queensland cane field in the late 1930s or mid-1940s.

and lasting twelve or fourteen hours, only ending when it got dark. There were many fights among the men and some deaths due to snake bites and the heat.

People who knew my dad in the 1930s and 1940s describe him as a quiet man, a good bloke, always smiling and a real people's person. And, to tell the truth, a bit of a larrikin in his heyday.

The few photos I have of him reveal more aspects of his character and his maturation from a young man to an adult. At nineteen or twenty he looked like an awkward, skinny kid all dressed up, but later photos reveal a fellow who seems to know what he's about. Whether wearing singlet and work pants in a Queensland cane field, an army uniform during

World War Two or nattily dressed for formal occasions in suit and tie, he has an air of confidence and sometimes an angled hat or half smile suggesting the larrikin side of his nature. In my favourite photo he looks like a movie star. I reckon if I had been able to meet my dad in those days, we would have become good mates.

My mother, Menka Stamkos[9], was born on the 6th of December 1923, in the Greek village of Armensko, about twelve miles from my father's village of Bitusha. As far as I know they never met in Greece, but they may have crossed paths in the nearby town of Lerin when they were young. She also experienced harsh economic conditions. But, unlike my father who had already emigrated to Australia in 1934, she endured the Italian occupation (1940) the German occupation (1941–1944) during World War Two and the Greek Civil War (1944–49).[10] I was fortunate enough to learn more about her life in Greece through the many stories she shared with me while I was growing up, as well as through a series of interviews I did with her for this memoir. Further information and insight about her came from interviews with relatives both here and in Greece.

Her father Tarnus married her mother, Lena (pronounced Leh-na) Koufis, and they had four children; my mother, Kata,

---

9   Stamkos is a Hellenised version of her original name of Stamkov or Stamkoff. Here in Australia, she and our family generally used Stamkos when discussing her maiden name.

10 Britannica – Greek Civil War. Some references state the Greek Civil War began in 1945 or 1946. It may have been a two-stage conflict, although it is generally agreed it ended in 1949.

Ordana, and another child who died very young. Tarnus was multilingual and could speak Maco (Macedonian), Greek, Bulgarian and Turkish, but Lena spoke only Maco.

Tarnus emigrated to America in the early 1900s aged about twenty. He was part of the first wave of mass immigration there at that time. Tarnus's brother, Chris, also emigrated to America in the 1930s, but disappeared and was never heard from again. One of my relatives told me he was a policeman and 'ended up in the Detroit River with cement boots' during the bootlegging gangster time of Al Capone.

In 1912 Tarnus returned to Greece to join the Greek army and fight the Turks during the first Balkan war. It was guerrilla style warfare in which Greece and its coalition of partners defeated the Turks in 1913. This war ended about four centuries of Turkish occupation in the Lerin area. Southern Greece was liberated much earlier in the 1820s.

During the next few years there were continual conflicts and upheavals in Greece. These included the short occupation of Lerin by the Bulgarian army in 1916 during the First World War and the Greco–Turkish war between 1919 and 1922, which the Turks won. The end of this war saw a huge population exchange in 1923, mostly forcible, between Greece and Turkey – 1.5 million Greeks from Turkey and 500,000 Greek-speaking Muslims from Greece. Some of these Greek immigrants from Turkey took over farms in at least one village and caused a deep resentment amongst the original owners, who were powerless to stop them because the Greek authorities allowed this to happen.

Tarnus decided to emigrate to Australia in 1927 for a better life and to earn enough money to send back, support his family

A wedding in Armensko, Greece about 1932. My mother and her mother are both in the crowd. This is the earliest photo I have of my mother, aged about 9, and the only photo I have of my grandmother.

and eventually bring them out here. He never returned to Greece and would never see his wife and two of his daughters again. My mother was three years old when he left and would not see him again for 22 years.

He never made enough money to bring the family out prior to World War Two and, even if he had, his wife Lena would unlikely have come because she wanted to look after her elderly relatives in Armensko. In those days, whenever Lena killed a pig for a feast with her family, she would set aside a plate for her husband and say, 'He's coming, he's coming, he's going to come next autumn.'

Many years later when Tarnus was in his late sixties he would often say, 'I wanna go back.' Velika[11], my mother's cousin, had the same yearning even though she had been in Australia for over fifty years. She said this was a common view of the early female arrivals of the 1930s. In this extract from her 1989 poem 'Mother's Grief', dedicated to her mother, she wrote:

I left my beloved village
not by choice or free hand ...
I have never come to terms with moving,
miss my native language and customs.

Tarnus had similar traits to my mother. He was described as a calm person, sometimes soft, and he rarely argued with anyone. He also shared my mother's persistence and generosity of spirit. During the depression in the 1930s many immigrants were discriminated against but, despite the prejudice, Tarnus found menial jobs to survive. He worked long hours and, in one job as kitchen hand at the Regent Theatre restaurant here in Melbourne in 1939, he secretly fed many fellow countrymen who did not have jobs or enough food to eat. He would grab scraps or left-overs from the kitchen and distribute the food at 10:00 am when he was taking out the rubbish. He would also hand out food at lunch time and at night-time. If it weren't for Tarnus's generosity many of the men would have gone without food for a day or perhaps days at a time.

---

11 Velika also wrote a memoir and sent the manuscript – the original and only copy – to a publisher, but somehow it was lost. As far as I know, she never published it.

While Tarnus was in Australia, his daughter Kata died in 1942 at the age of 30. My mother had gone to bed about midnight when she heard Kata yell, 'I can't, I can't.' My mother got up and found Kata dead of a heart attack. She leaned on the stairs and moaned, 'Oh god, what have you done to me.'

Four years later, Tarnus's wife Lena also died. Their daughter Ordana had already married and lived in another village further away, so only four remained in the household – my mother, aged 24, with her nephew Tom and nieces Magda and Sofia, all aged between ten and twelve. This would have been very hard for my mother, the only adult remaining, to manage the household chores and care for the children – unlike in the 1920s and 1930s when up to eight or more family members lived together.

There were about 150 houses in Armensko. My mother's house, built by her father and uncle, had a red tiled roof, clay and rock walls and a large wooden front door. It consisted of three rooms: a storeroom, a bedroom, and a multipurpose room that had a wood stove and was used as both bedroom and kitchen. Three sisters slept in one room and up to six family members and relatives slept in the other rooms. There were no beds, just hay-filled bags with blankets underneath and on top. There was no running water or a bathtub in the house and the family washed their clothes at a riverbank, just up the road from the village. The bank had iron tubs under which wood was lit to heat the water.

Below their house was a stable so the smell of goats, chickens, a pig, and a donkey pervaded the house. On a strip of land just outside the village, they also owned a horse, eighteen sheep, a bull and a cow.

Across the footpath from the house was a public drinking tap, and two doors down were the village square and the local school. At the edge of the square and up a steep hill stood a church and a small cemetery. From that high point you could see the village, surrounding farmland, the nearby mountain range and a monastery that was a 15-minute walk from the village square. It was very picturesque, and my mother and her family and relatives would go to the monastery on religious days and for picnics.

My mother attended the church, which was full on Sunday mornings, and she remembered both her uncle and a priest singing. Years later when she told me this, she began to sing, 'Christos Anesti' (Christ has arisen).

She also remembered running around as a child at the many gatherings, dances and weddings, where her brother-in-law played the trumpet really well as they danced and sang, and her father happily waved a hanky above his head as he danced.

She would play outside her house because there was no space in her backyard, and at night she'd go outside to talk to other kids from the village.

There wasn't much meat available, and they usually ate it during winter because it would keep longer than it would in summer. They slaughtered goats and cattle for meat, though my mother would run away to avoid seeing the animals killed. Elderly villagers would then prepare the meat with salt and cook it over a wood fire. All this food came from animals they raised and crops they grew themselves. They couldn't afford and didn't need to buy any food.

She ate a lot of baked peppers, cheese, zelnik and velnik (Greek pastries) and vegetables. They baked bread made from

*My mother in her village dress, which we still have.
Photo taken late 1930s or 1940s in Greece.*

flour and wheat, baking twenty loaves of bread in one week in a large oven to feed her family. They also ate cauliflower soaked in vinegar and lep (bread) and munja (a stew that usually consisted of meat, potatoes, tomatoes, and rice).

Wild animals made it dangerous in the village and around the strips of farmland nearby. Wolves killed sheep and howled at night, frightening many children who cuddled their mums crying. Across the road large brown bears would stand up to their full height, roar and come up to the front door. They were vicious and would usually appear in the morning and just before dusk. Village houses had high doors and fences to keep the bears and wolves out. Men carried rifles to protect themselves and guard children as they played. As added protection they twirled handheld windmills and rang bells to frighten the bears away if they came too close.

Women made their own clothes, and nothing was store bought. They wore skirts, as dresses were not made in those days. Women worked more than the men. They worked on strips of land outside the village, as men did, but also at home for the three or four months that they were snowed in. When it snowed, the men, who had nothing to do, would wander on down to their local clubs before coming home for a meal at lunchtime and going back to the clubs for the rest of the day.

During summer, villagers rose at 6:00 am to start work on the family plots of land. These were about the size of a paddock, and an hour's walk away. They ploughed and planted seeds of wheat, potatoes, corn, peppers, tomatoes, and watermelons – and sold corn at the market in Lerin. Eventually people left the village because there wasn't enough productive soil to go around.

To earn extra money, my mother and her cousins would walk for half an hour to the nearby hills to gather wood and store it at home. When they had enough, they would tie the wood to either side of a donkey and travel to Lerin to sell it. The journey by foot took between an hour and an hour-and-a-half. They didn't make much money, just enough to buy sugar and salt while they were there. On the way home they rode the donkey.

My mother attended school in the village square with her two sisters and cousins until she finished 8th grade, at the age of 15 or 16 and left to work at home and on the strip of farmland.

A school day started at 9:00 am and ended at 4:00 pm, with a 30-minute lunch break when they ate bread with peppers and cheese. Occasionally they had lunch at home. During morning and afternoon recess the children played outside and a boy would ring a bell to signal time to return to class.

Downstairs in the three-storeyed school were the smaller grades, and if you didn't pass a grade, you stayed down.

Classrooms had desks that seated three to four children and in the drawers were lead pencils, coloured pencils and chalk. When students entered the room they sat, took out pencil and paper from a drawer and wrote down what the teacher taught.

There were about fifteen to twenty students in each grade and physical punishment occurred often. If you were cheeky, talked in class, didn't sit still, or couldn't answer a question you were hit with a stick on an open palm. My mother was very quiet because she was scared but, even then, she could not completely escape punishment so was hit with a stick and 'cried later'.

One day a teacher really lost her temper. A girl next to Fania, my mother's cousin, was reading a text aloud to the class and the teacher said stop, called Fania's name and told her to read the rest of text. Fania couldn't find the place to read from so the teacher walked over, grabbed her by the hair and banged her head against the desk. Fania screamed in pain as two inches in diameter of her hair was pulled out of her scalp. Fania's mother took the teacher to court in Lerin. The woman got off with a warning that if she ever did this again, she would be thrown out of teaching. She apparently learned her lesson and never repeated it.

A vicious teacher was not the only creature to be wary of. Dogs in the village could also attack without warning. My mother was once walking along a path when she came across two dogs fighting. Suddenly the white bluish one turned and bit her on the shin and she ran away. At a safe distance she sat down and cried because of the pain and also because she knew there were no doctors close by to treat her wound. Dogs were usually tied up to safeguard a guest. However not all dogs were mean. She owned a dog and taught it to shake hands.

She had another lucky escape with an animal when she rode a black horse home from her family's farming plot. As she entered the village a noisy car scared the horse and it bolted. My mother hung on and somehow managed to jump off it without injuring herself. Villagers who witnessed this were stunned and couldn't believe she wasn't thrown to the ground and hurt.

Just before she turned seventeen her life was dangerously disrupted when Italy invaded Lerin on 28th October 1940. It was the beginning of World War Two. The Italians were driven out in a few weeks and on 6th April 1941 Germany invaded. They remained until October 1944 when the Allies liberated Greece and drove the Germans out.

She and her family experienced many hardships under the occupation of her village. She had to tolerate two Bulgarian army sergeants who came to occupy her crowded family house. Bulgaria was allied to Germany at that time.

She heard bombs launched and explode nearby. Not so lucky was her cousin's wife who was killed. 'It was terrible, we hid in the stable, slept on hay, not washed or fed, we were scared.' She said, 'You are lucky, Chris, you have never seen or experienced this.'

When the Germans marched into the village looking for partisans, they scared my mother. She was very nervous and hid, never speaking to the tall soldiers dressed in green.

Later, in a comical situation, a man ran towards my mother and her cousins, yelling the Germans were shooting at him. What had really happened was that he had panicked and kicked up stones as he ran, which to him sounded like gunfire.

Nick, my cousin told me two stories about his mother's and father's experiences in and near the villages, which showed how dangerous it was under German occupation. When the Germans raided the house where his parents lived, only his mum's grandmother was there sitting on a chair. Underneath the chair was a trap door where two family members were hiding in waist deep water and keeping quiet. If discovered, they would have been taken away. In another dramatic incident, Nick's mother and father travelled to town on a horse and cart with other friends. There were people in about three or four carts altogether and they would take turns to lead the group because of landmines. On one trip, his mum and dad were due to lead the group but for some reason another horse and cart led the way, and that group was blown up and killed.

The Second World War ended in 1945 but then the Greek Civil War raged on until 1949. The Greek army, backed by the UK and USA, fought the combined forces of the National Liberation Front (EAM) and the National People's Liberation Army (ELA) which combined in December 1946 to become the Greek Democratic Party (DSE). The DSE was backed by Albania, Bulgaria and Yugoslavia, but ultimately was defeated.

Again, my mother was in considerable danger, in yet another war. She was a 23-year-old woman and the partisans in the area were forcing men, women and children to fight with them in the DSE. At this stage she was living in the family home looking after her two young nieces and a nephew as all her other family members and relatives had either moved away, emigrated, or died. Over the next two years it became more dangerous, and they were very afraid of the partisans so children in the area including her nieces and nephew were evacuated by trucks to Thessaloniki, a distance of 121 miles away in the eastern part of Greece. She was now alone in the house.

During the early days of the civil war my mother was engaged to a local boy for a short time until he was forcibly recruited into the partisan army. He said to her, 'Men are killed like flies here in the hills of Armensko. Not many survive, you'd better look for your love elsewhere.' My mother was devastated, frightened and thought she'd end up an old maid.

She never told me this story – I only found out about it when my cousin told me recently. I'm not sure if the young

My mother, back row, second from right, aged 26. Photo taken in Thessaloniki, Greece, 1949. She was on her way to Australia visiting Thessaloniki to say goodbye to her nephew Tom Missios, standing to her right, and her niece Magda, standing next to Tom who emigrated to Australia in 1956. She did not see Magda again until 47 years later when she visited her in Armensko. We still have the handbag she is carrying in this photo.

man was killed, but my cousin said she didn't push it to find out because she knew my mother only talked about private matters when she wanted to. This is another trait I shared with her. I must admit I was very surprised and sad to hear this story, as I always thought she had told me everything about the war. But I suppose many people don't reveal everything about themselves – and if they have a very painful experience they would be even less inclined to talk about it. Just like my father, who revealed very little about his wartime experiences.

It was becoming very dangerous in Armensko so my mother escaped the village with her sister's help, leaving only with the clothes she wore because there was no time to gather any other possessions. She somehow reached the safety of Lerin and stayed there with her aunt. While all this was happening her father, Tarnus, was convinced by his brother to get her out of Greece because of the war. Tarnus paid for my mother's fare so she could emigrate to Australia and join him.

My mother began the first leg of her 9,460-mile journey to Australia from Lerin, travelling for three hours by bus to Thessaloniki and staying there for three weeks. While she was there, she met up again with her nieces and her nephew Magda, Sofia, and Tom, who had all been looked after by the authorities. They had attended local schools in Thessaloniki since they were evacuated from Armensko in 1947. Before my mother left Thessaloniki, she went to the school to say goodbye to the three children who had lived with her in Armensko. Tears flowed as they embraced, she walked away, paused, and looked back at them one last time until Magda yelled, 'Go, go.' She would not see Tom and Sofia until they emigrated to Australia a few years later, and it would be over 45 years before she saw Magda again when she returned to Greece for a visit in 1996.

After my mother left Thessaloniki, Tom, Magda, and Sofia were finally reunited with their father in 1950 after three years. Their father had been in the army and imprisoned on an island after he was accused of being a communist. When he came home to Armensko he discovered his children were in Thessaloniki, travelled there to see them, and told them he'd return to fetch them. He came back soon after, signed

My mother's Greek passport issued to her 1949.

official documents for their release into his care and returned to Armensko with them.

The next leg of my mother's journey was a 319-mile bus ride to Athens from Thessaloniki, taking almost seven hours. The long trip was made bearable as she had a friend, also named Menka, to chat away the time with She stayed in an Athens hotel for two weeks and waited for a ship called the *SS Cyrenia* to take her to Australia.

When she arrived at the dock in the morning she was scared by the size of the ship because she had never seen one so big before. She eventually boarded with a huge crowd and made her way down to a two-bed cabin with her friend Menka. During the six-week journey the time passed very slowly and she kept thinking 'when will we ever land?' At times she was miserable because she was seasick, vomited a lot and the meals were only 'okay if you were hungry'. She also didn't speak to anyone unless she knew them, and apart from her friend Menka, there would have been very few from her village to talk to anyway because the passengers were from all over Greece.

She and Menka explored the ship and were surprised to discover a swimming pool. However, she never used it because she could not swim. Even if she could, she would never have worn a bathing costume because she was a bit of a prude and disapproved of the bathers worn in those days. They revealed too much flesh, and she would often say, even in my adult life, 'nerma-strum' (no shame). When she said that my sister, Lorna, and I would jokingly say to her, 'Oh, you're just jealous.'

On the ship she enjoyed listening to the music and watching people dance at night. It brought back pleasant memories of the music and dancing in Armensko she had so much loved. And it reminded her of the happy times she experienced during her teenage years, as a member of the village dancing troupe, which had once travelled to Athens for a festive occasion. The dancing and music also made her homesick, and she wondered if she would ever see her relatives and friends in Greece again.

The *SS Cyrenia* arrived in Melbourne in September 1949. My mother disembarked with only one suitcase of clothes and was greeted by her father, Tarnus. Very few words were exchanged apart from 'how are you?' and 'how was the trip?' She never did describe to me how she felt when she stood there looking at her father. Nor did I find out how he felt about seeing his daughter for the first time since she was three years old. The only connection between my mother and her father over the

My mother (on the right) and her cousin Velika Mitchell. Photo taken in 1949, the same year my mother arrived in Australia.

previous two decades had been through letters and the little money he could afford to send back to the family.

Tarnus took her to his rooming house in Carlton where he rented a room, and she stayed overnight. There wasn't enough space for the two of them to live there so he arranged for my mother to stay at Nomcher's (his brother's farm) in Werribee South, where she could live and work for a wage. When she arrived on the farm she saw chickens and vegetables and was surprised to see women working in the field digging and planting. She thought women in Australia didn't work. She was also shocked at the isolation of working and living on a farm in Werribee South, because there weren't many people around as there had been Armensko. She was used to working on a farm, but back home when she had finished work she could walk to her family home in the village. She felt lonely. Some of my other relatives who worked in factories had a different experience – they felt they were in an open gaol because 'everything is done by the clock'. They all shared the common belief that life was more open and free back home.

Ironically, she would experience that same sense of isolation when she retired in the 1980s to live in the outer eastern suburb of Boronia. There wasn't the same sense of community as there had been in Armensko and, apart from a couple of good neighbours, people generally kept to themselves. My mother was a very sociable person and loved to mix with people, but Australian suburbia reduced her opportunities to do so. To be fair, her basic command of English may also have been a factor, but that didn't stop her from trying to get along with people.

Tarnus had a different experience at Nomcher's farm, because he had been around for a few years and considered the farm a wonderful escape from the suburbs. It provided him with a sense of belonging and over several years he would stay there for short visits over a weekend or a week to help out. He'd clean all the cobwebs from sheds and machinery, chop wood, and work every day while he was there.

My father and mother met for the first time on the Werribee South farm in 1949, soon after she arrived in Australia. He was 35 years old, had a strong desire to get married and told my cousin, 'Now you and your sister are spoken for I'm going to ask for Menka's hand in marriage. I'm sure she is good, and besides she's from Armensko and people are nice there.'

A relative acted as matchmaker and organised a meeting between my father and mother on the farm. He stayed for the weekend, they got to know each other a little and decided to get married. My mother's first impressions of him were that he was 'nice' and he was 'tall'. She confided in my cousin, 'After everything I've gone through, I should be so lucky to marry him.' In a short time, she grew to love him and would do anything for him.

After they were engaged, she decided to leave the farm and live and work with my father in his fish shop in Fitzroy. He rented the fish shop and, earlier in 1949, had purchased the good will of the business and plant fittings from Michael Popovich for the sum of £600 (which is about $35,475 in today's money).[12] So he must have been doing okay financially.

---

[12] I guess my father saved this sum from working on the Queensland cane fields after World War Two. I also have the original document – Konstantinos Goulopoulos with Michael Popovich Agreement – 4 April 1949.

My parents' wedding in 1950. Photo taken at Allan Studios in Smith Street, Collingwood.

Next to my mother, the bride, stands Tarnus, my maternal grandfather. He was aged about 62. His stern expression in this photo is what I remember most about him, as he rarely smiled.

My mother moved into the fish shop for practical reasons. It would have been too crowded if my father had decided to live with her on the farm, and the long hours he worked in the shop would have made it almost impossible for him to see her during the week because train services were inconvenient and infrequent.

However, when my mother arrived at the fish shop, she initially wondered what she was doing there. She didn't speak English and had no prior experience working in a shop or dealing with customers and money. She was frustrated and blamed herself for being incompetent. But gradually she learned basic English, learned how to cook and how to deal with customers.

They were married in a Greek Orthodox church in Melbourne in 1950. About a year and a half later my sister Lorna was born, and I came along on 18th December 1952.

The Centre of My Universe

I grew up in the 1950s and 1960s in Fitzroy, which at that time was a rough, working-class suburb. It was established in 1839 as Melbourne's first suburb. My playground was inside the rectangle formed by Victoria Parade, Smith Street, Alexandra Parade, and Nicholson Street.

Fitzroy had everything a decent or indecent citizen could hope for: schools, churches, shops, factories, a library, a town hall, a cop shop, pubs, brothels, sly grog and illegal gambling, as well as its fair share of criminals, ratbags, and homeless alcoholics. But above all it had a sense of community. What it didn't have was money; most people just got by on a basic working wage.

Going way back, Fitzroy originally belonged to the Wurundjeri people of the Kulin Nation. When the suburb was established by European settlers in the mid 1800s, it was regarded as a 'pleasant place'[13]. That dramatically changed

---

13 *Fitzroy Melbourne's First Suburb*, Cutton History Committee of the Fitzroy Historical Society

Roy Boy

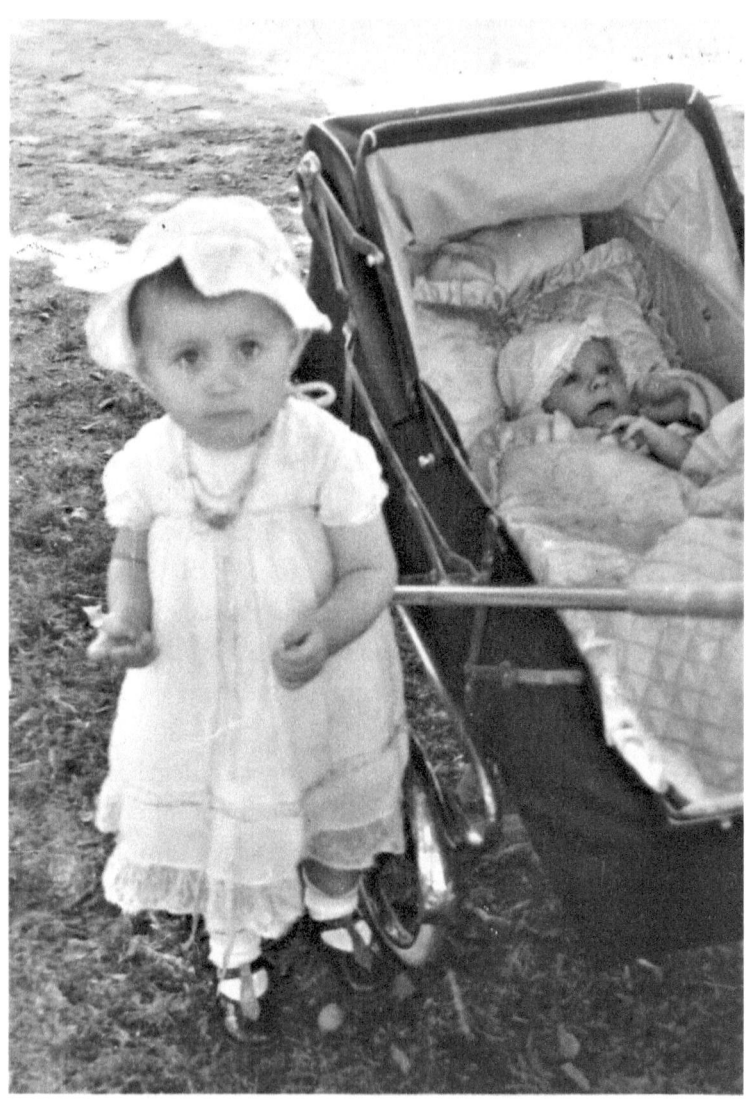

I was too young to get out of the pram, but my sister, Lorna, was up and about. Photo taken in 1953.

during the 1890s depression. It became a slum area over the next few decades and was considered the 'haunt of criminals and prostitutes'[14]. During the 1950s the government drew up plans to clear the slum and between the mid-1960s and 1971 a whole block of Fitzroy was demolished and replaced by a housing estate of four high-rise blocks of flats.

As a kid I didn't know or care about the history of Fitzroy. It was just a fun place where I lived and played. The centre of my universe was 357 Brunswick Street, the fish shop in which I grew up, three doors down from Kerr Street. Our neighbours on either side were Violetta Florist and Penders cake factory. The florist shop was eventually bought out by the Evelyn Hotel on the corner. Brunswick Street was one of the main commercial strips of the suburb, with most shops between Alexandra Parade and Victoria Street.

If you stood outside the fish shop in the middle of the road and looked towards the city you could see St Patrick's Cathedral spire. If you turned around to face the opposite way you could see the spire of St Luke's Anglican Church (now the Hungarian Reformed Church of Australia) at the other end of Brunswick Street, in North Fitzroy. Both spires pointed high in the sky like long extended fingers threatening God's retribution if you misbehaved or sinned. There were a lot of sinners in Fitzroy, though maybe not on a Sunday morning if they were church goers.

The fish shop was a two-storey Victorian building with a flat metal awning extended over the footpath. Above the awning were two large narrow rectangular windows with white lace

---

14 *ibid*

That sooky baby is me trying to bail out of the tin tub. Lorna sits calmly in the other tub as my mother looks on. Photo taken in 1953, in the backyard of our fish shop.

curtains. I would climb out of our second-floor window onto the awning for something to do. But someone would often dob me in so my old man would come storming out of the shop, stand in the gutter, look up, wave his arms about in anger and yell, 'Get off the roof, you idiot.' I suppose he was concerned about the awning collapsing under my weight, or that I would be electrocuted by the live power line dangling below the window ledge. But as a kid I didn't worry about trivial things like that. It was the challenge and the view that motivated me to do this dumb kid thing. I'd stay out for only a few minutes; just enough time before my old man could discover I was up there again.

There were two display windows in front of the shop, separated by a small, recessed area where the entrance was – a narrowly framed wooden fly-screen door with an inbuilt wire screen in the top half of it. The screen was only partially successful keeping the flies out because this door was constantly opened and closed by customers. Any fly unlucky enough to enter and buzz around didn't last long though, because it was attracted to our fly paper traps – long thin strips of sticky fragrant coated paper hanging from the kitchen ceiling and elsewhere. The fly would land on the strip of paper, get stuck, wither away and die. Each fly trap was replaced with another when it was dotted with dead flies.

Behind this fly-screen door was a solid wood-framed glass door, kept open during business hours. One night a drunk tested the strength of the locked door by kicking the base of it with his heel several times. The noise woke my father and he yelled at the drunk who in turn swore at my father before shuffling away. Luckily the door remained intact.

The small display window to the left of the shop measured about three feet by six feet. It was curtained off and rarely used for displaying anything apart from the signage, in red capital letters the words FRESH FISH at the top and CRAYFISH at the bottom. Behind the larger window, to the right were various flat metal trays containing seafood, such as live eels, flake, couta, Murray cod, whiting, and occasionally crayfish. KG FISH SUPPLY was painted in red capital letters on a white background in the top third of this window. Below that was a drawing of a fish and on the bottom third of the window was painted HOT FISH & CHIPS also on a white background. Black painted brick bases, about three feet high were below both windows.

One day there was a surprise addition to the display of sea food. It was a three-year old me. Somehow, I'd managed to climb into the display area wearing only my underpants and was sitting on a tray of fish – presumably contaminating them, so they weren't sold. I don't know how I managed to get into the window area on a workday, when the fish were on display. On Sundays it was easier to lie about in the display area because it was empty and nobody around apart from a few passers-by who probably looked at me and thought, 'Stupid kid'.

The large window also served as another plaything when I was in my early teens. My mate and I would stand outside and crack each other up with laughter when we discovered it could be used to create an optical illusion. I would stand in the doorway, press my nose against the edge of the window, make a silly face and wave my right arm and right leg up and down. My mate watched me from about six feet away and the reflection in the window gave the illusion that I was waving both legs and arms up in the air at the same time. We always looked for an opportunity to have a laugh – especially when it didn't cost us anything.

As you walked into the shop onto a concrete floor, to the right was a long wooden countertop – high enough for most customers to rest their elbows and for parents to perch their kids. The business side of the shop was on the other side of the counter, where a narrow walkway divided it from the cooking area, consisting of a twin-pan gas fryer that heated the oil for cooking fish and chips. There was no central heating or air conditioning, so the heat from the fryer raised the temperature of the shop area considerably, making it a welcome relief on cold winter days but only just bearable during summer. A canopy above the fryer allowed the smoke to escape naturally into a brick chimney. In one of the photos I have, the canopy has a picture of a British and Australian flag below with two lines below them reading:

EMPIRE DAY 1954
YEAR OF THE ROYAL VISIT.

On either side of the fryer were wooden benches. One contained an old-style basic scale, consisting of an inverted U-shaped pipe frame. It supported a clock-like weight indicator hooked to another inverted U shape steel wire that held a flat tray to weigh the seafood. From a distance the inverted U frame looked like an ideal bird cage holder. Later my parents bought a smaller box-size scale which was easier to use. Above the other larger bench were two-tiered wooden shelves containing various small jars of mussels and pickled onions. My mother also placed three vases of plastic flowers on the shelves to give the shop a homier look.

Once the fish and/or chips were cooked in a wire basket, my parents would turn around and empty the contents onto a newspaper that lay on the bench behind the counter. They would add Skipping Girl vinegar or salt or a pickled onion if requested. I loved the taste of Skipping Girl vinegar on my chips and still do. I'd also practically overdose on the huge, beautiful onions and usually devoured one too many, feeling queasy for a while – though when that passed, I'd raid the jar again.

Below the bench was a wooden drawer with wooden dividers that separated various coins and notes. The drawer was far enough away from customers to stop any ratbag reaching over and knocking off the money. We also had a commercial chrome-plated flat rectangle fridge beside the bench that kept our seafood fresh and cold.

As a kid the only things that interested me about the front of the shop were the unlimited supply of free fish and chips, and the penny-operated chewing gum game machine.

Entrance to the back of the shop was either through a door on the customers' side of the counter or through an archway on the other side. I used the door every day to come and go, though rarely used the archway except to grab a free pickled onion.

At the back of the shop on the ground floor were two work areas, our kitchen and the backyard.

The first work area had a concrete floor and housed an electric motor, which powered the commercial fridge. I could often hear the motor humming in the background – it was the pulse that had to be maintained or the fridge would stop, the fish spoil and the fish shop eventually grind to a halt. Once in a rare while the motor would pack up, but my old man, who was not mechanically minded, would have it fixed by a repair man.

In the same area were large hessian bags of spuds stacked vertically against the wall. The 90–110-pound bags were delivered by the potato man, who parked his truck outside the shop, and used a hand hook to lift the bag over his shoulders. He'd walk in hunched over so I rarely saw his face. Next to the bags was a black forty-gallon drum of flour. A few feet away was a worktable used to batter fish and an entrance to the kitchen.

About twelve feet away from the worktable was a wooden door that opened to a recessed storage room with a steep angled ceiling supporting the stairway above it. On the floor of the room were stacked and tied bundles of newspapers bought for sixpence a bundle from kids who wanted to make some pocket money. Each sheet of newspaper was cut to a smaller size and used to wrap fish and chip orders. On one wall of the room were shelves to store empty jars and other bits of equipment.

Part of this first and larger work area doubled as a rest and social break spot when there were no customers in the shop. My parents would sit on chairs just behind the wall, have a yarn and rest. Occasionally my father would have a beer and smoke with a mate who had come for a visit. It was a convenient spot because there was a shelf, within reach, that held a beer bottle, beer bottle opener and a couple of glasses. There was also a small cutaway in the wall about a foot square, next to the door, where they could see if a customer came in to the shop. You could even see through the cutaway from the kitchen behind the work area.

An open entrance to the left of the first work area led to a long and narrow second area. This was the heavy-duty engine room of the fish shop where all the cutting, peeling, slicing and chopping, occurred. There was a long bench, sinks, taps and various cutting implements to prepare the fish and chips. On the concrete floor there was also a long wooden board to stand on, which reduced the chance of slipping on the often-wet floor and was more comfortable when working at the bench for long periods of time.

My favourite bits of equipment to watch were the potato peeler and the hand press chip cutter. My father would place a handful of spuds into a cylindrical machine about three feet high and two feet in circumference. He'd close the little door, flick the power switch and WHOOSH – the little buggers would rotate and bump into each other on a rough metal disc. When enough rumble time passed, any spuds not fully stripped were given a once over with a small knife. The old man would then place a spud on the criss-crossed bladed base of the chip cutter and pull a long lever down, forcing a metal plate to come crashing down on top, and out would come several sliced chips. My dad would do this several times a day and it was just another job for him. But for me it was show time whenever a spud magically turned into chips.

I wasn't the only one excited by the goings-on in the work area. One day Lorna watched my father expertly slice a shark into strips and suddenly shrieked when a dead baby shark fell out. He was about to throw it away, but Lorna pleaded, 'Give it to me, give it to me.' He handed it to her, and she gently held the baby shark, hurrying off to put it in a jar of water to revive it. But to her disappointment it remained dead.

Towards the back door was a gully trap that was hosed down regularly to keep it clean. When the shop was closed, my father would occasionally use the gully trap as a urinal because he couldn't be bothered to go to the toilet outside. When he did this, I'd yell, 'Go to the bloody toilet you lazy bugger!'

A corrugated iron roof covered this second work area and included a couple of see-through sheets to allow daylight in. This was possible because our second storey building resembled an 'r' shape with the area above this roof exposed to the elements. At the end of this work area was a door leading to our backyard, and to the right of that door were slatted windows above a sink used to wash clothes. Beside the sink, in a recessed area, was a large copper tub used to heat water by lighting a wood fire under it.

Two sides of our kitchen were framed by our work areas and a lace-curtained window helped hide the larger work area. A table where we ate our meals was pushed up against the wall in front of the curtained window and four chairs seated our family. Three standard chairs were for my mother, sister and me and the other chair, a large based one, was for my father who was a big and heavy bloke in those days. Once, as a little kid, I pulled a chair away from my father before he was able to sit down, and he fell. I copped a real serve and was not very popular for a time after that cheeky prank.

Next to the table was an old single bed with steel springs, a mattress, blanket and pillow. My dad rested on it occasionally and later in life he used the bed to sleep overnight when he had great difficulty climbing the stairs to his bedroom because

My dad the fishmonger with his usual smile inside our fish shop in 1954. He was a big bloke in those days.

My mother in 1954. She was the other half of our popular fish shop known to the locals as Kon's.

of a crook back and bad knees. Just above the bed was another small window, which was very handy because you could see if a customer came into the shop.

 The kitchen also had a small gas oven and grill that sat on a wooden base, a sink and one cold water tap. Next to the sink, in a recessed area, was an old-style wood furnace and flue that kept the kitchen warm during the winter. Beside the furnace was a cabinet to store our cutlery and dishes, which had a set of coloured plastic canisters for rice, tea, and coffee on top of it. There was one canister where my father stored bills and paperwork. My favourite item in the cabinet was a large black-and-white photographic book of World War Two and I would often flick through the pages to gaze at the dramatic pictures. It was an ideal read for a little kid because it didn't have too many words. The book disappeared over time; I wish I still had it. The cabinet proved to be sturdy for several years until this one time when I leaned on it and brought it crashing down. I could feel it give way but was not quick enough to steady it as it toppled over. I somehow managed to pick it up, with Lorna's help, and place it back into position – a hard bloody job, because it was taller and heavier than I was at the time. I got a real serve from my mother and father for my clumsiness and never leaned on it again.

 Our concrete backyard was more of a junk yard than one where a kid could play. The only concessions to the ugliness were the potted plants my mother spread along a portion of a wall and on a ledge that bordered the florist shop next door. Another eyesore was the outdoor sink where my father sometimes stored empty fish crates. There was no escape from the fish shop even in our backyard.

The back border of the yard was just a wall of rusted corrugated iron sheets separating the laneway from the shop. There was a tin roof attached to it so it looked like an empty shed when viewed from the laneway. To add to the visual pollution, the towering twenty-foot-high brick wall of Penders cake factory dwarfed our yard. There was a tiny space available in the middle part of the yard where I could ride my tricycle in a very narrow circle. The space also allowed my mother to bathe us in a tin tub when Lorna and I were toddlers. Just above the tub area a wire clothesline hung across the yard.

Our outdoor brick toilet had a concrete floor, a wooden seat and bowl and a cast iron cistern with a chain attached so it could be pulled down to flush the toilet. Our toilet paper consisted of small pieces of newspaper pages spiked on a nail in the wall. Once in a while the toilet would pack up, and then it really smelled like a shit house.

Next to the toilet was a short walkway, about five to six feet in length, leading to a high wooden gate opening to a small cobbled-stoned lane, which led to Kerr Street. The laneway was an open access area until the pub built a huge gate across the Kerr Street entrance, about twelve to fifteen feet high, for security reasons. The big gate also had a small door in it that was kept locked, though we had a key so we could have access to the street.

The ground floor of our premises held the business, while the second floor was our home. Though the kitchen provided some respite from the shop after business hours from Monday to Saturday, the only time I could feel completely at home in the kitchen was on a Sunday.

Sixteen wooden stairs next to the kitchen led to our living room, bedrooms, spare room and bathroom. As soon as I was old enough, I'd run up and down these stairs – I rarely walked. It was a challenge to see how fast I could go up or down. At first, I'd sprint one step at a time and then, as I got older, cover two steps at a time. Occasionally I'd stumble but that never stopped me from the challenge. Customers in the shop must have thought a herd of elephants was stampeding when I ran up and down those stairs. I remember one day I sprinted down the stairs and the vibration nudged forward a large jar of pickled onions sitting on the last step. It toppled over and smashed into the concrete floor where it exploded, flinging pickled onions, bits of glass and vinegar in every direction. Before I got to the bottom of the stairway, I knew I was in big trouble, and sure enough, the old man cracked the shits at me and I had to apologise. The next day I continued my sprints and over the next few years would often hear my parents yell, 'Slow down!' I still sprint up and down any stairs, though not as fast as I used to.

Upstairs, the wall-papered living room contained a table, chairs and eventually a television. It also had the odd decorative items on a mantelpiece. Two windows faced Brunswick Street, the right-hand one was rarely opened, but the other was often opened to freshen the room and I would stick my head out to see what was going on in the street. I used that window so often that the sash cord in the side of it broke and I had to use a piece of wood to keep it open. It was quite some time before the window was repaired.

Near this window was a single bed and one night Lorna was sleeping in it and got the fright of her life. A portion of the ceiling above her sagged and suddenly came crashing down with bits and pieces of debris spread over her, the bed, and the floor. Fortunately, she was unhurt, but she never slept in that bed again. A leaky roof had allowed water to accumulate until the ceiling could no longer support the weight. As I got older, I slept in that bed and would occasionally look up at the ceiling thinking, 'Don't come down ya bastard.'

Next to the living room was the bedroom where Lorna and I slept when we were little. We slept in one bed 'top and tail' and, as we got older, we each had a single metal-framed spring bed on either side of the room. The bed where I slept eventually sagged as the springs loosened and it became uncomfortable. Bed bugs that lived in the coiled springs would sometimes venture out to bite me. We had to spray the springs with a commercial solution every now and again to kill the bugs.

As I got older, I had to move out of the bedroom because of the lack of space and the fact that the dresser and wardrobe were painted pink. That was far too girly for me, so I had no choice. I moved my bed to the living room or, at one stage to the tiny spare room between my parents' bedroom and the bathroom. The spare room was the smallest room in the shop, and my first and only personal space. It had everything I could want – a bed, white painted dresser, a window and space for my toys and marble collection. However, it was sometimes awkward at night as I had to pass through my parents' bedroom to enter or leave. Their bedroom was the largest, furnished with a double bed, a dresser and two wardrobes – one small and the other larger. There was also a window that faced the backyard. When I saw their bedroom again, as an adult researching this memoir, it looked so small, and

I wondered how all the furniture could fit. That was also the impression I had for every other room and other parts of the former fish shop.

Our bathroom was not really a proper bathroom. All it contained was a partially rusted bathtub, bath taps, and an old curtain covering the window. There was no hot water. It looked more like a storage area than a functional bathroom and I rarely used it. We washed ourselves with soap and hot water from the copper tub downstairs. I would use a soapy hand towel to wash myself and a large towel to dry off. Eventually my uncle installed a shower in the bathroom, with a four-foot-high cylindrical gas hot-water unit positioned above the end of the tub. A thin pipe extended upward from the unit with a shower head attached to it. To heat the water, you'd turn a lever near the bottom of the unit to release the gas and poke a lighted match through a slit to ignite it. I was rapt when I had my first shower at home at about the age of ten.

My parents worked between eighty and ninety hours per week, six days a week, day and night. This included work during opening hours of the fish shop, as well as work done before and after hours. The only extended holiday they had each year was a two-week break when the shop closed over Christmas. Their workday started at 6:00 am and one of their first jobs was to tip a tin of oil into both twin pan fryers and turn the gas on to heat them. Two or three mornings each week, before dawn, my father would walk to the corner of Brunswick Street and Johnston Street and wait to be picked up in a ute by a fellow Maco, who owned a fish shop in Smith Street, Collingwood (the neighbouring suburb). They would drive to the fish market in Footscray to buy supplies, returning at about 10:00 am to unload crates into the back of our shop. By this time my mother would have prepared the shop for opening.

My father would then slice the new supply of fish into thin strips, put them into the fridge and make a batch of chips. My mother made batter by mixing flour and water in a large dish, battered strips of fish stored the day before and cooked the fish and chips in the fryer. They placed battered fish in one panel of the fryer to cook for a while and then put them in the other panel to cook thoroughly. When a customer came in and ordered they'd reheat the fish and chips again ready to be served.

Once in a while, usually in the afternoon, my father would duck into the pub next door with a mate for a quick beer. If he stayed too long my mother would jokingly tell Lorna, 'Go and get Dad from the doctors.' On other occasions he would have a short nap.

Their workday ended when the fryer was turned off at night. One night my father forgot to turn it off and a passer-by pounded on the door, because we had no doorbell, to warn him the fryer was still on. My dad thought the person banging on the door was just another crazy drunk who had stumbled out of the pub. At first, he ignored the noise until he eventually decided to go and confront the person making it. When he opened the door and was told the gas was still on, he was shocked at his carelessness because he was usually very thorough in his work. He was also relieved and thanked the bloke who warned him. When my mother found out she was also shocked and ever after was obsessed with checking and rechecking the fryer to make sure it had been turned off. She'd always say to my father, 'Did you turn the gas off?'

The fish shop served a variety of sea food and treats including pickled onions, potato cakes, flake, whiting, couta, crayfish, mussels, chiko rolls, chips, prawns, and pickled gherkins. In those days, potato cakes were a penny each and fish about a shilling, though whiting was a little more expensive. My father always checked the fish thoroughly and if they weren't up to his high standard, he'd throw them out. My mother would complain and say, 'Don't throw them out we'll lose money.' But he insisted only the best fish was used because, 'If we serve poor quality fish, we'll lose customers and more money.'

Lunch times were busy when people came from various factories to pick up their orders, and evenings were also busy, especially on a Friday and Saturday night. On those two nights, customers would buy their fish and chips on the way to and from the Regent picture theatre in Johnston Street or from a pub nearby. It got even busier after 10:00 pm with more people enjoying a night out. My mother loved watching people go to the pictures, but she and my dad never did because they didn't have the time.

There were tough times. Sometimes my father struggled to pay the bills when prices increased for fish and potatoes but he somehow managed to find the money. And it was tough on my parents to get a good night's sleep on a Saturday night because of the noise made by the pub next door after 10:00 pm when it was closed to the public. Private parties in the back rooms of the pub caused a racket for some time and my father would shout 'turn it down' to no avail. There was no respite from work on Sunday when my parents washed greasy floors and the counter from 8:00 am to 9:00 am, so they never had the opportunity to sleep in. Once that was done, my father would go up the road to the local male-only Maco club. He'd come home for lunch before heading back to the club for the rest of the day. It was something men did back in the villages in Greece, so the old man was following a male Greek tradition.

My mother rarely had any time spare on a Sunday because she had to cook meals, wash clothes and look after Lorna and me. She would sometimes open up the shop for a short time to make some extra money, even if she had a visitor. Velika, her cousin, would sometimes visit her on a Sunday and have a yarn in the kitchen and occasionally my mother would excuse herself to serve any customer that came into the shop. She would proudly tell Velika, 'I've made two pounds!'

I remember Mum telling me she sometimes felt dizzy going out because of all the time spent in the shop. She did have the occasional break when we visited relatives and attended Maco social functions as a family. Sometimes on a Sunday she would also take Lorna and me to the park so she could rest for a bit. Years later, Mum told me she resented all the added responsibilities. But in those days, it was a strongly male orientated society. Men focused on making a crust and women did the housework, cooked, and looked after children. Men did not do what they considered 'women's work'. Some women, like my mother, helped run a business or worked in factories, shops, and pubs as well as do all the 'women's work'.

She also did a 'man's job' occasionally, for example when she decided to paint the inside of the shop, upstairs and downstairs. She nagged my father to do it but he never got around to it. So, one day my mother walked up to Smith Street several blocks away, bought tins of paint and then prepared all the walls, washing off any stains that had accumulated from the steam and smoke. She applied an undercoat and then two coats of paint to complete the huge job. She laughed when she told me she got up on a table using a long stick with a paint brush attached to paint the high walls and ceiling. As she did this, two Macedonians walked past and the wife said to her husband, 'See how much work she does. You do nothing!'

My father and my mother were popular with customers. Mum was known as Mary to the locals. Many people would say hello to her when she walked down the street. And kids would tell their parents, 'Let's go to Kon's,' because they knew they would always get a free potato cake or extra chips.

My cousin Sam worked in the fish shop part-time on a Friday and Saturday night, and he said people used to come from several suburbs away so the shop would be jam packed. My parents gave customers very large servings of chips and Sam would ask my dad, 'Why are you giving out huge amounts? No one else does.' My father would reply, 'What do you mean, it's not much.' He would also tell me and Sam to work hard, save your money, trust very few – advice I've followed over the years.

In 2015, I posted pictures on a Facebook group of my smiling parents in the fish shop during the mid-1950s. They drew many responses from people who fondly remembered my parents as very generous and the effect that generosity had on them as kids. I'm still getting positive responses to those photos.

As a kid I didn't realise how popular the fish shop was or how well regarded my parents were. All I knew was that they ran a fish shop and worked hard. Looking back now as an adult and reading the various interviews I have conducted with my sister, extended family members, and friends, I can fully appreciate and admire their work ethic and generosity of spirit.

My parents lived and worked together virtually twenty-four hours a day for forty-five years of married life, rarely apart for more than a day. Though they had their differences and arguments like any married couple, they remained devoted to each other – and didn't throttle each other. An impressive achievement.

More Early Memories

When I was a little kid, I buzzed around like a blue-arsed fly and couldn't sit still for too long before getting into some sort of mischief.

I was also a cheeky little bugger and rebellious, which would tire my mother both physically and emotionally. Outside the shop I'd break free from my mother's hand and sprint up the street with her chasing me down. She could barely keep up with my shenanigans and she always worried I'd get run over and killed. I loved the freedom of running around the streets and I became a street kid, though not in terms of what a street kid means today – homeless and sleeping rough. I had a home to go to. I roamed the streets day and night, when I was not in school, because it was an adventure – my backyard was too boring and small to contain me.

I was not the only one running away from my mother. Lorna took off one day unnoticed and was found wandering around the Exhibition Gardens several blocks away. Someone spotted her and told my mother, who then had to close the fish shop and go get her.

*My dad on the right at a dance or wedding hall in the 1950s.
As he aged, he got heavier.*

In the 1950s and 1960s it was normal for kids to play in the streets as long as they were home before dark or teatime. I did so more than most kids, because I could slip out unnoticed while my parents worked in the shop.

I much preferred to run around on my own than walk with my mother. I remember she would take me by the hand and we'd walk to the Isabel Henderson Kindergarten, just across the road from the baths, several blocks away from the shop. After half a block of walking I'd carry on like a sook, 'I'm tired, it's too far, carry me, please, ah come on.' I'd drag my little feet and she'd pull me along a few yards until she'd had enough and lift me up.

More Early Memories

At times I could be a bit of a pest. I remember teasing and upsetting my grandfather Tarnus, when he was sleeping on the kitchen bed. He woke up and chased me around the kitchen. My five-year-old legs were quicker than his and I dived under the table where he couldn't reach me. He yelled but I stayed there for a while until it was safe to come out. Pushing things for fun was something I often did. Usually, I could get away with it – though occasionally I'd come undone by going too far.

Other early memories I have are about fun at various Maco gatherings. Just about all families who attended were either immigrants from the different Lerin villages in Greece or, like me, children born in Australia of these immigrants. When some of my relatives arrived in Melbourne in the 1920s and 1930s there was little support for them, so over several years they gradually re-created the social gatherings they'd had in their villages. This played a crucial role in maintaining the Maco culture and provided a support system for family members and friends here in Australia.

One of my favourite get-togethers, as an eight-year-old, was the Maco club in Brunswick Street, Fitzroy, near Gertrude Street. Every Sunday my dad visited the club and would sometimes invite me to come along. It was a refuge for him after working long hours. He would wash up, shave, comb his hair and dress in his going-out clothes, which always consisted of a dark-coloured suit and tie, a white shirt, black shoes and hat. He would secure his gold metal-banded, brass-plated rectangular watch to his wrist. This watch, minus the band, is one of the few possessions I still have of his. He'd then grab his essentials; a packet of fags and a box of Redhead matches, because he smoked like a chimney. A visit to the club was one of the very few occasions we shared father and son time outside the fish shop. But that never worried me because we'd see each other every day at home.

I was full of beans on those days and couldn't wait to get out of the shop with my old man and walk up the street to the club. We never caught a tram because they were as rare as hens' teeth on Sundays.

When we arrived, we were always warmly greeted by fellow Macos who were inside playing cards, reading a Greek newspaper, talking, playing the soccer machine, smoking, or drinking coffee. While there I drank normal coffee but some of the blokes illegally added a bit of alcohol to theirs, which put a smile on their faces.

'Kar-corsi, Kosta?' (How are you, Kon?)

'Doorbra.' (Good.)

'Kar-corsi, ti?' (And how are you?)

'Doorbra, doorbra.' (Good, good.)

'Doysh, doysh, senni toa' (Come, come, sit here)

One of his mates would say to me, 'Itsaw! Kar-corsi?' Itsaw is the Maco word for Chris. He stretched the two syllables of my first name into a single shout that lasted about five seconds. He belted it out in a low, friendly tone, with the 'saw', reaching a crescendo followed by raised eyebrows and a smile.

As a young kid there was no way I was going to sit still and listen to the oldies talk. I had ants in my pants and had to move about. So, I'd very quickly eye off the soccer table game on the other side of the room. I loved playing it, especially against an adult.

This wooden soccer table was similar in shape and size to

a cafe pool table. About four feet high, three feet wide and six feet in length. I could just see over the top of it. The hard plastic surface was marked with soccer field lines and surrounded by six-inch-high walls. At the base of the machine was a slot where a sixpence was placed to release six one-inch wooden balls that all tumbled into a tray below. After all six balls were played, the game ended. The goal areas at each end of the table were small 'n' shaped cutaway sections that allowed a ball to disappear into the base of the table. Above the goals were single row abacuses used to keep score. I loved moving a bead across after I scored, because it was a silent way of yelling, 'Goal. Ya bloody beauty!' A polite way of not rubbing it in for your opponent. The last thing I wanted to do was to act like a smart arse after scoring a goal.

Each team had eleven hard plastic, armless figures – a goalie, two defenders, five midfielders and three forwards. The figures were mounted on a square base so the ball could be struck and were fixed and threaded on a total of eight rods. Each rod extended across the table and through the sides where hand grips allowed a player to grip the rods. They could be rotated clockwise or anticlockwise to kick a ball or pushed slightly forwards or backwards so the figures could move from side to side.

I could never work out why the figures were armless. I suppose if they had arms there may have been all sorts of arguments about illegal 'hand ball' and the game could go on forever. They were all dressed neatly wearing painted singlet, shorts, and socks and almost looked real except for the fact that their ankles were moulded into a square base, so they looked like their feet were stuck in a cement block.

In my day, the game started by throwing a ball between the row of midfielders and it had to bounce off the opposite wall before it could be struck. Striking the ball before it hit the wall gave the thrower or opponent an unfair advantage, because it could be struck without warning. If that happened the culprit would get a dirty look and the game would restart. A player could also get a filthy look from the owner of the club and blokes waiting to play the next game if he grabbed the ball after a goal was scored, stopping it from disappearing into the base of machine. That prolonged the game unnecessarily, a no-no rule, though I'd do it when no one was looking – the temptation was too great not to.

I didn't have any money so my father would give me sixpences to play, or I was occasionally shouted by an opponent. I had to make the most of my time as there was a limit to the free sixpences on offer. My first few games were exciting, and the oldies let me win, but I soon developed skills where I could hold my own against most of the blokes and sometimes beat them. One or two players were almost impossible to beat but that made me more determined to win.

Regardless of the score, I never gave up. It's something I learned at a very young age – 'it's not over until it's over'. My attitude was, and still is, that if you want to achieve something important just hang in there and keep going. Playing the soccer game against adults was very important so I hung in even if it was impossible to win. If I lost, I wasn't a sore loser; I just waited until the next game.

The soccer game required good hand and eye co-ordination, quick wrist reflexes, excellent timing, and sometimes yelling, 'Yes, No, Shit,' or 'Jeezus.' The noise annoyed the card players while other blokes would smile at my intensity, but that didn't matter to me; I was playing for the World Cup.

The game could be played against one opponent or in doubles. In a doubles game one player controlled the back lines and the other the mid and forward lines. Sometimes doubles teams would arse about and switch positions during a game, but I never did that because it could cost you a goal or even the whole game. If my opponents switched, I'd focus on scoring a goal before they could get back into position. And if I did score against the switchers, I felt terrific because they ended up looking like rabbits caught in a headlight. Served them right.

I learned other skills from the old blokes at the club. One of them was always to keep my hand on the rod that controlled the goalie, so I could quickly deflect the ball from the goal. My hand gripped the rod like it was stuck on with Tarzan glue. Opponents who let go of the goalie were usually caught out of position and could not get back in time to stop the speeding ball heading towards the goal. Another, the tap-tap skill, was very handy to get past my opponents' figures. I'd tap the ball from side to side and wait for my opponent to react. If he didn't, I'd flick my wrist so one of the figures could hit the ball past his. The only way an opponent could stop this was to mirror my movements and close off any gaps. It was like a cat and mouse game to see who would fall prey. However, the most impressive skill was to score a goal with your goalkeeper. This was incredibly difficult to do, because there were twenty-one other figures that could get in the way of a ball travelling the full length of the table. Once in a blue moon I succeeded, and my opponent's mouth would drop

*I'm sitting next to my paternal grandfather, Borsher.
This photo was cropped from a larger image of my cousin
Peter's wedding group in the late 1950s.*

open in disbelief. I'd keep a straight face and act as if I could do it any time.

The only occasions I didn't enjoy playing was when an opponent kept spinning his rods in the hope of scoring a goal. When this happened I'd just pause, wait for an opening and whack the ball through for a goal. Sometimes one of these lunatic spinners would score a goal and piss me off, because that was pure arse not skill.

When the money ran out to play soccer – and that was always too soon – I'd get fidgety because there was nothing else to do in a men's club. Sitting still was never an option and something I was never good at – even now I get up and move around after sitting for a while. As I got older, I continued to play the soccer machines at various cafes but by then I had to use my own coins to play games.

Sometime between the mid-sixties and 1971 the Maco club was demolished along with over 120 houses and more than sixty shops, to make way for a new high-rise public housing estate. A whole block of old Fitzroy vanished between Brunswick, Gertrude, Napier and King William Streets. Unlike many other old buildings in Fitzroy, there is no trace of the club left and I can no longer stand there and reminisce unless I close my eyes. I feel sad a chunk of Fitzroy was ripped out to make way for concrete towers, but it did get rid of the slum and provide accommodation for 3,000 people.

Maco weddings were fun to attend but, jeez, the church services were boring. Church was for adults, not for little kids like me who hated being dressed up. I felt like I was in a land of bustling giants, where I had to behave. And there was no fun in behaving.

I was always up to something. Here I am during a photo session for a wedding, playing with a long ribbon behind me. Check my mohawk haircut and sailor suit – what a combination. To my right is Lorna and above her are my father and mother holding hands. Photo cropped from a wedding group taken at Allan Studios, about 1954.

After a marriage service, which seemed to take forever, we'd all wander down Smith Street nearby to attend a photo session at Allan Studios. It's where many Maco wedding groups headed if they were married at the Greek Orthodox church. I remember anywhere from 60 to 125 adults and children being herded into a room for photos. Sometimes there were double weddings, which accounted for the large numbers. Little kids like me sat on the floor in front of the bride, bridegroom, wedding party and close relatives, who were all seated on chairs. Standing on three or four tiered benches behind them were the rest of the relatives. Each row would have had between fifteen and 25 people.

I can still feel the warmth of the crowd and the heat given off by the large lights in the room. The photographer worked hard to get everyone to smile by squeezing a plastic toy yellow duck. He was only partially successful because few people smiled; some stared at the camera and some looked grim. My father and mother always smiled but my grandfather, Tarnus, never did. He looked like an old man weighed down with age and painful memories, which I suppose he was.

In one wedding photo I see my mother holding my father's hand, though I don't remember ever seeing them hold each other's hand in public. If they did, my mother would have initiated it, never my father. He didn't express his emotions in that sort of way.

Later wedding photos are sepia toned, with the odd black-and-white one among them. Most are large prints, some mounted on an Allan Studios cardboard backing with a thin front and back cover. Others are missing covers.

I have all our old photos scanned and stored digitally in

Lorna and me outside a church wedding service in Victoria Parade, East Melbourne. I styled my own hair by rubbing my hands through it after my mother combed it.

case they get lost or damaged. They are easily accessible on my computer of course but there is something special about holding the original photos in my hands and feeling the texture of the covers. It sometimes makes me feel more connected to my family.

I treasure the several original Allan Studios wedding photographs I have of my parents and relatives. They remind me of the vibrant Maco community I lived in as a child. Most of the adults were born in the Lerin area and here they are together again, just as they were at weddings back in their old villages.

When I recognise a face, often glimpses of the past come to mind and I relive the stories. Most of these adults and some of the children have passed away but they all still live on in my memory.

After the church service and photo sessions it was time for the fair dinkum fun to begin. We'd walk to the Fitzroy Town Hall, a few blocks away, for the reception. To the adults it was a wedding reception, but to a kid like me it was all about food and mucking about with the other kids. Receptions were held on the ground floor at street level. It's now a library, but when I walk past the bluestone walls, I can still hear another young kid belt out a song starting with, 'Ker-vretch-a-yamer' (We are going to eat). Back then, as I sat listening, I thought, 'Bloody hell, get on with it, I'm starving.' Thankfully, he put me out of my misery when he finished singing.

The next ordeal we kids had to endure was long speeches made by various adults until finally it was time to eat. It was a Maco's food paradise. A main meal of either chicken or red meat was served and side plates of olives, Greek cheese,

My family at the back of a dance or wedding hall in 1956. I'm holding Lorna's hand to my left and above us from the right are my father, mother, and Tom my cousin.

salad, ham, and lollies. Slices of wedding cake were offered and, though it was a bit too fruity for me, I still gobbled it up because I was starving. There was also plenty of booze for adults and soft drinks for kids. I always gutsed myself with food before mucking about and having fun with the other kids who were also raring to go. I remember being told off for being too boisterous, which slowed me down only briefly.

The Maco community also gathered at Maco dances, held on a Sunday evening, every two or three weeks, starting at 7:30 pm and finishing at 11:30 pm. They were usually held at the Fitzroy Town Hall or sometimes at Cathedral Hall in Brunswick Street, near Gertrude Street. Other locations included the Richmond Town Hall, Northcote, and Clifton Hill. The whole Maco community was welcomed so it didn't matter from which village people had come originally. I always looked forward to these Sunday night dances, which were ideal for my family, who worked in the fish shop every other night of the week. During the 1950s and 1960s, up to several hundred people would turn up.

A traditional Maco dance was led by a male or female adult, usually waving a handkerchief overhead. The leader was then joined by several people, all holding each other's hands, to form a line. As more people joined the line it would become a huge circle around the dance floor and eventually spiral inwards. When I joined in, I always had to concentrate to get the steps, half turns and rhythm right. I can still hear the trumpet and clarinet blaring out the Maco music. As a kid I didn't like the sound but as an adult, when I hear it now on ethnic radio or TV, I appreciate it because it instantly takes me back to my childhood.

The Fitzroy Town Hall was my favourite dance location because it was within a short walking distance from home and there were more places for me to muck about compared with other dance halls. Sliding up and down the wooden floors in the hallways with other kids was fun until we got told off by an adult. Then we'd go and play outside on the concrete steps stretching across the front of the Town Hall. My favourite plaything was a six-foot-high concrete divider wall outside the entrance. I'd jump off the ledge to land on a small patch of lawn below, and then go round the wall, walk up a few steps of a concrete stairway and have another go. I vaguely remember the lawn being replaced with concrete, which meant fewer jumps to avoid the sensation of my knee joints fusing with my ankle joints on impact. But, like most kids, I considered fun before safety.

Maco picnics were great and another way of bringing the Maco community together. Everyone would meet early Sunday mornings in front of the Exhibition Gardens, on the footpath in Nicholson Street, just across the road from where the Gertrude Street tram turned left and rattled towards town. A row of pre-booked buses would be parked along the street, ready to take us somewhere out in the sticks or to the Eastern Beach in Geelong. There were the usual latecomers who arrived after the buses were due to leave and we had to wait for these stragglers, which took forever for a kid excited to start the adventure. Why couldn't those buggers get there on time like we did? We'd walk all the way from Brunswick Street, which seemed a million miles away, yet we'd still manage to get there on time – despite my mother taking ages checking and rechecking the front door of the fish shop to make sure it was locked. We'd try to hurry her up by walking away up the street, but she would always check at least one more time before hurrying to catch up.

When we finally reached the buses, our names would be marked off a list and we'd hand over our bags to be stored in the luggage compartment. I'd nervously climb aboard to make sure I had a window seat, because it would be absolute torture if I got stuck sitting between two adults. If that happened, I felt trapped not being able to stare out of a window without hindrance. The bus would eventually pull away from the curb and I'd press my face against the window to watch Fitzroy slowly disappear. We would roll through several suburbs to reach our destination and it felt great to spend a day away from the asphalt streets and factories of Fitzroy. As our picnic bus arrived somewhere, as far away as the other side of the black stump, my excitement would ramp up. Ironically one of those distant picnic destinations was Kalorama in the Dandenong Ranges, just down the road from where I live now. In those days it was about a one-hour drive from Fitzroy to Kalorama on a Sunday.

It always took ages to get off the buses as people shuffled along the aisle towards the door. I would have sprinted if I'd had the chance to do so. Finally, we'd disembark, grab our picnic baskets and bag and then search for a flat grassy area to lay our blankets, as did all the other families. Food would be spread out on the blanket and then I'd be off like a shot, running, yelling, exploring, and playing with other kids until it was lunch time. My parents would kick back with other relatives to have a yarn and for one day escape the relentless grind of their working week.

When it was lunch time we'd sprint back and devour the delicious Maco food. Throughout the day we'd be invited to other relatives' spreads, so food was available all day. I believe the generosity of offering far more food than you could eat stemmed from the experiences of my parents' generation growing up in poor villages where food was sometimes very limited. One thing about the Maco community was that food was always available and, regardless of how full you were, you were always offered more.

I remember during one of the picnics a car was bogged in a muddy area. The driver accelerated to get out of the mire

Here I am having fun making noise by pounding the keyboard. Obscured behind me is Lorna. Photo taken in the mid-1950s.

but only managed to spin the rear wheels. He stuck his head out of the window and called out to a few blokes, including my father, to push the car from behind. He accelerated again as the men pushed the car, and again the wheels spun. My dad yelled, 'Hey, stop, stop' as mud splattered over his clean white shirt – now a polka dot shirt. The driver climbed out of the car and apologised as my dad muttered a curse or two. Someone found a wooden plank to place under the rear wheel for traction and on the next attempt to get out of the bog the driver was successful, though my father watched from a distance.

The Geelong Eastern Beach picnic area was one of my favourite destinations. It had an enclosed swimming section where I swam, dived off a diving board and slid down a giant slide into the water. I wasn't keen on the taste of seawater; I preferred swimming at our local baths. But I tolerated the sea because it was fun just mucking about in or near it with other kids.

I enjoyed visiting our relatives who mostly lived in the Northern suburbs or on farms in Shepparton and Werribee South. When they arrived in Melbourne from Greece, many lived in the inner suburbs or on farms. A few then moved to the northern suburbs and then to the more affluent eastern suburbs. Our relatives would visit us on a weeknight or a Sunday, but we'd visit them only on a Sunday because of my parents' restrictive work hours. The Werribee South farm visits were fun and travelling by train was exciting. As a kid I'd always get to the window seat so I could watch the buildings and backyards fly past as the train left the city and travelled through the suburbs. These soon disappeared and the terrain changed to open country as the train rattled on to Werribee station. There was plenty of space to play on a farm, and no sooner had I arrived than I was tear-arseing around. I remember picking peas on the farm, eating as much as I could, and how quiet and empty it felt compared with Fitzroy. I certainly wasn't a farm boy, but I enjoyed our visits.

The longest train trip we ever made to visit relatives was to Queanbeyan, near Canberra. My mother, my grandfather Tarnus, my sister and I travelled together without my father. I can't remember why he wasn't with us but I guess he decided to stay home to mind the shop. We travelled on a Victorian country train from the city to Wodonga before hopping off and catching another train to Queanbeyan, because Victoria and New South Wales had different railway gauges. This problem was finally resolved in 1962 when the gauges were standardised.

I remember the leather cushioned bench seats on the train, which sometimes had a tear in them, or a patched-up tear, courtesy of some ratbag's knife. In the compartment, two bench seats faced each other, with a curved metal luggage rack above our heads. The luggage rack was big enough to scramble into if you were a little kid. There was a panel of small wooden-framed windows below the racks, and usually a picture in a frame. There were also leather arm rests below the glass panels of the doorway. A sliding door separated the compartment from the corridor. It felt like I was in a luxurious mini mansion.

I can still see Tarnus, who was then in his mid-sixties, gripping a handrail, half hanging out of the last carriage, frantically waving to get the driver's attention to stop the train. I think it was at the border of Victoria and New South Wales when he suddenly thought, mistakenly, we had boarded the wrong train for the second leg of our journey. The drama ended well when he finally realised we were on the right train, so sat back down sheepishly, and we continued our journey to Queanbeyan.

Though our whole family visited relatives, we never visited our Aussie friends for a social get-together nor invited them to the shop. Lorna and I visited friends almost daily, but my mother and father never joined us. There was very little time available to do so because of the hours they worked. However, they did get on well with my friends' parents and would say g'day or have a little yarn when they met in the street, the pub, or our shop. The home I lived in wasn't a home. It was a fish shop, a place of business. It was not a place where Aussie friends were encouraged to visit as a family. Our friends the Burkes – John, Joyce and Denise – did occasionally pop in to see Lorna and me, but I don't remember them ever staying for tea. Upstairs was out of bounds for our friends, so we caught up with them in the kitchen or backyard. The only social get-together at home with the three Burke children and our family occurred when they were invited to celebrate Greek Easter with us, in the kitchen.

We celebrated Greek Easter each year. One of the rituals was to dye boiled eggs red, which symbolised the resurrection of Jesus Christ, and play the traditional game of cracking eggs. This game involved two people smashing their eggs together. The egg that cracked would be declared the loser and would be claimed by the winner. My mum loved telling us the story of one Easter in Greece, when she was a little girl. One kid

Roy Boy

Photo taken in 1962. Back row, from left to right are Lorna, Joyce, John, and me. Denise is in front.

kept winning all the contests and nobody could work out why he was so lucky. They discovered he had made a wooden egg and painted it red. Wood beats shell every time. He was banned from further competitions for that particular Easter. I briefly considered making a wooden one and painting it red, but no. It was more fun, challenging and satisfying when I won fairly. I always hoped I'd find an invincible red egg but that never happened.

Most of these childhood experiences were typical of many children born to Maco immigrants and so were the smells and sounds of a working-class suburb like Fitzroy.

The smells could either delight you or hit you for a six. There were some sections of streets and laneways I could have identified while blindfolded just by sniffing.

Among the first smells I encountered, after I left The Royal Women's Hospital in Parkville as a newborn baby, were most likely from the fish shop. I can't remember that far back but the smells would have been the same as those throughout my childhood: cooked fish and chips, raw fish, dripping, the gully trap, vinegar, hessian bags full of potatoes, the pungent additive used to pickle onions in jars, bundled old newspapers in our storeroom, rubbish in our metal rubbish bins and our outdoor dunny. These were accompanied by heavenly smells that always put a smile on my face, and came from the cake, potato chip and chocolate factories. One whiff of freshly baked Penders cakes next door lifted me higher than the twenty-foot brick factory wall and also briefly masked the constant fishy smell of the shop. I also loved the smell of potato chips coming from the Colvan potato chip factory in Rose Street. If you hung out long enough outside the factory you could get a free bag of chips from a worker inside. MacRobertson's chocolate factory in Argyle Street was the home of the legendary Cherry Ripe and Freddo Frog chocolates. If the chocolate aroma didn't send you into seventh heaven you were not right in the head. Kids would also hang outside this factory to get free chocolates from a worker.

The chlorine odour from the Fitzroy Swimming Pool, which everyone called the Fitzroy baths, wasn't a particularly pleasant smell but it did arouse my sense of fun as I walked along Young Street towards the pool. Breathing the chlorine felt like I was already in the baths – swimming, diving off the diving board and mucking around just enough not to get chucked out.

The absolute stinker smells included the cheese factory near the Town Hall. Jeez, that smell could destroy your nostrils and any living creature within several blocks. You could only survive if you held your breath and walked past it quickly. The locals who lived close by and those who worked in the factory, may have got used to it, but I never did. The stink of horse manure could also make you turn your nose up and grimace. And there was plenty of it from the stable in the laneway, around the corner from the fish shop. The stable housed up to ten draught horses along with their harnesses and other tackle. Sometimes my mate John and I would hang about near the stable to watch a bloke shoe a horse. We'd be so engrossed in watching him work we didn't really notice the smell.

If the horse shit didn't get to you, the smell coming from the pub toilet and the laneway next door to our shop would. Some drinkers pissed in the urinal or, if that was full of blokes, go outside and piss against the wall or on the cobblestones in the laneway. When I walked by, I'd quicken my pace and almost run this pissy gauntlet to get it over and done with.

Another assault on the nostrils were the half-open garbage bins on collection day. Even the covered ones were smelly. Our garbage bin was a shocker with all sorts of fish scraps, and I wondered how the garbos who collected the bins could put up with the smell. They either had nostrils of steel or they'd got used to it.

The sounds and noises of old Fitzroy also still echo in my head when I think about them.

The green and white W-class trams rattled up and down Brunswick Street between the city and Preston at the other end of the line. The sound of one tram was loud, but two trams passing each other sounded like a roar of thunder. I'd watch these metal monsters from the footpath or from our upstairs living room window. The trams were powered by overhead electric cables and were occupied by a conductor, a driver, and passengers who would sway gently with the motion of the tram.

The noise of a rattling tram would occasionally be punctuated by the clanging bell the driver would ring to warn slowpokes crossing the road to hurry up, and warn cars to move on if they got in the way. Louder and more frequent clanging was the driver's way of saying, 'Get out of the way, you bloody idiot!' Those who ignored this warning also got a further mouthful of abuse from an angry red-faced driver. My sister recalls seeing a drunk man on a tram start to shadow box when he heard the bell ring. I don't know how long the imaginary round lasted or who won the fight.

Noisy cars and vans competed with trams for space along busy Brunswick Street from Monday to Saturday, but on

Sunday it was dead quiet. You could just about fire a cannon down the middle of Brunswick Street and not hit anything, apart from an occasional tram that ran on the Sunday schedule.

The bottle yard in Fitzroy Street, near Kerr Street, was usually noisy with the cascading sounds of empty beer bottles being handled, stored, loaded, delivered, and sometimes accidentally dropped, smashing to smithereens on the concrete ground. The bottle yard would send someone to the stable most mornings to hitch the horses to a cart and drive it around the streets of Fitzroy to collect empty beer bottles. The driver would yell, 'Bottle-O!' occasionally to let residents know he was nearby.

The clippity-clop sound a draught horse made as it ambled out of the stable along the bluestone cobbled lane and onto Kerr Street always grabbed my attention. It would be harnessed to an open tray cart guided by an old bloke sitting on the edge of the cart, flicking and pulling on the reins. The horse didn't really need a reminder of what to do as it had made the same journey many times. When I heard the sound, I'd stop what I was doing and wait until it appeared so I could marvel at the size and wonder of the animal. I'd stand outside the pub on the corner of Brunswick Street and wouldn't budge, even if the horse shat in front of me.

One sound I looked forward to hearing came from the Salvation Army band that marched and held sermons around the streets of Fitzroy on a Sunday. Both women and men wore uniforms, with the women in bonnets and the men in peaked caps. I loved the BOOM BOOM BOOM of the bass drum and could hear it a mile away. The brass instruments blared, and the tambourine player shook her wrist, vibrating the bells on the rim of the tambourine, and striking it by tapping with her fingers, fist, or palm. It was the sound and spectacle that always drew me to the band, not the religion. The Salvos were a vibrant bunch who firmly believed in God and preached His message, but I didn't really listen to the words. The preaching was just a pause between music and the songs. The Salvation Army band was almost as popular as the Mr Whippy van that cruised the streets during summer, selling ice-cream to kids. When I heard the van pipe out 'Greensleeves', I knew it was ice-cream time, if I had any pocket money left.

Closer to home, the Evelyn Hotel next door made a bit of a racket on busy Friday and Saturday nights; I could hear chatter, laughter, yells, glasses clinking, as well as the occasional drunk who staggered out of the pub swearing and trying to remain upright so he could stumble home, into our fish shop or to the next pub down the road.

And I could make a bit of noise too if I didn't get my way. I remember when I was about four years old and overheard my father talk about going to the fish market in Footscray the next morning. Without discussing it I decided I was going too, so the next day I was up at 4:00 am – but my dad said, 'Go back to bed.'

'No, I'm going to the market with you.'

'No, you're not.'

'Yes, I am!' I continued to carry on like a pork chop until he gave in.

My dad and I were joined by my 20-year-old cousin Tom, who emigrated from Greece in 1956 and lived in the shop for a brief time. We walked to the corner of Brunswick Street and Johnston Street waiting to be picked up by my father's Maco friend, a fellow fish monger, in his ute.

When we walked into the market warehouse it was a smelly fish wonderland, packed with sellers, buyers, a smorgasbord of fish jammed into open crates, and loud voices booming across the open area. The fresh fish lay there, some with their mouths open just like mine. I stared at their eyes hoping they would come alive or at least blink but of course they didn't. I was tempted to run around but decided not to and held my father's hand, rather than get lost among all the fish.

My father and his friend selected supplies of fish for their fish shops and loaded the crates into the back of the ute. They and Tom had a long yarn with a few blokes before we headed for home. I wanted to go right away, not to get home but to ride in the ute again, and I had to wait impatiently until the grown-ups finished gas bagging. Jeez it took a long time before they decided to move on; to a four-year-old, it felt like they talked all day.

On the way back my father and his mate decided to have a quick beer in a pub near the Queen Victoria Market. Tom said, 'I've got some shopping to do, I'll take Chris with me, and we'll see you back at the shop'. Tom probably guessed the quick beer would become a long beer, which it did, and he wanted to get on with things.

Tom had come prepared with a netted shopping bag, and he held my hand as we crossed the busy road to disappear into the market. It was another adventure land of noisy people selling, buying and bustling along shoulder to shoulder. Crates and displays of fresh fruit lured me into fruit heaven as we walked by. I excitedly yelled, 'I want that banana. I want that pear. I want that apple.' I wore Tom down and he bought me what I wanted, just to shut me up.

More Early Memories

After Tom had finished buying fruit, we walked towards Lygon Street to catch a bus home. But as we neared the bus stop, I managed to break free of his hand and sprinted towards the city. As Tom chased me, I was making good ground along the footpath until my shoe slipped off and I ran back to get it. By this time Tom had caught up and grabbed me so I yelled, 'You bloody bastard', which startled people walking by. He gripped my hand and, as we boarded a bus and sat behind a copper, he whispered, 'If you play up again, I'll give you to the policeman.' I didn't say a word for the rest of journey, but when we reached our stop in Johnston Street, I broke free again to run home about two blocks away. I burst into the shop yelling, 'I'll kill the bastard', headed for the backyard, picked up a stick and waited outside so I could clobber Tom. He arrived, managed to grab the stick out of my hand and gave me a smack. My mum saw this and cried out, 'Why are you hitting my boy?' Tom was quick to explain what had happened and that settled my mum down.

I don't know where or how I learned to swear by the age of four. It may have been from my parents but that's unlikely as they rarely swore in English. When they were angry or frustrated they did let out a Maco swear word or two such as sheep-en-ski (shit) or vorcar-to-yayou (may the devil eat you). But I can't remember swearing in Maco myself as a kid. It was always in English. I may have picked up swear words from customers in the fish shop. I do remember 'bastard' was my favourite one. As I got older my swearing vocabulary expanded but 'bastard' was my go-to word. It was so versatile – you could use it as a friendly jibe like most kids and blokes did in those days, or as a threat if you were really pissed off with someone.

You could even elongate the word 'baaaaaaaaaaastard' for maximum effect. Sometimes I'd add 'bloody' or 'fucking' before it, just to give the word a real boost. If I caught myself in time, I could water my swearing down to 'bloody hell' which was more acceptable for most people.

As a kid I discovered that swearing at a person could cause a range of responses: a smile, a frown, being ignored, a smack in the mouth or a fight. The reaction would depend on the tone, the time, the place and who you swore at. Swearing at a copper could automatically get a kid or a bloke a kick up the arse, a belt in the mouth or free ride to the cop shop for some re-education. I saw a drunk swear at a copper once, and he was rammed into the side of a divvy van. There was no age discrimination with the police. Sometimes, when I was very angry, I'd let fly and suffer the consequences. But never at a copper. I wasn't suicidal.

Most kids and blokes swore. Some ockers littered almost every sentence with 'bloody' 'fucking' or 'fuck'. But usually only to other fellows. When I was growing up, swearing in front of females was frowned on and could get you into trouble. If you did slip you would often be told to, 'Mind your language' and often the response would be, 'Sorry, excuse my French.' The ockers really had to mind their Ps and Qs in mixed company. I remember playing in my primary school yard one day when a kid upset me, so I yelled, 'You bastard!' He dobbed me in and a teacher told me off. I was then a marked man because the teacher asked other kids to let him know if I swore again. Sometimes I'd slip and get into trouble again. But how could I avoid telling an annoying kid he was a bastard when he was acting like one? When I reached the ripe old age of about six or seven, I still swore but never directly at an adult. If an oldie pissed me off, I'd hold off and either swear inwardly or use the word when telling other kids what someone had done to me.

I remember being forced to go to the barber up the road because my mother decided I needed a haircut. I didn't think so but as an eight-year-old I had no choice. I tolerated the barber messing with my hair but not my mother, who combed my hair every day. I would mess it up almost immediately, which frustrated her.

The old-style barber shop had all the equipment a little kid could marvel at: leather chairs, razors, scissors, clippers, brushes, hair shaving cream lotions, leather straps to sharpen a razor, and a large mirror. I waited for my turn, sitting next to a small table that held various magazines like the *Australasian Post* and racing guides. I flicked through them looking for cartoons. When it was my turn for a haircut, I climbed up onto the leather chair while the barber swept away a pile of hair tufts on the floor.

He was a friendly bloke, who looked a hundred years old to me but was probably in his sixties. The cut started well as snips of hair flew off my unruly mop. He then lathered the back of my neck and under my ears with a soapy brush so he could shave those areas. I squirmed when I saw the razor and sat very still in case one of those strokes cut my neck and went too deep.

Then it happened. He nicked me and drew blood and it hurt. He apologised and dabbed the cut with a paper towel to stem the blood. But I silently yelled, 'You bastard.' That's all I could do because I didn't dare yell out loud to a man holding a sharp razor against my neck.

I was pissed off and, when I returned home, said to Lorna, 'The bastard nearly cut my head off!' I swore I would never go back again but of course I did – the next time I needed a haircut.

My Family

My father was usually quiet at home but outside the family he was talkative, jovial, friendly, and popular with customers, relatives and many others who knew him.

If I played up, he'd become angry and raise his voice to yell at me, but he rarely ever completely lost it. The only time he really went off the deep end happened one night when I was watching a movie called *House of Wax* on TV. It was late and Lorna, my father and mother were in their bedrooms trying to sleep. Lorna complained first about the noisy TV and then my father yelled, 'Turn it off.'

I turned the sound down to eke out a few more minutes, but no such luck. The complaints continued even though I could hardly hear the TV. I was determined to watch the show because I was only halfway through so couldn't possibly bail out.

Finally, the old man had enough and roared, 'Right, that's it!' He burst into the living room and I immediately jumped up from my chair, but he was so pissed off he yelled again and moved towards me with a raised open hand. I kept edging around the table so he couldn't reach me. After a couple of attempts to grab me, he gave up the chase turned off the TV and stormed out. I waited until I felt it was safe and decided to go to bed rather than risk getting belted if I turned the TV on again. I had missed half of the show and it would be several more years before I was able to watch it completely – and it was terrific. But, on that night, I definitely wasn't going to tempt fate.

I had very few deep conversations with my father, though we did generally get on well and there were hardly any major problems between us. We didn't avoid each other – we had the odd chat here and there as we each went about our own day-to-day activities. His focus was working in the fish shop and mine was either watching TV or going out to play.

There was little opportunity to discuss much during evening meals because there were only two or three meals each week where the entire family sat down to eat together. My father or mother would usually still be working in the shop until late. Besides, my father was mostly too tired to engage in a long conversation anyway. And there were very few after dinner chats because once the meal finished, I'd be up and about.

Probably, the only deep conversation we had was when I asked about his war experiences but, even then, he would only describe some of the things that happened to him – never the emotional impact they had. But there was one story he loved to tell that connected his time in the army with something that happened much later.

There were regular health inspections of the fish shop and my dad was always worried they would find something wrong and he'd either end up in court or have to close. One day a health inspector did find something wrong and cited my father for a health infringement. My dad went to court to defend the charge rather than pay a fine. During the court case my father had a character witness, and he couldn't have selected a better bloke to testify on his behalf. During World War Two, while on patrol in New Guinea, my father had saved an officer from being killed by a Japanese sniper hidden in a nearby tree. This officer was the character witness.

I'm sure the witness impressed the presiding magistrate, but I believe the turning point was when my father's solicitor questioned the health inspector.

'What did you discover when you opened the fridge door?'
'Smelly fish.'
'Do fish smell?'
'Yes.'

The magistrate threw out the charge for what he said was really a trivial matter and should never have gone to court in the first place.

Over the decades the health regulations became tighter. My father eventually closed the shop in 1981 and retired, because he couldn't afford the cost of replacing major equipment required by the health department to run a fish shop. Towards the end, I do remember a health inspector making several demands and my father becoming emotional. He was almost crying and pleaded for a 'fair go'. I decided to step in before it got out of hand and firmly said to the health inspector, 'Just tell me what needs to be done and we'll do it.'

That eased the situation – the inspector told me what was needed and left. He may have been overzealous and was probably just doing his job, but I was glad when the prick left.

He'd really upset my old man and I hated to see that happen.

I remember a shared moment I had with my old man when I was eight as I curiously watched him shave rough stubble off his face with a long-bladed razor, like the ones used in a barber shop. I stared in fascination as he wet the shaving brush in a cup of hot water, swiped it backwards and forwards over a bar of soap, and raised it to lather the sides of his face, jaw and the front of his neck, producing a thick coating of soap. Then he expertly moved the razor about until the stubble disappeared and he was clean shaven.

As he was shaving, he gave me a few tips on how to do it correctly. My chest puffed up with pride as he shared this grown-up moment. I still have his old wooden handled brush with some strands of fibres left and his silver razor with the burled handle, which he would unscrew to place a blade into the curved head. When I started to shave several years later, I followed his advice and I still shave the same way he did, though with a plastic-handled Gillette razor.

My father wasn't a physically expressive bloke when it came to his emotions. There were no hugs or kisses in our family that I can remember – which doesn't mean to say we didn't love each other. We were just not a touchy-feely family. The best I could expect was a handshake from him, and that was fine with me – it's just the way we interacted. And I don't remember exchanging gifts at Christmas either – it was not something he would do. He wasn't stingy, it was just that he had no interest in Christmas. He did care, and he probably loved me. He never said it in words but there are things he did that showed he cared. He and my family supported me throughout my Turana experience and many other difficult times when I was growing up. I didn't fully appreciate his support at the time, but I do now.

Although he was easy going, he could get physical if the situation warranted. I remember a ratbag in the fish shop swearing and carrying on, and there was certainly a threat of violence in the air. After a bit of verbal to-ing and fro-ing, my father had enough, grabbed a long-handled broom, waved it about and started to move from behind the counter towards this fellow. The bloke took one look at my father, thought better of it and darted out of the shop before my old man could get to him. A wise decision.

When I was a kid, I rarely saw my old man vulnerable. That would happen much later in life when he was elderly and ill. But I do remember one time when his back was giving him heaps of trouble and he was lying on the bed in the kitchen. Someone came over to help fix him. I don't know if this fellow was qualified to help or if he was just a mate. As he manipulated my dad's back, my father screamed in pain, which scared me and I felt helpless. I wanted it fixed and I wanted him to stop yelling but I couldn't do anything. He was a big bloke and could look after himself, but in this moment he was also helpless. It was the first time I saw him this way.

We talked in English or Maco depending on the moment. A sentence could contain words in both languages. My old man's English was basic though he could be understood. I can't remember how well he could write or read in English, but he could sign his name far more neatly than my chook scribble. Some of my relatives' English skills were poor or virtually non-existent, even after spending decades here in Australia. Usually, my female relatives were in that category, as they were homemakers and had limited contact with English speaking people. Whereas my male relatives were out and about, working and mixing with fellow English-speaking workers, so they picked up the language as they went along. Just like my dad did.

The thing I hated most about my father was that he'd sometimes yell at my mother in frustration over something or other while they worked in the shop. His outbursts would severely embarrass her and some of our customers. One customer didn't hold back and said, 'Shut up Kon, you've got a lovely wife.' And another customer told me, fifty years later, that she is still distressed over the memories of those moments. I never saw him physically abuse my mother, but she confided in me much later that he nudged her arm with his elbow once when he was angry and that upset her. He was a big bloke, towering over her, and she momentarily felt threatened and shocked that he would do that to her.

In private, my mother, Lorna and I would have a go at him for the way he acted. He'd have three voices admonishing him and would say, 'Alright, alright, alright.' There was never any apology, just an acknowledgement he was in the wrong.

Perhaps a few things contributed to his outbursts and frustration: the excessive alcohol he often drank, working eighty-to-ninety-hour weeks, struggling to pay the bills, working and living with my mother for virtually twenty-four hours a day, and maybe traumatic memories of his wartime experiences. These are not excuses for his bad behaviour but possibly reasons.

I remember when I was about ten, my parents were arguing while preparing fish in the work area at the back of the shop.

I opened the kitchen door, threw a thong at his feet and yelled, 'Leave her alone!' They both looked at me and burst out laughing. So, they did have a sense of humour about their argument on this occasion. Apart from the usual husband and wife squabbles and these kinds of moments in the shop, they got on well together and worked as an efficient team. My mum loved telling me the story of my father's attitude to arguments. He'd say, 'If I'm right and you're right then who's wrong?'

I suppose seeing those outbursts from my father influenced the way I deal with anger or frustration in public. I tend to go quiet and wait for a calmer moment. I've always regretted the rare occasions I've publicly gone off my head. The reason I try not to get angry with someone in public is because I don't want anyone to feel the way my mother did, or the way I felt when I saw what she went through. Even if I feel my anger is justified, that's still no reason to embarrass someone or make them feel uncomfortable. Nowadays if I'm angry with an ignorant, selfish or prejudiced person I usually don't bother reacting because it's a waste of energy to try to change other people's attitudes. I'm glad those sorts of people can't read my mind because they'd hear, 'What a dickhead.' The silent swearing habit I picked up as a kid is still keeping me out of trouble today!

Another thing I've learned over the years is to try not to be judgemental of someone. That's not easy because I do tend to judge people on their attitudes and actions, but I try to remember there's more to the story – just as there was more to my father than his angry outbursts. I try to avoid a final judgement until I learn more about the person and the reason why they are behaving in a certain way – if it's worth the effort.

My father wasn't into religion even though he was officially Greek Orthodox. I don't know whether he believed in God as we never had those sorts of discussions. He only attended church with the family for weddings or funerals. The only thing he was religious about on a Sunday was attending the Maco club up the road. I was never religious though I did attend Sunday school for a short while as a kid. It wasn't the religious aspect that attracted me to Sunday school, it was the social interaction. I became bored with religious instruction and left. The only other religious experience I can remember was my christening in a Greek Orthodox church when I was about four years old. Somehow my parents never got around to do it when I was baby so there I was, an old timer, in front of a priest who was spraying water over me. Being a late starter, just like with my christening, has seemed to be a feature of my personal and professional life over the years.

My old man smoked cigarettes every day and rolled his own tobacco. He never smoked while he was serving customers in the shop but there was usually a lit fag lurking around in an ashtray somewhere. When we were out on a social occasion, he'd usually be smoking a fag and drinking a glass of beer, with a smile on his face. After many years of smoking roll-your-own tobacco, he switched to a packet or two of Turf then Craven A, most days. Much later in his life he got crook one day from all the smoking and gave them up. It wasn't a gradual decision – he just stopped. I never saw him smoke another cigarette again. He loved his booze and would drink Fosters beer either from a glass or a can virtually every day. Later in life he drank wine and I remember going down the road to buy him a flagon of wine from a liquor store near the corner of Brunswick Street and Westgarth Street. I think the old man possibly developed his smoking and drinking habits either during his army years, perhaps more likely during his Queensland years as a cane cutter – apart from long hours working there was nothing much else to do but suffer the heat, smoke, drink, fight and look out for snakes.

Though I didn't know this until much later, when a relative told me about it, one other vice he had was gambling. He regularly lost a fair bit of money playing cards at a Macedonian cafe during the late 1950s. One night he lost all the shop takings, came home after midnight and argued with my mother about the missing money. I don't know how long his gambling lasted, as I was never aware of it when I was young.

He was a generous man and this extended beyond giving kids a free potato cake or chip in our fish shop. He and other fellow Maco fishmongers, originally from nearby villages in Lerin, pitched in to help run another fish shop in North Fitzroy when the owner, Chris, a Maco, fell ill with rheumatic fever and was hospitalised. My old man and his mates helped Chris's wife by buying fish from the market and filleting some of it. I knew and liked Chris and his wife, as we'd visit him and they'd visit us. He and my father would share fish purchases at the market if a box was too expensive. My old man did another good turn for Chris when he rang and warned him of a con man, impersonating a health inspector, who had just swindled my dad out of £20 by threatening to report him.

My father was active in the Maco/Greek community in several ways. He was a foundation member of Alexander the Great Melbourne Soccer Club in the late 1950s. The club later became Heidelberg United Football Club, which plays in the

National Premier League. In 2016 he was inducted into the Hall of Fame along with his cousin, Marcos Economides.[15] In 1960 my dad was on the supreme supervisory committee of the Ethnikos Pammakedonikos Organismos (National Pan-Macedonian Organisation). He was also involved in organising dances. As a kid, I wasn't fully aware of his involvement in the Maco community. It's only during my research for this memoir that I discovered how active he was. I don't know how he found the time to be so involved.

He revealed very little about his childhood and young adult life to me. It's only through research, official documents, interviews with my extended family and some of the stories my mother shared with me about him that I have an idea of who he was. He wasn't a secretive man; he just didn't voluntarily talk about his past. It's one of several traits I shared with him until I started to write this memoir.

In one major way my father was different from my mother. She enjoyed reminiscing about her childhood in Greece and her life in Australia – he didn't.

My mother was a shy, gentle, warm-hearted, caring lady who tried to keep me in check when I was a kid. I caused her a lot of grief with my Turana escapades, which I regret, but she supported me in every way she could. She had a good sense of humour and I inherited her funny one-line observations of people and events. It was a friendly type of humour designed to get a laugh and help make people feel at ease. We both used humour as a way of overcoming our shyness in social

---

15 I was delighted to discover this during my research, and it makes me proud his past efforts were honoured by the club.

situations and I have also used it as a way of deflecting any probing questions about my life that I haven't wanted to share in public such as my migrant background. I still do that to this day, although not as much now as I'm more open about my past.

As I got older, my mother and I developed a banter that always made us both smile. It stemmed from a relative who always complained about life and had a 'woe is me' attitude. If my mother was experiencing a difficult situation, I would say to her, 'You know why you are ....' 'Why?' 'It's because you are a Stamkos' (my mother's family name). The inference was that only a Stamkos has bad experiences and no one else does. The banter always got a laugh, and it helped my mother briefly cope better with any difficulty she was experiencing. One of her strongest characteristics was her resilience in adverse situations, a resilience probably developed over the years she spent growing up in Greece and dealing with various hardships such as wars, prejudice and poverty. She worried about me because I was always up to something and tear-arseing around. She worried about many other things as well, but when she faced any difficulty her quiet determination would see her through.

She rarely ever lost her temper with me and I can only remember one time she snapped at me for some reason. Of course, we had arguments, as mothers and sons do, but on this occasion she completely surprised and stunned me. I couldn't say anything after her outburst. I believe she must have been very stressed about something else because it was so out of character for her. Though I do remember two other occasions when she really lost her temper in public. Once I had just walked into the shop and heard a male customer who was arguing with her yell, 'I'll smack your son.' She fired back with, 'Get out!' and he stormed out. I kept walking, opened a door and headed for the kitchen. On another occasion in 1995, my mother, Lorna and I were walking along a footpath on holiday in Thessaloniki, Greece, when suddenly a motor bike roared between us and my mother yelled in Greek, 'Pou pas trelo?' (Where are you going, crazy?). Raising her voice in public was a sure sign she was extremely upset.

My mother always tried to please everyone and generally avoided conflict. Usually, I'd stick up for her if I felt someone was treating her unfairly. More than once a pushy relative gave her a hard time telling her what to do and I'd jump in using humour to deflect the situation. I remember my mum was always keen to ask for advice from others so she could decide about something that worried her – she was very much influenced by what others thought. And that left her open to being told what to do because some of the well-meaning advice from others came across as a demand rather than a suggestion. I suppose we are all guilty of that at one time or another.

She never smoked cigarettes, which was a relief for me because I hated the smell of smoke and I still do. The old man's continuous puffing was more than enough for me to tolerate and I'd try not to breathe in the haze when it wafted towards me. Unlike the old man, she rarely drank alcohol apart from a small glass of wine when it was offered on social occasions.

She also loved to have a yarn with anybody and she always had a smile on her face when she was engaging with customers in the fish shop. Her English was very basic, though most people could follow what she said. She could understand it more that she could speak it. We spoke mainly in Maco though sometimes there would be an odd English word thrown into our conversation if I couldn't think of a Maco word for what I was describing. And I still do that when I speak to my relatives.

When I was little my mother would tuck me into bed every night, but that changed when I turned twelve. One night I rebelled, ripped the blankets off and angrily stomped downstairs to the kitchen to sit on my father's chair. She was shocked and followed me down to find out what had upset me. My old man did the usual thing and said, 'Just leave him alone.' She sat next to me and asked what was wrong. I said, 'You're always doing that, I'm not a kid anymore.' That was the last time she tucked me into bed.

I loved glancing over at my mum when she was watching professional wresting on TV after our Sunday roast lunch. She'd be animated, tense and would occasionally throw her arm out in front of her as sign of disgust when a villain cowardly attacked a hero. When the hero got the upper hand she would yell, 'Ha, what did you expect, serves you right!' I would stir her and say, 'It's not real, they're not really hitting each other.' She would take the bait. 'What do you mean not real, can't you see, he's hitting him, look, look, there.' Watching the wrestling was one of the very few times my mother was able to enjoy herself at home.

If I could talk to my mother today about the past, I reckon she would end the conversation with 'taka-besheh' (that's the way it was). Also, when reflecting about the old days she would often say, 'heyda, heyda, ennor den' (one day it will all end).

I don't remember my dad and mother calling each other by their first names. He would sometimes use the Maco word for 'missus' – 'morree' (the r's rolled) – when talking to her, but I can't remember how she addressed him.

As kids Lorna and I didn't use the words mum, mother, dad or father in either English or Maco when talking directly to my parents. For example, we'd say instead, 'kar-corsi' (how are you?) or 'shorpraysh?' (what are you doing?) when greeting them. Though, I'd use the words mum, mother, dad and father when describing them to others.

Lorna and I would refer to our parents as 'the old man' and 'the old lady', which were common expressions in those days, but we rarely used these words in their presence. I remember our mother overhead a discussion Lorna and I were having which included the words, the old lady. My mum said, 'What do you mean, old lady!'

When Lorna and I were kids, we had more arguments than my parents did. We fought like cats and dogs. When our brand spanking new TV arrived in 1964, we found something else to bicker about constantly – which program to watch. We were at each other's throats and one day we carried on so loudly that my father stormed up the stairs to sort us out, but we scattered and hid before he reached the living room.

We both attended George Street Primary School. Lorna was a year ahead of me and we both visited our friends, the Burkes, in Argyle Street, almost every night and at the weekends to watch television together – that was before we bought our TV.

We met the Burkes at the same primary school; Joyce became Lorna's friend and John was mine. He was a year ahead of me at school and we became good mates and hung out together most days.

My Family

Apart from those common interests, Lorna and I rarely went out anywhere together – she knocked around with her friends and I knocked around with mine. The only times we'd go out together would be to various family functions or when my mother took us, and sometimes the Burke children, to the Fitzroy baths, to a park or the beach.

Lorna had a determination to get things done and overcome any obstacles, as we all did in our family. We share the same characteristics as our mother and father – friendly, sociable, kind and humorous. And of course, we lose our temper on occasions, although those moments pass quickly. Unlike my mother and me, Lorna is not shy and has a natural and inviting manner with strangers and friends. I tend to be reserved until I get to know people before engaging in any serious conversations.

As teenagers we never had the normal Maco/Greek upbringing where boys usually had more freedom of movement than girls, who were strictly supervised when it came to associating with the opposite sex. Lorna could get out and about and had dates and boyfriends, though admittedly she never told my parents about such relationships. That changed when she was fifteen-and-a-half and met Harold. After a year of secretly going out with him she suddenly disappeared for two days with him. I don't remember why she did this – she may have had a blue with our parents when they found out. The joy of seeing Lorna again when she came back overrode any negative emotions our mother experienced, though it must have had an impact on her. Lorna became engaged to Harold at seventeen and they married a year later. Over time he developed an easy-going relationship with the rest of our family.

As Lorna and I grew older we no longer had kids' spats and over several decades we have rarely had an argument. We certainly have disagreements from time to time, but our conversations are calm and friendly – rarely with raised voices. We stay in touch on a regular basis as she lives only fifteen minutes away by car, though it's mainly by phone because we both lead busy lives. We don't often have in-depth conversations about serious issues; our conversations are usually about catching up and finding out 'what's new'.

She jokingly told me that the only thing she had against me is that when she was eleven years old, we swapped beds one night and when she woke up she couldn't move. She had rheumatic fever and ended up in The Royal Children's Hospital in Parkville for several weeks. When the doctor diagnosed the fever, Lorna was convinced she'd got it because she slept in my bed.

We each had a very different work ethic when we were young, because Lorna worked part-time at Eve's toy store up the road and helped in the fish shop. I rarely worked in the shop and the only job I had as a teenager was delivering newspapers for a brief time. This changed when I entered the work force full-time; it had to because no work meant no pay. When I started my business later in life, I had to work even harder to earn a crust. So, I evolved from bludger into a fair dinkum hard worker over time.

Lorna's experience working in Eve's toy shop helped her develop a flair for retail shop presentations. So, when she worked in fruit shops for over 20 years, she had a natural instinct for displaying fruit in a way that was attractive and enticed customers to buy. Like my mother and father, she loves engaging with customers – not only as an employee but as a friend.

She is a devoted mother, grandmother, cares for her family and I admire her resilience in bouncing back from any major problems she has had over the years.

As our parents aged and became frail, we both supported them by visiting their home in Fitzroy, then later in Boronia, and running errands until they passed away. I'm forever grateful to Lorna and her current husband, Rodger, for allowing our mother to live in a granny flat on their farm in Silvan for the last two years of her life. I'd visit at least two or three times a week, but Lorna provided virtually full-time care and companionship.

She sometimes introduces me to others as 'my little brother' even though I'm six foot one and she's four inches shorter than I am. We have never expressed our feelings physically, no hugging or pecks on the cheek. We communicate our feelings verbally or with silence if warranted. It's taken me over 50 years to feel comfortable hugging or kissing a female friend on the cheek, whereas in the past it was always done with a handshake. It was never an aversion but an uncomfortable habit that developed. Even as a kid I'd respond but never initiate that sort of physical contact. I'd usually greet people with, 'G'day' or 'How are you?', shake their hand and say either, 'See ya later,' or 'Catch ya later,' for goodbyes. This behaviour was typical of the whole family – 'taka besha' (that's the way it was).

Over the years I've come to an even deeper appreciation of my relationships with my father, mother, and Lorna. As I matured, I realised how important family was and still is, even though my parents passed away several years ago.

And those relationships played a crucial role when I was separated from my family in 1960 at the age of seven-and-a-half. For the next six months I lived at Turana boys' home and then at an orchard farm in Toolamba.

In Exile

Turana boys' home was not a good place to be. A 2016 report by the Royal Commission into Institutional Responses to Child Sexual Abuse revealed there was evidence of sexual abuse, cruel punishment, poor management, and inadequate supervision in many such institutions, including Turana.

Boys like me were not just placed in care; we were placed in danger. I was lucky. Though I could have experienced abuse, I never did. I can't help wondering how my life might have turned out otherwise, and just thinking about it makes me angry. Some of the boys who served time in Turana got into further trouble with the law and ended up in Pentridge Prison in Coburg, an adult prison sometimes known as the 'blue stone cottage' or 'the college of knowledge'. Ironically the former prison is now a luxury development – housing a very different type of client.

The official name of the boys' home was the Turana Reception Centre (1955–1968), part of the Children's Welfare Department. It was previously called the Royal Park

Depot (1890–1955). I imagine around 1955 some bureaucrat decided to change the name from 'depot' to the more pleasing term of 'reception'. Both words were technically correct in describing the institution – it was a depot and a reception centre that stored children before they were dispatched to other destinations decided by the authorities. Neither word sits well with me – 'depot' is dehumanising when referring to children and 'reception' is bland, almost implying it was a pleasant place, which it certainly was not.

Turana was in Royal Park, Parkville, about two and a half miles from my home in Fitzroy, and it seemed a million miles away. The word Turana is believed to be a local Koori word for rainbow but for me the only pot of gold at the end of this rainbow was getting out of the place and coming home.

In 2011, I obtained official records from the Department of Human Services under the Freedom of Information Act and learned more about what happened to me both at Turana and in the six months following my release. Thirty-four pages mailed to me covered events from May 1960 to November 1962. The records included reports, statements, interdepartmental memos, notations, letters and inspector reports from Turana Reception Centre, Children's Court, Children's Welfare Department and Victoria Police.

Before I saw these documents, I always thought I had been about ten years old when I was sent to Turana, not seven-and-a-half. I was surprised but not shocked, perhaps because this happened over sixty years ago and time has blunted any emotional reaction I might have now. However, when I told my sister, friends and relatives they were stunned; they couldn't believe a kid of that age could be sent to a boys' home. Maybe

I should be upset about this, but I've always had a 'taka besha' attitude with negative experiences. This may be a coping mechanism to deal with unpleasant memories, but it works for me and I guess that's all that matters. Just saying the words 'taka besha' usually defuses a fleeting bad memory until the next time it enters my mind. Thankfully this doesn't happen often, and I don't dwell on the past, even though I have been thinking about it while writing this memoir.

I only have fragments of memories about events leading up to Turana and my time spent there. I remember sitting in a small waiting area with my mother at court. I was laughing and restless, so she gave me a furious look, smacked my arm and told me to be still. I had no idea that by the end of the day I would not be going home. I also remember the first night in Turana, sitting in an office being interviewed, crying for several nights before bed, playing in a dirt pit with a toy truck and attending school classes. My parents and Lorna visited me on weekends, and on one occasion, two kids told me my parents had arrived, which was a lie. They lied to get me out of the main room and into the corridor so they could accuse me of stealing, which I denied because it was not true.

I do have one vivid memory of the time I tried to escape. I had only been there a few days. It was early evening, about teatime, when I snuck out of the main building using some bushes nearby as a cover. I kept very low so I couldn't be seen and edged slowly to freedom, home where I'd be safe, away from all the strangers. I had no idea how far home was or how to get there, my only thought was to get out. As I crawled further along past the bushes a strong aroma of cooked chops and sausages drifted towards me from the kitchen. It was overpowering and I was hungry, so I decided to go back for tea. That ended my great escape attempt.

According to the documents, I was admitted to Turana on the 9th of May 1960 and was described as 'clean, appears healthy', with clothing in good condition and carrying no cash or property. My religion was noted as Greek Orthodox and my surname was continually misspelled in various notes as 'Goulonoulos' until corrected later. I did not know about this at that time, nor would have I cared, but now it pisses me off because it's sloppy recording of a fact.

Perhaps one error, if corrected during the court proceedings, may have altered my sentence. My birthday was recorded as 18-12-51, which made me eight-and-a-half years old, not seven-and-a-half. Had the court known my real age it may have been more lenient and placed me on home probation.

Even if my birthday had been noted correctly, I wonder if the outcome might have been different if my parents were not blue-collar workers, of a migrant background with limited command of English. Or if they had not lived in Fitzroy, considered then as a slum area, and not been caught up in a justice system that was predominately Anglo-Saxon. Perhaps I may have got off with a slap on the wrist if my parents were from a wealthy suburb like Toorak, whose residents had all the resources available to help keep their kids out of trouble with the law and court system. I also sometimes wonder how many kids there would have been left in Fitzroy if every kid who was caught nicking something was bundled off to Turana. But I have never blamed anyone or anything for the mess I got myself into. I take a simple view of what happened. I stole – I was caught – I was punished.

To add to the confusion, my father called the Children's Welfare Department two weeks after I was admitted to Turana and was recorded as saying my birth date was 18-12-53. Another stuff up – this time for a year after my actual birthday. The person who recorded the date either misinterpreted or misheard the date, because my dad knew the correct one.

Soon after I was sentenced, my dad asked the Department to consider three options because of my age: that I could return home, be placed on probation, or go to my uncle's farm in Toolamba, about eleven miles from the country town of Shepparton. An official supported the option of probation if my birth date could be proved, and noted: 'The parents who make a very good impression [...] are distressed that their small son should be in an institution.'[16] However another official wrote: 'Owing to the short period since he was admitted to the care of the Department, I consider it would be unwise to allow this boy to return home. Enquiries could be made at Shepparton with a view to the possible placement of the boy with his uncle.'[17]

So, behind the scenes my parents, uncle and the Department were organising my transfer from Turana to my uncle's farm at Toolamba. I had no idea this was happening and thought I was stuck in Turana for ever.

A handwritten page in my file from the Children's Welfare Department notes that someone from the Department called my uncle and noted: 'the person speaking was a man with good command of English and an Australian rather than

---

16 Children's Welfare Department – Turana – Memorandum – 23 May 1960
17 Letter from Director – 25 May 1960

Greek accent.' The caller asked my uncle if he would allow me to stay at the farm in his care for a while, provided it was okay to inspect the farm first and allow the police to make any necessary inquiries. My uncle said yes to all the requests and I was almost on my way. The farm was inspected and it was arranged for me to attend Toolamba Primary School. My uncle was also informed: 'From time to time, an inspector will call at your home to ascertain the boy's progress.' A policeman from Mooroopna police station said the Goulopoulos family was very much respected in the district, and he would keep me 'within his notice' as he often visited the primary school.

So, in 1960 in a period of just over three weeks, I was ripped off the streets by coppers, interrogated at the Russell Street police station, taken to Turana then to the Children's Court, made a ward of the state and returned to Turana. I was then exiled to my relatives' orchard farm in Toolamba, 112 miles from my home in Fitzroy. All this at the tender age of seven-and-a-half.

I don't remember leaving Fitzroy for Toolamba or the effect it had on me, but it must have been a very emotional time for my family. I was probably told I was going to stay on the farm for a while – but that 'while' lasted six months, from June to December of 1960. I do remember a rare father-and-son moment, away from the fish shop, when my father took me to Eve's toy store up the road to buy a going away present. Inside the toy shop, he said I could have anything I wanted so I excitedly looked at all the possibilities, eventually choosing a cork pop rifle. The cork was attached to a string, which was secured near the trigger. I loaded the rifle by jamming the cork inside the end of the barrel and pulled the trigger. The cork exploded out of the barrel like a bullet. I repeatedly loaded and fired again. I loved the popping sound the cork made as it flew out of the barrel. I now had a rifle with an unlimited supply of bullets – the cork was my repeating bullet within reach – wow!

In early June it was time to leave for the farm. The Children's Welfare Department continued to keep tabs on me; the official reports contained further facts, reviews, and errors.

One report, dated 3-10-60, stated: '28-9-60 visited Chris. He appeared to be well, cared for and happy, although as far as I fathom from some very broken English he is fretting for his home in Carlton. I informed Mr Goulopoulos before any thought of Chris parole was considered this Dept must be consulted.' It's unlikely the official who wrote this report was referring to my skills as I was born in Australia and had a good command of English. And I did not live in Carlton. I lived in Fitzroy. I was a Roy Boy. This report I believe was the catalyst for my eventual return home, as it was officially referenced two months later, noting I was fretting for home.

I wasn't completely separated from my family because they visited me every two or three weeks. They would catch a tram to the city then a train to Shepparton – about a three-hour trip – then my relatives would drive them from the train station to the farm in Toolamba. The visits to the farm must have been a huge burden on my parents because of the hours they worked. Sunday was the only day they could leave the shop and, if you take six hours out of the day for travel, there wasn't much time left for a family visit.

I don't remember those visits but, looking back now, they showed my parents loved me and never gave up on me. Ironically, as my parents became older and frailer, it was my turn to look after them with Lorna's help. I wasn't a full-time carer, but I'd pop in about three times a week to do any errands, spend time with them for a meal and keep them company. I remember taking my mother for a doctor's visit where we chatted with someone we knew and that person said to me, 'Oh, you're a good son,' which completely surprised me as I was only doing what I considered was the right thing – look after my family. After all, how could I do otherwise? They had looked after me when I was a kid.

The orchard farm where I stayed was across the road from a railway depot and covered about nine acres. Set back about 100 yards from Toolamba Road, the large weatherboard farmhouse was clean and tidy, with nine rooms, including five bedrooms. Three generations of the Goulopoulos family lived on the farm, ranging in age from one year old to eighty-two. There were eight adults and four children including me. This was like the many families who lived in the Lerin villages in Greece, where three generations of one family often lived together. My cousin Nick, who also lived there, later told me his parents were encouraged by other relatives to, 'Come to Shepparton, it's a thriving community, you'll make a lot of money buying a farm.' His family stayed there for four to five years before moving to the northern suburbs of Melbourne.

My first impression of the farm was how quiet it was, especially on a Sunday. Unlike the noisy, bustling world of Fitzroy, occasionally a crow would punctuate the silence with an 'aaaaaark' during the day but that was about it. There were no lolly shops, baths, cobbled laneways or traffic – just a huge empty space that went on forever and could suck the life out of you. I felt like I was on the moon. A long, long way from home. But I eventually adapted, and the farm became a huge playground.

I remember breakfast times when all the adults and children would sit around a long table eating and chatting away. Plenty of food was served, in the usual Maco tradition. There was also plenty of toasted bread on the table, its delicious smell wafting across the room. Other memories I have of life on the farm include the day I discovered some books I owned had been damaged. I asked my five-year-old cousin, 'What happened?' She said, 'A cow came in and sat on them.' Bloody hell, that would never have happened in Fitzroy. I also remember deciding my slippers were too old and that I needed new ones, so I deliberately wrecked them and said, 'I need new slippers, these are no good.' The adults saw through my deception, told me off and I was made to continue to wear the old pair. That was a hard lesson to learn but I certainly gained an appreciation of the value of things every time I had to drag those wrecked slippers around.

I was still a cheeky bugger. I remember playing in the front yard near a mound of dirt with my one-year-old cousin, Nick, while my eighty-two-year-old grandmother was bent over gardening nearby. Nick and I drifted off behind the dirt mound where we could not be seen, and I started chucking small pebbles towards her. She let out a loud curse and continued gardening. I don't remember getting into trouble, but I certainly deserved a kick in the arse for that cheeky display. However, there was one episode where I did get into trouble, and I wasn't even being cheeky – just clumsy. I was given the job of carrying a billycan full of tea and some food for the adults who were working in the orchard. By the time I got there I had spilled half the billycan and was told off for being careless. I'm not sure if I was given billycan duty after that effort.

Though the adults worked long hours on the farm, they managed to attend social events as a family. I remember going to a soccer game that became rough, and I saw a player with blood streaming down his face. Those friendly soccer games were not always friendly.

Soon after I arrived on the farm, I began attending Toolamba Primary School, which was about two miles away on Toolamba Road, just over the railway track. It was a bloody long walk if I didn't get a lift to and from school. I was in a mixed grade and there was plenty of playing space in the dirt grounds around the school. We also played in and around the shelter shed. On one memorable day I spotted a dead snake near the railway track. I kept my distance just in case it leapt up and bit me. And just before Christmas, during the summer, I saw a bloke dressed up as Santa Claus and yelling, 'Merry Christmas.' He was clanging a bell while standing on a horse drawn cart, travelling along Toolamba Road towards my school.

On the first of December 1960, my father signed a document requesting I be placed in his care. A notation on this document read: 'Might be better to leave the boy where he is […] See report that he is fretting for home. Perhaps holidays would meet that need.' A few days later another notation appeared suggesting I be returned to Fitzroy after a home inspection. I don't remember being aware of any early moves to return me to Fitzroy and it's possible I wasn't told so I would not get my hopes up. It would have broken my heart to find out a request was made and denied, just a few weeks before Christmas, after spending five months on the farm.

An inspector visited my home on the 13th of December and reported the place was clean, the rooms were generally bare, with only the essentials in furnishing. He also observed the whole home seemed geared towards the shop business. He said we were a typical Greek-type family – very industrious and well-knit under the old man's leadership. He also commented that Lorna appeared to be well behaved. My mother told him I had never been in trouble until I met my mates and that I had attended school regularly. The Department decided to give me a trial at home, but if I caused any more trouble, I would be returned to my uncle in Shepparton. Another written note on this report said my parents were not able to give close supervision but expected that I would be more subdued after being away from home.

One day after my eighth birthday my father and uncle received a letter from the Department: 'It has been decided to allow the above-named to return to your custody under department supervision … From time to time an inspector from this department will call at your home to ascertain the progress of the ward.'[18]

You'd think some bright spark in the department, after approving the custody request from my father in the first week of December, could have made sure I was home for my birthday on the eighteenth. But probably due to either bureaucratic process or lack of sentiment, it was not meant to be.

Sometime between the 19th and 23rd of December in 1960, I arrived back in Fitzroy. Although still a ward of the state I was now officially a free boy.

---

18 These were the Acting Director's exact words – 19-12-1960

That skinny kid standing to attention is me in front of our fish shop. About 1962.

Back Home Again

After my return home, the Children's Welfare Department kept an eye on me for the next two years. At the end of January 1961, a few weeks after my return, an inspector's report said: 'Visited Chris swimming at baths 26-1-61. Visited Mr and Mrs Goulonoulos (sic) and Chris seen. He is a nice-looking little boy – said he is very happy to be home again. The parents appear to be very hard-working homely people, anxious to do the right thing by the children. Chris will commence school on Feb 7th at George Street State School – does not know which grade he will be in. Parents are keeping him well occupied during the holidays with swimming – he spends most of his time at the baths. Accommodation above the shop is very clean, sparsely furnished. Conditions satisfactory.'

I settled down over the following two years and a social worker reported that I had been no trouble, was more mature, and attended school regularly. The report concluded, 'Discharge to father recommended.'

So, on the 5th of November 1962, I was officially discharged as a ward of the state, a few weeks before my tenth birthday.

Yet again, my surname was misspelled in the document. It seems ironic that earlier official documents misspell my name, it's corrected in some subsequent reports then misspelled again in the later correspondence in December. The misspelling and mispronunciation of Goulopoulos would continue until I changed my surname many years later.

I stayed out of trouble and out of a 'life of vice and crime' because I no longer knocked around with my former mates. No doubt the experiences with the law, the boys' home and being away from my family were also contributing factors, because I knew I could be ripped away from Fitzroy if I played up again.

Ah Fitzroy. My home. My playground.

With Turana and Toolamba behind me, over the next four years I experienced some of the best times of my childhood – adventure, mischief and fun mixed with the occasional ugly, sad or mad time, as was the case for most Roy Boys and Roy Girls growing up in Fitzroy during the 1950s and 1960s.

After I'd returned from the farm, I spent most of my time at the Fitzroy baths during the school holidays. It was magical and a wonderful transition back to normal life. I loved the outdoor pools – a welcome relief from the endless hot summer days, and an oasis from the surrounding factories, shops and traffic of Fitzroy. The pool was open from Monday to Sunday, and I'd go there just about every day with my best mate John Burke. I fondly remember John's parents. His father's name was Raymond, nicknamed Slim because of his thin build, and he worked on the wharves. Ivy, John's mother, worked as a cook at the Evelyn Hotel and Tankerville Arms Hotel nearby. I called them Mr Burke and Mrs Burke, never Raymond or

Ivy. Kids in those days never called adults by their first names and if you did you were told, 'Mind your manners.'

John and I would meet up outside the fish shop and walk down Brunswick Street towards the baths, on the corner of Young Street and Alexandra Parade, a few blocks away. We both wore our shorts over our bathers, slung towels around our waists or necks, and had enough money to get into the baths and buy a drink or ice-cream afterwards. Sometimes we'd wear thongs, our favourite summer footwear, which would often stick to the steamy asphalt footpath after a few steps. Other times we walked barefoot, always a challenge as there was very little shade we could dash into to cool the burning soles of our feet. The searing heat from the roads and footpaths felt like we were jumping in and out of a heated fry pan. Each time a bare foot hit the ground we would yell, 'Ow, ow, ow!' We'd sprint across Brunswick Street to minimise contact with the hot road, carefully jumping over each of the four tram tracks that threatened to burn our feet to a crisp. We'd time our dash to avoid being collected by passing trams and cars. Occasionally we'd mistime it and get stuck in the middle of the road as traffic sped by on either side of us. We would jump up and down on the spot trying to relieve the burning sensation of the hot road and, when there was a break in the traffic, we'd dash across to the nearest cool spot in the shade. Sometimes we'd make the risky split-second decision to run when a clanging tram was heading towards us. If there were two trams coming from either direction, we'd run like our arses were on fire.

Once across the main road, we'd turn right down Westgarth Street and walk pass the ice works. I remember the three-shilling coin operated machine that would release a huge block of ice down a chute. It came thundering down like a rocket to hit the end of the chute, often chipping bits off the ice. John's sister, Joyce, was sometimes sent by their mum to pick up a block of ice using a pram. She would struggle to lift the ice block, but once she managed to place it into the pram she'd gather the chips of ice that had broken off the block and drop them in as well. She'd then cover the block with a hessian bag and push the pram home, though much of the block would have melted from the summer heat before she got there. The block of ice was then placed inside an ice chest, roughly the size of half a fridge, which kept food and drinks cold.

As John and I walked past the ice works we'd turn left into Young Street and walk a further two blocks until we saw the baths' high brick walls with bits of glass embedded on the top to deter people from climbing in for free. I don't know how anyone could scale those high walls, but someone would have found a way; this was Fitzroy and overcoming obstacles was a way of life.

The entrance was around the corner in Alexandra Parade. We'd line up with other kids and adults waiting to get in and slowly edge our way forward. The entrance fee was about sixpence, then about ten cents after decimal currency arrived in 1966.[19] You'd pay a bit extra for a locker key but get that money back when you returned it. The key was attached to

---

[19] I remember the cartoon advertisement on television explaining the conversion. It had a snappy jingle to the tune of the Australian folksong 'Click Go the Shears' with the voices of Kevin Golshy and Ross Higgins. The 'Out with the old and in with the new' song, lyrics by Ted Roberts. (source Reserve Bank of Australia Museum – Dollar Bill Turns 50 Years Old)

a numbered metal tag, which had a large safety pin, and we would pin it to our bathers for safekeeping.

As we stepped into the pool area, the sun's rays bounced off the blue water and dazzled my eyes. Once I regained my sight, I could see I was in the middle of an oasis of fun. I would turn around towards the lockers and not even the overpowering presence of the two huge gas tanks, visible from the baths across Alexandra Parade, could spoil the view. These monster, cannister-like structures were several storeys high and the metal panels surrounding the frame would rise or fall depending on how much gas was stored. Nearby was the Gasometer Hotel. There was always a pub across the road or down the street.

Joyce, me and Lorna near the corner of Brunswick Street and Alexandra Parade. In the background is one of the three gas towers, partially full.

The main pool was one hundred and sixty-four feet in length, and I would swim up and down until I was too tired to go on. The thick black painted lines on the bottom of the pool were my guideline to swim straight. The pool was eighty-two feet wide, and I remember getting my Herald swimming certificate for making it across the pool without sinking or drowning. The pool's depth ranged from three feet at the shallow end to about seven or seven and half feet at the deep end. Two diving boards were located on either side of the deep end. I loved bouncing up and down on a diving board and trying to maintain my balance before diving into the water. Too much bouncing meant I could fall off the board and look like an absolute dill, which was enough motivation to get the bounces right. The only frustrating thing about diving was waiting in line to have my turn. Sometimes a long line of kids and adults would make the waiting time seem forever. Other times when it wasn't so busy, I'd just dive and dive until I was exhausted.

Behind the diving boards on the brick wall were the words DANGER DEEP WATER and below AQUA PROFONDA. Those words in thick black paint covered most of the wall. Aqua profonda is Italian and roughly translates to 'water deep', though the correct spelling of 'aqua' is 'acqua'. I don't know why it was misspelled but I do know the story behind the sign. Apparently back in the 1950s, a pool supervisor got tired of pulling out Italian kids who struggled swimming in the deep end because they couldn't read the English warning sign. So, he organised the sign to be painted in Italian as well to warn them. I not sure what happened to kids who were from other countries and couldn't read English or Italian. But I suppose if they painted signs in every other language spoken in Fitzroy, all the walls would have been covered in paint.

Hot days drew large crowds to the baths, especially during the school summer holidays when the pool was filled with people of all ages and sizes. It was busier than Bourke Street and at times difficult to swim without getting kicked in the head by a swimmer.

A four-tiered concrete grandstand also ran the length of the pool. Sometimes I'd sit on the highest tier and watch the crowd of people swimming, sunbaking or sitting on the side of the pool with their legs dangling in the water. Some people sun baked on the concrete grandstand or in two other smaller areas. These smaller areas were about twenty feet square, one at the end of the grandstand and the other across the pool in the right corner where there was a six-foot high exit turnstile that led into Young Street. If you fell asleep while sun baking, you'd end up redder than a crayfish in our fish shop front window. I rarely used suntan lotion and was careful not to nod off. If I got too hot, I'd dive into the pool to cool off and return to sun baking. Occasionally I'd be caught out and become painfully sunburned.

I can still remember the sensation of plunging deep into the water and swimming towards the black lines on the bottom of the pool to look up and see the flaying legs and arms from swimmers above me. It was invigorating at first, followed by a sense of calmness as l glided through this silent world underwater. The only thing that could disrupt the calm was swallowing a mouthful of water. Then the pleasure would turn into terror as I'd desperately struggle to the surface, gasping for air as I emerged. So, it was a good lesson to learn – keep your mouth shut when you dive into a pool. I also learned early on it was also wise to keep your mouth shut if you walked past a ratbag in the streets of Fitzroy.

Once I'd absorbed the views of our oasis, I'd walk with John to the dressing rooms, which was full of green lockers and wooden slatted benches. We'd quickly change and shove our towels, shorts and shirts in our lockers. We didn't muck about; we'd lock the lockers, pin our keys to our bathers and hurry out. We ignored the toddlers pool on our left, though sometimes we would stand on the bench seats there with our backs to the wall to cool off late in the day.

Outside the lockers it was on for young and old. I'd chase John to the edge of the pool and a lifeguard would yell, 'No running!' We'd slow down, not because we knew it was unsafe and you could easily slip on the watery edge of the pool and injure yourself, but because we didn't want to get chucked out.

On one occasion a kid beside us did a 'bomb' and it was a beauty, splashing water on several people nearby. It was a perfect bomb. He jumped high into the air, crouched, folded his knees into his chest, held his knees with both hands and hit the water with his backside. Then the bomb exploded. So did the lifeguard. 'Hey, you, Cut it out. no bombs or else!' It was going to be a long day for this lifeguard, and he'd certainly earn his pay.

John would dive into the shallow end of the main pool and I'd dive in after him. He was a stronger and faster swimmer than me and would soon outpace me. He'd then turn, wait until I caught up and splash water at my face as I got closer.

'Cop that.'

'Ah, ya bastard.'

I would laugh and splash water back at him until we were both engulfed in sprays of water. He'd swim towards me, grab the top of my head and dunk me before swimming away. I'd race after him, but he was always too quick; I could never catch him once he took off.

Some kids did belly whackers, a dive that had gone wrong. Instead of diving in on a downward angle, inexperienced divers would hit the water in an almost horizontal position. The result was pain and a red mark on their stomachs.

One kid dived into the pool in front of us and accidentally did a perfect belly whacker as soon as he hit the water. He surfaced and rolled over in pain holding his stomach.

'Ah, fuck, jeez, my guts, my guts.'

'Whoa, what a belly whacker,' I said.

John laughed, 'Yeah, what a dag.'

Belly whackers were painful and we all knew what it felt like, but it was always funny when someone else did one. We regarded belly whackers as dickheads even though we were guilty of doing some when we were little.

After several hours we'd go home. In those days the baths were open from 9:00 am to 7:30 pm, closing at 6:30 pm on a Sunday. We certainly got more than our money's worth of fun.

By late afternoon the footpaths had cooled off and we no longer had to hop step into shaded areas to keep our feet cool on the way home.

I can't remember the very first time I went to the Fitzroy baths, but it was probably when I was very young. My mother would take Lorna and me to make sure we didn't play up. I know she would never have gone in for a swim because that was not the done thing for a Macedonian mum. She would have stayed by the poolside watching us play. Going to the baths with us was one of the very few times she could get out of the fish shop and relax. My father never went there as he had neither the time nor the interest. He'd rather go to the Maco club up the road.

We almost lost the Fitzroy baths in 1994 when the City of Yarra council decided to close the 86-year-old baths for financial reasons. This caused a community uproar. A 'Save our Pool' group was quickly formed and organised thousands of locals and other pool users to march to the Brunswick Street Oval (Fitzroy footy ground) in protest. There were also mass sit-ins in the empty pool for six weeks until the decision was overturned.

I can't imagine walking past the site now and not seeing the iconic Fitzroy baths. It was the pulse of Fitzroy during the summer days of my childhood.

Up to Mischief

I settled into my old life as a Roy Boy and stayed on the right side of the law. But I still got up to a fair bit of mischief.

I remember the chewing gum game machine my parents hired from Mr Scott, who ran Burke Scales a couple of doors down from our shop. He hired out various scales and weighing machines, and lived above his shop with his wife, two sons and two daughters. We were friendly with the Scotts and Lorna and I spent one Christmas Eve there. Mr Scott was a tall bloke, with a large gut, and got on well with my dad. He was also big-hearted, looking after homeless people who slept in the front outdoor recess of his shop by taking them to the fish shop and buying them a meal.

The chewing gum machine was a sideline earner for our shop and I spent heaps of my parents' pennies playing it. I loved that machine. It measured about five feet high, two feet wide, and one foot deep. The top third of the machine had a glass pane covering a circular metal plate with several metal spikes attached to it. This circular plate could be moved clockwise or anticlockwise by turning a knob on the machine. Below the metal plate, about half a foot down, were three small metal chutes, spaced apart. I'd drop a penny into the slot located at the top right, and this would release a small steel ball above the circular plate allowing it to travel downward around the spikes. I controlled the path of the ball by turning the knob to the left or right and tried to manoeuvre it into one of the three open metal chutes below. If the ball went into a chute, I'd win a small packet of Wrigley's PK chewing gum, which was released near the base, just like a vending machine. If it missed the chute, I'd end up wasting a penny.

I won the odd chewie pack every now and again and started to wonder if there was a way I could do it without spending a penny. Breaking into the machine was not an option because it wasn't the right thing to do. Even if I had that inclination, I'd get sprung because the machine was in a public space – the fish shop. And I'd learned my lesson from my Turana days that knocking stuff off was wrong. But in my little brain I figured if the machine gave me a chewy packet for free without breaking into it, that would be okay. So, there had to be an easier and better way.

My first brainwave was to use a washer the size of a penny and insert that. It went down into the slot, but it failed to release the ball – bugger. I racked my brain for more ideas and then it hit me like a ton of bricks. I thought if the penny dropped down to release a ball maybe I could use a long wire thin enough to fit through the slot and push it down to free the ball. There was only one problem with this theory – what if the wire stuck when I pushed it down? So, I figured I would have to be very careful on my first go and not get caught with a 'smoking gun' in my hand – in this case a 'smoking wire'.

Theory was one thing, but the question was would it work? Especially when the stakes were so high – a free chewing gum packet.

Time came to test the theory. I found an old wire lying around, straightened it out and waited until Sunday when the shop was closed. I cased the joint so I could try my experiment without being sprung by Lorna or my mum. My dad had already left for the club, so I didn't have to worry about him. I grabbed my long piece of wire and excitedly approached my dream machine. I edged the wire into the slot, gently pushed it down and jiggled it so the wire would not jam. It hit the release mechanism and out came the ball. You bloody beauty! I was about to enter chewing gum heaven. All I had to do now was navigate the ball into a slot to win a chewie packet. It didn't matter if I missed a chute because I'd simply push the wire down again for another free game and repeat the process until I won.

After spending about twenty minutes on the machine, the thought occurred to me that if I won too many chewies and there were not enough pennies in the machine to justify the wins, Mr Scott would become suspicious when he emptied the penny tray below each week. I still remember the huge bunch of keys he carried around with him to empty the various machines he owned. So, I paced myself to avoid suspicion. After winning two or three chewie packs, I stopped playing and waited until the next Sunday came along to continue my splurge.

Then one day the machine was gone. I was devastated. No more free chewies. I now had to go to the milk bar and pay for them. I don't know why the machine disappeared, but perhaps

Mr Scott found it was not as profitable as it had been. So ended my reign as the kid who cracked the code and won big time. The chewing gum machine was my favourite machine of all time and now there was just empty space where it once stood.

Climbing onto roofs by myself or with my mate John was another fun, mischievous activity. One of the first roofs we climbed together on a boring Sunday afternoon was the corrugated tin roof of an automotive garage behind John's place. No one was around because it was closed, so there was little chance of getting caught. It was an easy climb because we used the end of the side garage wall, which had a gap between each brick making it an ideal ladder. Adjoining the brick wall, about halfway up from the ground, was a wooden fence enclosing a backyard of overgrown grass. The garage was about one-and-a-half storeys high and when we reached the roof, we made sure we walked on the nailed sections so our weight could be supported.

One day we decided to up the ante and see if we could get into the garage. We found a loose window at the back, near the roof, and pried it open. We slipped inside and climbed down onto the floor. There was a heavy smell of oil and grease as we wandered around, but we didn't spend much time just in case we were caught. Technically you could say it was a break and enter, but we didn't break or steal anything – we just entered and pissed off quick smart. I remember the thrill, the nervousness of being in a place where we shouldn't be, although the excitement was dampened by the smell of the place. After that experience we still climbed the garage roof on a Sunday but never again went inside. As kids we were always looking for thrills and adventures, but the inside of that garage was too smelly and boring to bother with again. And besides, if we got sprung, we would have been in big, big trouble.

Our next challenge was to climb and walk across a whole block of roofs. I'd already had a trial run by myself climbing onto the fish shop roof. Not an easy climb because I had to open my parents' second storey window, climb onto the ledge and then very carefully step to the right onto the steeply angled, sometimes slippery, tiled roof covering our spare room and bathroom. Once I had achieved that, I was ready to have a go at walking across several roofs along the block to Rose Street. However, I only managed three roofs before chickening out and coming back. Nevertheless, I was determined to succeed and convinced John to have a go with me. It wasn't practical for John to join me and climb our block. I wasn't game enough to smuggle him into my parents' bedroom and climbing to the roof from the backyard was impossible. There was always someone home and we would have been sprung.

So we decided to have a go at John's block – about twelve roofs – from Argyle Street to Kerr Street. John lived behind O'Brien's milk bar, which was the first building on the block. When no-one was around, we carefully scaled the wall at the back of O'Brien's to start our epic adventure. On the first attempt we almost made it to the butcher's shop at the end of the block but someone in an upstairs room spotted us and we hurried back. On our next try we were triumphant and felt terrific.

Sometimes on a warm night I would climb on top of the fish shop roof and sit on the ledge that separated the shop from Penders cake factory, next door. I'd sometimes put my feet up flat against our warm chimney and just sit there. It was probably one of the few times I sat still. It was very meditative and, for me, the quietest spot in Fitzroy. It was a temporary escape from the busy streets below and allowed me to be alone, to think and dream. I could stare up into a vast dark sky lit with endless stars. It was hypnotic and I would easily drift off to new imaginary adventures. Sometimes I dreamed of being Superman, gracefully flying in the night sky, occasionally twisting and turning in every direction, free and in control. When it was time to leave, I'd stand up and look around at the lights of the distant suburbs surrounding me, Carlton, North Fitzroy, Collingwood, and the city of Melbourne's buildings. Then I knew I was back in the real world.

I remember another cheeky adventure we had as kids. There was an old recycled tyre place at the end of Alexandra Parade, near where the start of the Eastern Freeway is now. A 44-gallon drum raft was chained up inside an open shed, next to the tyres. We tried to 'borrow' the raft several times by cutting through the chain with various tools, none of which worked. Our dream of sailing the Yarra in our raft never happened, though we tried like buggery to realise it. If we had been successful, we would have returned the raft to its original spot, because we weren't thieves.

I enjoyed telling jokes and watching my mates crack up with laughter. One of the most popular kids' funnies were the knock knock jokes:

'Knock, knock.'
'Who's there?'
'Boo.'
'Boo who?'
'Why are you crying?'

I also enjoyed telling other rib-ticklers. I remember visiting a schoolmate of mine who lived around the corner in Kerr Street. His mother was there and he insisted I tell his mother the joke I had told him. Well, I gave it my best shot and she smiled patiently waiting for the punchline. I can't remember the entire joke, but I do remember it was set in a church and there was a parrot involved. Finally came the punchline, a singsong from the parrot 'Sit down, sit down, for Christ's sake, the poor buggers at the back can't see.' I waited for the burst of laughter but there was silence. It was not the reaction I had expected and I froze, not knowing what to do. Then she exploded and yelled, 'Get out, Get out.' Looking back now I think she must have been very religious and my blasphemy was not acceptable. I didn't know what blasphemy meant back then and didn't understand why she'd been so angry – it was a bloody good joke. I was never invited back there again.

When I was very little I decided to 'borrow' some of the pennies in the fish shop. I grabbed a heap and placed them in a plastic bag. Once I had my bag of loot, I snuck out of the shop and ran up Brunswick Street. But just outside Tony's newsagency I dropped the bag and pennies scattered all over the footpath. I can't remember what the reactions were of people passing by as I didn't stop long enough to find out. I hurriedly gathered up all the pennies and ran back to the shop.

Another time, almost in that exact spot, I came to grief again. I was running towards Gibbs' hardware store, my flailing arms and skinny legs propelling me forward faster and faster. I ran between two men who were facing each other about six feet apart and felt a tremendous force slow me down. I had no idea what had happened and was stunned, I staggered a couple of steps forward and looked around to discover I had just run through a large sheet of glass these two men had been holding. Both eyed me in shocked disbelief. In what seemed like minutes, but was probably seconds, I realised what I'd done and sprinted away. It must have been fear and adrenalin that kicked in, as well as the thought I'd be in strife for breaking the glass panel, which was now in bits lying on the ground. I was lucky, I could have been sliced to pieces but only suffered a couple of minor cuts and bruises. I never ran past Gibbs' hardware store again; I walked and kept an eye out for invisible glass.

The evening of November 5th was the best time of year for a kid. It was Guy Fawkes night or, as we called it, cracker night. Guy was a pom who, back in the 1600s, on 5th of November, tried to blow up the English parliament and failed.

We were more successful than Guy because we blew up just about everything in sight, including our mates and ourselves. Fitzroy exploded with fireworks in various laneways, streets and reserves, as well as the median strip in Alexandra Parade. Probably the biggest bonfire was on the Smith Reserve oval behind the Fitzroy baths. People used to take all their old chairs, couches, tyres and other rubbish to throw on the bonfire. Lorna and I would join the Burkes outside their place in Argyle Street to celebrate cracker night. I'd save up my ha'pennies, pennies, thruppences, zacs and deenas so I could buy an arsenal of firecrackers from Tony's newsagency. I was very selective because I didn't have much to spend, so every penny had to count. I'd usually buy rockets, strings of small firecrackers, tom thumbs, penny bungers and sparklers.

Up to Mischief

Our bonfire was a rubbish bin placed in the laneway at the back of John's place. We would chuck our firecrackers in and watch them explode. Occasionally we'd chuck a firecracker at each other's feet, never with the intent to hurt but to get a laugh. One of my favourite tricks was to light the fuse of one and hold it in my hand for as long as possible before throwing it in the air or at someone. I did this to show off and leave little time for my intended victim to jump out of the way. Occasionally I'd mistime it and the bloody cracker would explode in my hand leaving a dirty big black powder stain, so the laugh was on me. I would never try this trick with a penny bunger, the ultimate firecracker, because if it exploded in my hand I would be blown to smithereens. Once lit, that monster was chucked as soon as possible. I loved the firecracker rocket. It was spectacular. I'd place one in an upright empty milk bottle, light the fuse and stand back. The fuse would burn quickly, ignite the cardboard packed with chemicals at the other end of the stick, and WHOOSH! Up it would fly into the night sky.

I remember one night John was standing about 30 yards away from me, across Argyle Street outside a factory, and I lit a rocket lying on the ground facing him. It whizzed over the road and hit John right in the guts. He doubled over, grabbed his stomach and groaned. For a moment I thought I had blown his guts away. I panicked and ran over to see if he was okay. What a relief it was when he said yes! It was a fantastic shot and a stupid thing to do. Injuries were not unusual when playing with firecrackers, but we only experienced minor ones. Some people weren't so lucky and serious injuries did occur, which eventually led to the ban of selling fireworks to the general public here in Victoria in 1982.

Sparklers were kind of fun but not as much as exploding firecrackers. Standing around waving a sparkler and watching the trail of light patterns was okay, but they were really a temporary distraction for a kid like me who wanted to blow things up. I remember the screams of delight from excited kids and the occasional crying or curse if a cracker exploded too close. When we ran out of crackers, we'd stand around the bonfire watching it burn to a crisp, occasionally hearing the last of the firecrackers explode in nearby streets until it was quiet. I'd then think about the fun we'd had and wished every night was cracker night.

Much less dangerous than exploding firecrackers, but just as enjoyable, was watching the late 1950s TV show *Circus Boy*, which starred a young Micky Dolenz, who later became a member of the 1960s pop group The Monkees. He played the role of Corky, who travelled with a circus. He'd ride a baby elephant called Bimbo in circus parades and played with all sorts of other animals. He mixed with the other circus folks – Joey the clown, trapeze artists, lion tamers and other performers. After watching the show, I wanted to be a circus boy and do everything that Corky did.

One day the circus did come to Fitzroy and I was absolutely rapt. What a dream! It was just down the road from where I lived. All I had to do was walk down Brunswick Street, turn right into Alexandra Parade and there it was – on a wide median strip of grass near the Fitzroy baths. I remember being inside the big tent for a show with a crowd of excited children and adults. During the show the ring master asked for volunteers to join the whip cracking demonstration. I hurriedly put my hand up, jabbing it upwards several times, just as I would if I was in school, eagerly wanting to answer a question from my teacher. At the same time a heap of other kids did the same and I was lost in a sea of arms. I was lucky enough for the ringmaster to spot me – he called me to the centre of the ring with about half a dozen other kids. We were asked to lie down next to each other while a performer cracked a whip backwards and forwards. It sounded like the repeating rifle Chuck Connors fired in the opening scene of the TV show *The Rifleman*. The whip cracker slowly edged towards us and I could hear and feel the whip get closer and closer. I tensed my body as the whip snaked over without touching our bodies before flicking back over the head of the whip cracker. The crowd gasped, thinking we would be torn to shreds and was relieved when we all jumped up smiling after the demonstration. I felt like the star of the show, just like Corky in *Circus Boy*.

I also remember being selected from the audience to ride bareback on a white horse that trotted around the circus ring. A safety harness was around my waist with a cable attached to it so, if I fell off, someone from a distance could pull the cable and I'd float upwards before being gently lowered to the ground. I was on the broad back of the horse for only a few seconds before I lost my balance and fell, finding myself suddenly hoisted up and floating through the air like a fair dinkum trapeze artist. Before I knew it, I was safely on the ground wanting more. Another kid who also volunteered to ride the horse was raised up in the air after falling and his shorts fell to his ankles. Of course, the crowd erupted in laughter. At least I'd kept my pants on.

Another thrill was jumping on a moving Brunswick Street tram foot-board and riding it for a few blocks. I'd do this at night to avoid being spotted by the driver. I'd walk from the footpath to the middle of the road as the tram approached and jump on the non-passenger board (right side). I'd then crouch down, gripping the handrail, and get off several blocks away when the tram slowed for the tram stop near the Brotherhood of St Laurence building. I'd cross the road and walk back down the street feeling terrific. After two or three separate times of tram hopping, I decided to retire because I didn't want to push my luck and get caught.

I wasn't the only cheeky bugger around getting into mischief. There were a couple of kids living near the fish shop who threw apples from their second storey bedroom into open doorways of passing trams. Lorna and her friend Joyce could be cheeky too. Lorna remembers sitting upstairs at Joyce's place, sticking their heads out of an upstairs window and calling out to guys walking by in the street, 'Hello, dreamboat.' The guy would turn around and Lorna and Joyce would then yell out, 'Not you, shipwreck!'

Boisterous, exuberant, cheekiness – that was part of being a kid in Fitzroy in those days.

Mucking About with Mates

John was my best mate and from the age of eight we hung out together most days of the week.

During the summer, we played cricket in a bluestone-cobbled laneway at the back of his place, the best place for cricket during those hot summer days. It was shaded, cooler and close to home. We rarely played on a field because we didn't want to get our brains fried by the bloody hot sun. We used an old, up-ended wooden crate as our wicket at the Argyle Street end of the lane, between John's place and the side brick wall of an automotive business I called the garage. Our bat was a flat piece of board with a crudely carved handle. A proper bat would come much later, when we could afford one. We used a tennis ball for our cricket ball, which soon lost all its fluff bouncing off walls and cobblestones. We measured a 22-foot pitch by taking ten to twelve long strides, the length of the garage wall.

It was difficult to bowl a straight ball because of the uneven cobblestones, and I avoided full tosses because John could whack the ball over my head forcing me to run down the lane

Clowning around in front of our fish shop while John holds me up. My mother is in the background. About 1965.

to retrieve it. By that time, he'd make three or four runs – utter misery for an average bowler like me.

The rules of laneway cricket followed the rules of normal cricket except for two additions. If the ball was edged or flew past the batsman into or over Argyle Street, it was a no ball. Occasionally it would travel across Argyle Street, but I don't think we ever hit a passing car. The other rule we added was that a batsman would be out if the bowler caught the ball one handed after it bounced off the wall. I loved batting. It felt so good to whack the ball past John to make a run or two. It was an even better feeling when I smashed it over his head and down the lane. Though on the other hand, it was a crappy feeling when he did the same to me, 'Ya bastard!' I liked the sound of my own voice, particularly the phrase, 'You're out!' Bowling was okay because I was always one ball away from getting John out. The longer he stayed in, the more it frustrated me because I got hotter and wearier, but when I bowled or caught him out it was brilliant because it was now his turn to chase the bloody ball.

Laneway cricket was terrific and so was playing footy. During the football season we played kick-to-kick footy in Argyle Street. Without money to buy a fair dinkum Sherrin football we had to improvise, just like we had to for cricket. So, we made footballs out of strips of newspapers rolled up together and bound by a thick rubber band. We'd kick the crap out of the one-foot-long paper football until shredded bits flew into the air and settled on the ground, just like the aftermath of streamers chucked onto a real footy ground by supporters. Once our footy had shrunk to a few bits of paper loosely held together, it was time to make another one. Usually it was just the two of us playing, but sometimes other kids would join in. Running, leaping behind the pack, and taking a speccy over my mate was terrific. Though that feeling could sometimes turn into terror if I mistimed my leap, was bumped while in the air and failed to catch the footy – I'd hit the asphalt ground with a dull thud.

After countless paper footballs were shredded, we bought a brown plastic football. They were much cheaper than a real leather football and lasted longer than the paper version. The plastic ball was fantastic, it looked like a real football though was almost weightless in comparison. We kicked the bloody thing until it too wore out like the paper ones. It ended up with dents on all sides so was useless as a footy. We went through quite a few plastic ones in a season.

A few years later, as young teenagers, we got hold of a fair dinkum leather football. I can't remember who bought it, or if it was a brand spanking new Sherrin football like the Victorian Football League used in matches. More than likely, it was a used leather footy because we probably didn't have enough money to pay for a new one. Our leather football was ideal for playing Aussie rules 'three goals in' on Smith Reserve at the back of the Fitzroy baths. The fair dinkum football didn't fall apart like paper ones and could travel further and higher than plastic balls. The game was easy to play on any size field and only involved three players, a footy and two jumpers spread about ten feet apart for goal posts. As in a real game, the full forward and full back would line up in front of the goals. A third player, about forty feet away, would start the game by kicking the ball to the full forward, the full back would stick to the full forward and try to win possession of the ball. The rules of football applied: if the full forward marked the ball he could go back and kick the ball without interference; the full back could mark, tap the ball away or legally tackle the full forward. The play ended if the full forward was tackled and penalised for holding the ball, dispossessed of the ball or failed to kick a goal. Players were rotated to different positions after each game. I preferred playing full forward because if I kicked it in to start the game, I'd end up standing there like a stale bottle of piss while the full forward and full back battled it out. Playing full back was my least favourite position because I had to chase the full forward all over the place to stop him. Though it was fun yelling 'Chewie on your boot' to distract the full forward from kicking a goal after a mark, and very satisfying when I tackled the bugger dumping him to the ground. We'd spend at least a couple of hours in the park playing 'three goals in' before leaving exhausted but exhilarated.

Aussie rules was the best. Another mate of mine introduced me to American gridiron football when I was a teenager. We played on the median strip in front of the Fitzroy baths, but the novelty wore off quickly. There was a fair bit of running and throwing, but I preferred to kick the bloody ball as much as possible.

John and I also played street tennis against a factory wall in Argyle Street. We'd whack the ball in turn with our old wooden tennis racquets. The strings occasionally had to be adjusted back into position after a few whacks of the ball. Sometimes we played tennis at the Exhibition Gardens, where there were two outdoor courts. The racquets we hired there had half of the strings missing so when we'd hit the ball hard it would go through them.

As well as playing various games together, we joined Saint Mark's Cubs, a junior section of the Scouts. It met in the evening at Saint Mark's Anglican Church hall in George Street, Fitzroy. I was nine years old and excited to be involved. I was proud of my uniform – a green cap, shirt top, shorts, a loose necktie secured with a large buckle, long socks and black shoes. It must have been a relief for my mother that I'd dress myself in the uniform. When we went to functions, she'd try to force me to stand in front of the kitchen mirror so she could comb my hair and tidy me up, but for Cubs I'd comb my hair properly, dress and transform myself from a scruffy-looking kid. I had to because I didn't want to be hauled over the coals by a Cub leader for being untidy. After I had dressed, I'd walk out of the fish shop and the occasional adult nearby would smile at me. I felt special wearing my uniform. I was no longer a street kid – I was a Cub.

When I stepped into the church hall, I became part of another world. A world of games, ropes, salutes, reef and granny knots, badges, greetings, fellow Cubs, leaders and friendly discipline. I learned the curious Cub saying of 'dib, dib, dib, dob, dob, dob'. Someone would say, 'Dib, dib, dib which meant, 'do your best' and we'd reply, 'Dob, dob, dob, which meant, 'we'll do our best.' One activity I enjoyed involved trying to navigate blindfolded through a bunch of others lying spread out on the floor. Another Cub would call out instructions to help guide me around the obstacles.

I also enjoyed saluting and I still remember the difference between a Cub salute and a Scout salute. Cubs used two fingers, forefinger and middle finger either apart or together with the thumb over the two remaining bent fingers. The

Scout salute used the first three fingers. As a new member, I'd salute the higher ranked Cubs, such as a first sixer, who had two yellow stripes on his upper-arm sleeve, and would salute a second sixer, who had one yellow stripe. And, of course, I saluted adult leaders. The only other salutes I knew about before I joined Cubs were two versions of a two-finger upward salute that said 'get stuffed.' I'd just raise my hand up or if someone was really being a pain, move my arm in a huge semi-circle so two fingers ended up above my head. The other salute on the street was the middle finger salute, which said 'up yours'. This too could be done with a short or a huge semi-circle gesture. The range of motion all depended how mad I was at the person who had just upset me. But I never used those 'salutes' at Cubs.

Over the two years I was there, I worked my way up to a one-stripe second sixer rank, of which I was very proud. John achieved one more stripe than me and became a sixer. I remember one night another school classmate of mine attended. It was his first and only session. He didn't like taking orders and when a sixer gave him an order and pulled rank by saying, 'I'm a sixer!' his reply was, 'I'll knock you for a six!'

The Cubs held a bob-a-job week as a way of earning money. Cubs would knock on doors and asked for a job for a bob, which was a shilling in those days. I remember in 1961 I washed windows for a bob. Though if I was asked to wash windows at home, I'd try to get out of it. That bob made all the difference in the world to me – more pocket money meant more lollies I could buy.

About the age of ten it was time to leave the Cubs and that was the end of my 'dib, dib, dib, dob, dob, dob' days. I did join the Scouts after Cubs for a very brief time but lost interest and left.

After our Cub days, John and I were still as thick as thieves. We continued to hang out together and had many more shared adventures. Some of these involved a shared passion for billy carts. We were proud of our first wooden one because we'd built it from scratch in John's backyard. It wasn't the bee's knees of billy carts, but it was ours and that's all that mattered. It was made from an old fruit crate that could fit one kid, providing he kept his knees scrunched up close to his chest. The crate was attached to a central plank of wood that we scavenged from somewhere. Two short pieces of wood served as axles attached to the central plank. For steering we used a rough rope, tied to each end of the front axle. Attached to this axle were two small steel ball bearing wheels, about four inches in diameter, with two more attached to the fixed short plank under the back of the cart. We shaved just enough off the ends of the axles so the ball bearing wheel could slide on, then secured it by hammering a nail into the wood on the outside of the wheel. We'd bought the ball bearing wheels from Gibbs' hardware store around the corner with the few coins we had. We didn't use pram wheels like some kids, who were either richer than we were or had knocked off the wheels. Apart from the wheels, all the other bits used to secure various parts together, including nuts, bolts and washers, were scrounged from junk in the backyard. Nails were pulled out of pieces of old wood that were lying around and straightened out to be reused. There were no brakes fitted and the only ways to stop were to crash, come to a natural stop or have your mate hold onto the cart.

In our first attempt to build a billy cart we had nailed the front axle onto the centre plank but discovered you couldn't steer. Jeez, now what? I couldn't figure it out because I was never mechanically minded and building things bored me. It was only the end result that interested me. John, or perhaps his father, solved our problem. We drilled a hole into the middle of the front axle and centre plank and placed a bolt through both pieces, securing it with a nut and washers. We allowed some free play in fastening the two pieces of wood so the axle could move left or right by pulling the rope attached to either side of the axle. Terrific! We now had our own fair dinkum billy cart that wouldn't travel only in a straight line.

Once we finished our rough masterpiece, we excitedly carried it for the first time to our racetrack – Argyle Street. I jumped into the billy cart, grabbed the rope and was raring to go. John pushed as hard as he could, propelling it forward. He jumped on the step board behind me, and we both rocketed down the street. Each time the cart slowed, he'd jump off, push, and jump back on again. The ball bearing wheels sounded like a jet engine as they spun along the road, leaving a trail of scratches. We both had turns pushing or riding and for the next few hours nothing existed but us, the billy cart and Argyle Street. Darkness and John's mum calling him in for tea put an end to our fun for the day. The next day, we were back at it again – and for many days afterwards.

We would speed up and down Argyle Street almost as fast as Jack Brabham, a champion racing car driver, and I reckon we had more crashes than Jack ever did. Crashing the billy cart into the gutter or wall was almost as good as speeding. A bit of mayhem every now and again was great fun. Sometimes after crashing the cart, we would need to be patched up from the odd cut or bruise. When speeding along the road the only thing we would give way to would be an oncoming car. These huge metal vehicles were scary when they came straight at you so to avoid being run over you either swerved or crashed the billy cart into the gutter. Thankfully, this didn't happen very often, as Argyle Street was narrower and quieter compared with busy Brunswick Street around the corner. Though on a Sunday we did play with our cart on Brunswick Street's smooth footpath when there was hardly anyone around. We never ventured more than a block away from John's place, where the cart was stored. This was more convenient than storing it at my place, and his side street was also far less busy than mine in Kerr Street.

Eventually we outgrew our billy cart and graduated to tearing around the streets on our bicycles. But I missed those billy cart days because it was so much fun.

Though I knocked around with John most of the time there were other friends as well. Daryl was a kid I met at George Street Primary School, where we were together in both first and third grades. I remember when I was invited for tea one evening by his parents who lived in George Street, near the Fitzroy baths. As a guest I had the choice of which TV show we'd watch after dinner. Well, my nine-year old brain automatically selected 'Superman', one of my favourite TV series. A big mistake because Daryl's teenage brother wanted to watch the rock n roll singer Johnny O'Keefe's show. I'm not sure whether, at that time, the show was called 'Six O'Clock Rock', which ended in mid-1961, or 'The Johnny O'Keefe Show'. Ironically, much later, I became a great fan of Johnny O'Keefe and I'm still a fan of the 1950s Superman series. Daryl's brother fumed quietly and I couldn't work out why he was upset. I didn't think much of it at the time and settled in to watch 'Superman'. A few days later Daryl and I were mucking about in his backyard when suddenly, an arrow whooshed by us. We both looked up and there was Daryl's brother standing on the roof, laughing and about to launch another arrow at us. We quickly ducked for cover behind a 44-gallon drum and the next arrow bounced off the drum. We weren't going to take any chances because the arrows he was firing were fair dinkum and not those rubber suction tipped arrows you buy in toy shops. I'm not sure why he was carrying on – it may have been revenge for missing out on watching Johnny O' Keefe, or maybe he was just acting like a dickhead.

I also remember Barry, another mate of mine who was in third grade with me. His sister Cheryl was a year older and a friend of Lorna's – they were also in the same grade together. Barry lived across the road from the fish shop and one of the memories I have of him involved tin can phones. I remember learning how to make a telephone by joining two empty tin cans together with a piece of string. I scrounged around the backyard and found two empty Rosella soup cans, cleaned them up and removed the labels so they would look half decent. I punctured a small hole in the centre of the base of each can and threaded a long string through each hole, tying a slip knot on each end of the string so it would stay secured.

Then the fun began.

Barry and I would hold our tin cans up, making sure the string was taut. I would speak into the open end of my tin can, so the sound wave travelled along the string and Barry could hear me by holding his open-ended can to his ear. So we had our tin can telephone. What a beauty! We could make as many calls as we liked without spending a zac at the local post office telephone booths. Our phone had the added advantage of no timed calls, which cost extra once you talked over a certain time limit. We could gasbag for ever and not worry about being cut off.

The first time we made a call to each other was grouse.

'G'day Barry.'

'G'day. Chris.'

'Watcha doing?'

'Ah, nothing much.'

We often had that same conversation without the tin phones of course but talking into these was exciting and made all the difference in the world.

One day I had the bright idea of connecting the phones between our homes, from our second storey rooms across Brunswick Street. I thought it would be great to pick up a tin can phone and speak to Barry whenever I felt like it. I couldn't do that back then because we didn't own a real phone. It would be about another 25 years before my parents agreed to install a phone in the shop – after they retired. The first part of my grand plan was fairly easy. Barry would hold onto one of the tin-can phones in his room and toss the other end down to me on the footpath where I'd be waiting, then he'd secure the phone in his room, run downstairs, and join me. We'd both then walk across the road to the front of the shop. I'd run upstairs, open the window and Barry could throw the phone up to me. He'd have to stand in the gutter so he could throw the tin can up over the awning, a decent toss! This couldn't be done from Monday to Saturday because it was too busy with people and traffic. It had to be a Sunday.

However, after working all that out, in theory at least, the next part of the plan completely stumped my brain. Once we managed to pull the string taut from our window, I couldn't figure out how to avoid tangling the string in the overhead electric cables that powered the Brunswick Street trams and the lines that provided electricity for the building, I couldn't solve the problem and so eventually had to resign myself to the fact it would be impossible to use our tin can phones between our buildings to make long distance calls. I'd just have to enjoy a short distance call with Barry from ten feet. As a kid I hated reality when it interfered with my dreams. I still do.

Another kid who I mucked about with was John W, who lived with his father around the corner in a rundown boarding house. One day I bumped into him and his dad outside Frank Dempsey's butcher shop. His father was probably around forty to fifty years, unshaven, slightly stooped, and about five feet eight in height. He had a shambolic presence and I remember his smile and kind eyes, but his boozy breath was enough to make me keep my distance. He was rather drunk. We chatted as I held a small wind-up music box that played 'Waltzing Matilda'. It was my prized possession and still is. The outside casing consisted of an aluminium-plated front, secured to a wooden backing board by two screws. A three-inch narrow tubular shaft extended from the back, attached to which was a triangular metal piece making a handle. Turning the triangular piece rotated the shaft and thereby wound the internal mechanism, ready to play. Inscribed on the inner casing over the spring motor were the words 'Made in Switzerland Thorens'. The music box is now over sixty years old. When John's father saw my music box his eyes lit up and he wanted to trade it for a sealed plastic camera he had with him. He was determined to convince me, but I held out and refused – a wise decision for an eight-year-old kid who thought the music box was more fun than a camera. It's in pieces now, with the casing and screws rusted, the backing board intact, the triangular handle missing, and the shaft of the handle jammed. But the internal mechanics are still functional, and it still plays. Just looking at it makes me smile because it's a happy connection to my childhood. I loved the sound of 'Waltzing Matilda' and would often play with the music box.

We had few possessions and bugger-all money during the 1950s and 1960s, just like most other kids and adults I knew.

But I had one of the most important things that made me happy – mates.

The Yabby Adventure

Another delight of my childhood was the excitement of catching yabbies with my mate John at the Exhibition Gardens during summer school holidays. It didn't cost us a penny. The Gardens were several blocks from home and inside them was the majestic Royal Exhibition Building, built in the 1880s, the site of our first Federal Parliament on 9th May, 1901[20].

Yabbies are tiny, brown, freshwater crayfish with two front pincher claws the size of their bodies. The ones we caught varied in size from littlies to biggies the size of my hand. We always got heaps and gave them away to John's parents and friends to eat. I never ate them because they were nowhere near as tasty as the expensive crayfish in our fish shop and I was also put off when they were chucked into boiling water alive to cook. I always politely refused to eat one – I was only interested in the thrill of catching them.

---

20 Parliament of Australia – No.2 – The Opening of Parliament – July 2019

We would walk along Argyle Street and turn left into busy Nicholson Street, which separates Fitzroy from Carlton. We'd go about three blocks then cross Johnston Street at the lights passing the Tankerville Arms pub, which is now considered a prime real estate location. About five years ago it was listed for sale and expected to fetch at least twenty million dollars[21]. But I reckon any pub in Fitzroy in those days was considered prime real estate by the many drinkers, boozers and winos who regarded the place as either a second home, hallowed ground, or a temporary male refuge from the missus and the kids.

A couple of blocks up the road I could feel the presence of a house called The Raven and I'd nervously cross the road to the other side with John rather than walk past it. The Raven, a name carved into stone high up in front of the house, was the residence of someone to be avoided. On one of our yabby trips we had found what we thought was a stray dog roaming the streets near The Raven. It was a very friendly black dog, so we gave it a few pats and checked its tag for an address. We decided to do the right thing and return the dog to its owner. I had called, 'Here boy, come on,' and the dog followed us back to The Raven. I knocked on the door, which was opened by a short, dark-haired old bloke who just stared at us.

I said, 'Mister, we found your dog.'

To our surprise the bloke abused the hell out of us, grabbed the dog and slammed the door in our faces. We stood there shocked for a moment before we walked away.

I said, 'What a bastard.'

---

[21] Adrian Ballantyne - Realcommercial.com.au - $20m-plus asking price for Fitzroy's Tankerville Arms Hotel – 6 September 2017

'Yeah, a fucking ratbag.'

After that episode I never walked past The Raven again – I always crossed the road. Even today when I see the word 'raven', I usually think about what happened back then.

One memorable yabby day we caught more than we bargained for. It started out as a normal day. I met John in the laneway at the back of his joint about 9:00 am and we checked all our equipment – a ball of string, a pocketknife, small bits of meat wrapped in a newspaper, net, a large metal ice-cream container, and sandwiches wrapped in a brown paper bag. I also checked to make sure I had a zac so I could buy a soft drink at a garage near the edge of the gardens on the way home. Drinking the icy-cold bottle of Passiona or lemon squash was a huge relief after a hot, busy day of yabbying. But this day we never made it to the garage.

We continued walking along Nicholson Street and saw the edge of the Exhibition Gardens about three blocks away. We tried to stay in the shade to escape the sun without much success. The ground, our feet and our bodies were hot. It was a relief to cross the road and finally escape the oppressive heat as we entered the edge of the green oasis, the Exhibition Gardens.

The temperature quickly dropped to bearable and gave us enough energy to play on the old, low concrete wall that formed an almost unbroken border between the gardens and footpath, all the way up past the Exhibition Building to the corner of Victoria Parade, five blocks away. We jumped on top of the wall, which was about two-feet high and quite narrow – it had just enough room to stand on. We stuck our arms out to balance ourselves and it felt like being on a high wire in a circus, except this was only two feet off the ground.

Occasionally we'd nudge each other until one of us fell off, then jump back on to continue the game. Sometimes the nudge would become a full push, but the rough housing was usually fun; it was all part of the game.

We finally edged past the tennis courts, which were surrounded by trees, and walked towards an open area that revealed the Royal Exhibition Building and the eighteen-foot-high French fountain of three semi naked children, each supporting a dolphin over their heads and, above them, three cupped scallop shells.[22]

Straight ahead was the big yabby pond, overlooked on the right by a much larger fountain, the Exhibition fountain, which was thirty-three feet high and three tiered, with large half-human figures, boys in various poses, fish, fauna and flowers carved into the structure.[23] The pond was rimmed by a narrow concrete path and had a small island in the middle. Nearby, adults, children, prams, and dogs were roaming along. A wino sat under a tree, sipping from a bottle of booze partially covered by a wrinkled brown paper bag. There were other kids yabbying so we hurried to our favourite spot where we caught most of our yabbies – the sunny spot nearest the Exhibition Building.

We dropped our bag on the ground, knelt, scooped up some water into our clasped hands and threw it over our faces and

---

22 City of Melbourne – The three historical fountains of Carlton Gardens. https://tomelbourne.com.au/historical-fountains-carlton-gardens/
23 I was sure this fountain was in front of the building. However, when I walked around the building during my research I discovered the fountain was to the side. On this occasion my memory failed me, although most of the time I found it has been accurate.

heads to cool down. Jeez that felt good. I grabbed the ice-cream container and partially filled it with water to keep the caught yabbies alive until we got home. John cut two four-foot lengths of string, firmly tied a small bit of meat at the end of each one and handed me a baited line. I placed the net between us so we could both quickly reach it when we hooked a yabby. Our original net was made of old pantyhose with a knot tied at one end to stop a yabby from falling through. The frame and handle were made from a wire clothes hanger. On this day I had brought along an old wire fish-and-chip basket my father had used in the shop, the equivalent of going from the stone age to space age in net technology.

I cast my line into the pond about three feet away from the edge to avoid the crevices below where a yabby sheltered. A line near a crevice was a home delivery meal for a yabby – it would just reach out and eat the meat. The only way I could stop the little bugger from eating all my meat was to pull the line forward and upward, but it would let go and swim back to safety because no self-respecting yabby likes to be jerked around. Once I cast my line the correct distance I waited until I felt a slight tug, which meant one had grabbed the meat. I raised the line slowly to the surface, reached for the net and swooped it under the yabby. Gotcha! The netted creature was dropped into the ice-cream container with the rest of its mates. I remember once I missed the container and it dropped to the ground, I picked it up with my hand and it reached back with its huge claws and clamped onto my fingers. 'Fuckin hell, bastard, ow, ow!' It took a while and a lot of pain before I could shake it off. After that experience I learned the best way to pick up a yabby safely was to place my thumb and forefinger behind its claws so it couldn't reach back. Once bitten twice shy.

When we had caught a few, it was time to wander over to the small pond where the giant yabbies lived. And that's when things really started to happen in a way that was unexpected and dangerous. The smaller pond down the end of the gardens was fenced in to stop kids like us from yabbying there. The area had large overhanging tree branches nearby stopping most of the sunlight and giving it a remote 'no man's land' feeling, which was terrific. It too had a small island and a stone arched bridge. We looked around to make sure we were not sprung by the park keeper, scrambled over the fence and set up our gear near a small concrete block on the edge of the pool. This was big time yabbying and not for faint hearts or amateurs. We had the guts and the right equipment to have another go at a monster yabby I called Claw. We could never catch it because it had out-thought us every time we tried. That pissed me off and I was determined to catch him this time.

Claw had only one claw and was built like a brick shit house. I remember the first time I tried to catch him. I had him hooked and slowly raised the string until there he was near the surface, I yelled, 'Fuck, fuck. fuck' – he was huge. Before I could net him, he let go and disappeared into the deep. I was left with a piece of dangling string that had shredded meat hanging off the other end. I yelled, 'You, bastard! I'll get you next time.'

On this particular day, we cast our lines and caught some little yabbies. After a couple of hours waiting for the big catch, John spotted a large 'goldfish' swimming under the stone arched bridge.

'Jeez, look at the goldfish. Let's catch it.'

Claw would have to wait. I followed John, who carried our yabby gear, wading through the three-foot-deep water to the island. I didn't muck about and waded very quickly because I was now in Claw territory, his home turf, and knew that he could bite my leg off if he had the chance to do so. We climbed onto the island and positioned ourselves over the bridge under which the big goldfish swam several times, while we tried to figure out how to catch him. A piece of string with meat was useless as fish didn't eat meat. John got the bright idea of tying some of the bread, left over from one of our sandwiches, onto the end of the string to see what would happen. He lowered the piece of string with the bread attached and waited until the fish swam by again. He was half hanging off the arched bridge, one arm around it and one arm holding the line. The fish swam by several times but ignored the bait. Just as we were about to give up it circled around again and bit the bread; John quickly pulled up the line with the fish attached and I swooped the net under it to catch it.

'You beauty! We got him! We got him!'

John grabbed the ice-cream container, opened the lid and scooped some more water into it so our prized catch could swim around. The little yabbies remained in the tin. I gently lowered the fish into the container and secured the lid so it couldn't jump out. It was one of our best ever yabby days. We'd caught several yabbies and a fish. We reckoned nobody had ever caught a fish before in this small pond and were absolutely rapt.

We waded back to the mainland and were about to go when I said, 'Let's see if we can catch Claw one more time.'

'No, come on, we've got enough.'
'Just one more go, it won't take long, come on.'
'Oh, orr right.'

I crouched down on the ground near where I had almost caught Claw previously and tied a fresh piece of meat on the end of the string. I lowered the line into the water and waited. It didn't take long. I felt a tug on the line and tried to lift it. It felt incredibly heavy, and I knew it was Claw. You could tell what size a yabby was when you felt a tug and raised the string. And this time the weight felt like lifting a ton of bricks. I was confident I had Claw and would make no mistake this time in landing this giant yabby. After what seemed like a lifetime, I could see him as he surfaced attached to the meat. 'Gotcha now ya bastard.' I grabbed the basket with my right hand as I continued to pull the string upward. In one quick swoop I came in under him and trapped him in the basket. And there he was. Claw. The biggest yabby on the planet. I held the basket up in air in triumph and John yelled, 'You got him, you got him!'

'Yeah, yeah, I knew I'd catch the bugger. Now he's all ours. What a beauty!'

After we had congratulated ourselves on the catch of the century, we realised there was no place to put Claw. We couldn't put him in the container because the fish was already in there and we had no other container with us. There was no way I'd throw him back into the pond. We desperately searched for another container lying around that we could use to keep it alive. We could find nothing suitable nearby, so we grabbed our gear, climbed the fence and started to search the park.

Finally, 'Look, over there, let's put him in that.'

I'd found an empty beer bottle and picked it up by the neck, holding it between my thumb and fingers. I figured if I could break the neck of the bottle, we'd have an ideal container to store Claw until we got home. It was a great idea but the execution of it was pretty dumb even for a ten-year-old like me. I smashed the bottle against a nearby rock and it shattered in my hand cutting the side of my thumb, forefinger, and the webbing between them.

'Ow, ow, ow, you fuckin bastard, shit, bastard!'

I jumped up and shook my hand in pain with blood gushing out in every direction onto my shirt, shorts and the ground. John just stood there in shock watching me carry on with pain. There was nothing he could do. I covered my gaping wound with my other hand trying to stop the bleeding. That didn't help much, so I took out my hanky and used it as a rough bandage to help stem the flow of blood. I knew this was serious. I had nicked a finger before with a pocketknife and that had hurt. But this was a much deeper, throbbing, stabbing pain – real intense pain that kept going and going. I had to get help, but home was too far away. I realised our family doctor was just down the road towards the end of Gertrude Street and said, 'Come on, I'm going to the doctor's, let's go.' John collected our gear and the ice-cream container, and we hurriedly walked through the park towards Gertrude Street. In all the drama, we didn't realise until much later that we had left Claw behind.

The walk to the doctor's clinic took forever. Longer than forever because I was in extreme pain. We finally reached his surgery and I knocked on the door. There was no way I was going to wait in the waiting room and bleed to death. Bugger that. The door opened and there stood Dr Bartak.

'I cut my hand can you fix it?'

He unwrapped the handkerchief and had a quick look at my mortal wound. Too quick for my liking. 'Hmm, go to the hospital and they will fix it up.' He closed the door.

I was stunned! I was dying and here he was telling me to go to hospital.

We hurriedly left the surgery and walked towards St Vincent's Hospital, up Brunswick Street turning right into Victoria Parade. Another forever walk, punctuated by throbbing pain from my wounds. We arrived in Casualty, where I went straight to the receptionist expecting someone to fix my hand immediately.

She took out a form and asked, 'Name, address, contact details ...'

I thought, 'For fuck's sake. I'm bleeding to death, get someone to fix it.'

I gave her my details and soon after that a doctor led me to a curtained off cubicle. It wasn't soon enough for me.

'What have you done to yourself?'

'Jeezus,' I thought, 'can't you see the bleeding obvious? I've cut my hand off.'

But instead, I said, 'I cut myself.'

He unwrapped the handkerchief, checked the wound, asked me to lie down on the bed and placed a board underneath my outstretched arm. He cleaned the wound and sprayed some freezing stuff over it until it was numb. He stitched up my thumb, webbing, and forefinger, and bandaged the wound, which now looked clean compared with my bloody hanky.

I walked out of the cubicle to the waiting room where John was sitting on a chair holding the ice-cream container, the fish noisily splashing around trying to get out.

It was quite a day. We'd certainly had enough adventure for one yabby expedition and walked down Brunswick Street to the fish shop. I can't remember explaining to my parents how I had cut my hand, but I reckon I didn't tell the full story. I probably said, 'I cut myself with a knife but it's okay now.' The less I said, the less trouble I'd be in. We offered the fish to my old man, but he said, 'No, it's a carp. Throw it out.' John took the fish home, but his dad said, 'Put it back!' and he had to walk all the way back to the pond. What a mongrel way to end the day. We lost our fish and to top it off we had lost the catch of a lifetime, Claw.

I never saw Claw again and still wonder how he ended up. I hope he managed to crawl back into the pond and have a good life – he deserved it.

Roy Boy Antenna

Roaming around the streets of Fitzroy as a kid helped develop my Roy Boy antenna for danger. After several close calls I could usually feel if the environment or people around me were not quite right, and would take evasive action.

One of those earlier close calls happened when I was about nine or ten years old. I remember one evening a stranger approached me in Brunswick Street, just across the road from our fish shop. He seemed friendly and asked me questions as we walked towards Rose Street, about half a block away. He offered me an ice-cream and gave me money to buy two from the milk bar across the road. I bought two, returned and gave him one, after which we continued to walk along the footpath eating our ice-creams and chatting away.

Several blocks away from home, we crossed Alexandra Parade and kept walking up past the Fitzroy football ground. I felt safe because I thought he was a friendly chap and, besides, he'd bought me an ice-cream. Past the footy ground he turned, and I followed him into the Edinburgh Gardens. It was poorly lit – a place I normally would not enter at night.

We walked further into the park where it became even darker as we moved off the pathway.

He said, 'Let's sit down there on the grass.'

I said, 'Okay.'

So, we sat near each other in the dark and talked some more until I felt his hand rest on my thigh. Within seconds I jumped up and ran away across the gardens while hearing him yell, 'Don't go.' I kept running, not looking around. Somehow, I had the presence of mind not to run in the direction we had walked just in case he decided to follow me home. I ran about thirty-eight blocks at full speed without looking back until I reached home safely.

I never told anyone about what had happened. These days this bloke would be classified as a paedophile, but back then he was considered a 'funny old man', funny meaning weird. As kids we were warned about staying away from them, but for some reason I hadn't heeded that warning. Maybe it was because I had no idea what a funny old man was until that experience, but I learned quickly.

About three or four years later I was sitting in the Athenaeum Theatre in town on a Saturday afternoon waiting for a movie to start. There were only a few people scattered in seats across the theatre when a man walked in and sat beside me. The lights dimmed and the movie started. I was totally immersed in watching the film, when I suddenly felt a hand on my thigh. It was that bloke's hand. At first, I froze, but managed to gather my senses and grabbed his hand, wrenching it off me. I can't remember if he got up and left or I did, but either way there was quickly a distance between us. That was the second time a 'funny old man' tried to grope me. After that experience my Fitzroy antenna was even more finely attuned to possible dangers in confined spaces when people were around.

Even now, when I go into a theatre, I automatically scan the area, the seat I'm heading towards and the people sitting nearby. It's not because I'm fearful; it's just a wariness I have. When it feels right, I can relax. On the rare occasion when I feel a person or a group is not quite right, I use my peripheral vision every now and again to keep a check.

I wasn't the only kid who experienced this sort of attention. Lorna told me when she was about nine years old, a car pulled up near her as she was walking along a footpath in busy Brunswick Street, about a block away from home. The man inside the car offered to take her home but Lorna refused and kept walking.

Another close call happened to both of us at the back of the fish shop. Lorna and I were heading into the laneway, and I had just closed our six-foot high wooden door behind me when, suddenly, a drunk appeared. He was almost within arm's reach and had us cornered. We couldn't move backwards because the door was closed and there wasn't enough space around him to escape. The two of us froze. I could smell his boozy breath as he hovered over us, unsteady on his feet, I looked down and saw him holding his exposed dick, and mumbling, 'Cut it off, cut it off, it's useless.'

I didn't know what to do but, after what seemed like forever, I said, 'I'll go and get some scissors.' He seemed to accept that, which gave me the opportunity to run back inside, grab the scissors and return to where Lorna and the drunk were standing. I remember moving the scissors closer to his dick but stopping my hand in mid-air. After a moment or two

Lorna and I somehow managed to escape by running back inside and slamming the door shut behind us. I have no idea or memory of why I didn't raise the alarm and tell my parents – maybe I was just a little kid obeying an adult, even though this adult was pissed out of his mind.

I was always wary of drunks in Fitzroy. They were all over the place. Perhaps I'm exaggerating a little because I lived next door to a pub and only one block away from another pub. There were several others spread out along Brunswick Street between Alexandra Parade and Gertrude Street as well as on other main streets and side streets. Two of the roughest in Fitzroy were the Champion and the Rob Roy, on the corners of Brunswick Street and Gertrude Street. They were diagonally opposite each other. Gertrude Street had a history of being rough, though I wasn't aware of it when I was a kid. There were at least a dozen pubs in Fitzroy, heaps for the smallest suburb in Melbourne. It was heaven if you were a drinker or a boozer. But not for me. I had nothing against alcohol but hated what excessive drinking could do to normal, rational people. It could turn them into abusive or violent ratbags.

There was no better example of excessive drinking in those days than the six-o-clock swill, a slang term used to describe a law stopping a publican from selling alcohol after 6:00 pm. The law in Victoria was introduced in 1916 and repealed in 1966. It was designed to encourage working men, who usually knocked off from work at 5:00 pm, to go home instead of spending the evening in a pub. What happened was that, just before closing time at 6:00 pm, some blokes would line up several beers and scull them one after the other. Many would stagger out of the pub half or fully pissed. The odd drunk would stumble into the fish shop and incoherently order fish and chips from my mum and dad. He'd lean on the counter so he wouldn't topple over, reaching into his pockets for loose change to pay for the order. He'd stare at the coins in his hands for a long time trying to figure out how much he was handing over. My parents would often have to count the money as it took ages for him to do so.

There were all sorts of drunks stumbling around in the streets day and night, some aggressive, some comical and some just trying to stay upright and protect their most prized possession – a bottle of booze wrapped in a brown paper bag. I rarely felt threatened because I was quick footed and could dodge around them if they came too close. Only one of them scared me, Jim the drunk. He was a drinking mate of my dad's and was aggressive when drunk, even though quiet when sober. He'd have a regular beer with my dad in the working area of the fish shop. I rarely ever saw him sober.

I was always wary of Jim after the day I bumped into him outside the Evelyn Hotel in Kerr Street. He was unsteady on his feet and had a sullen expression. He saw me walking towards him, carrying a toy bow and arrow, and he bailed me up. I can't remember what he said but I do remember his nasty tone of voice. I simply answered his stirs and waited patiently until he eventually staggered on home. My mum told me later he would just sit in bed, smoking and drinking all day. After closing time, from our living room I sometimes heard noisy drunks and peered out of the window to watch them. I'd make sure I was behind a curtain in case they looked up and spotted me. Their cursing and carrying on was sometimes frightening.

Even today my Roy Boy antenna kicks in when I walk past a pub or inside one for a meal. I rarely go to pubs by choice because I don't feel entirely comfortable when booze and blokes are around. Almost the only time I go to a pub is when invited to join friends for a meal or when I'm travelling and it's the only option for a good feed.

Another thing I think has fuelled my aversion to pubs is an incident that happened when I was about twenty. I was outside the fish shop cleaning my CB 175 Honda motorcycle and an eleven-year-old kid I knew from the youth basketball group at St Brigid's in North Fitzroy stopped to have a chat. A few days later he was shot dead in a pub. According to a newspaper story at the time, his father had ordered fish and chips at our fish shop one evening and decided to go for a walk with his two sons to the Moonee Valley Hotel across the road to buy drinks for his friends. While there, they were having a drink themselves when a man burst in firing a gun at another man. The shots not only killed the intended victim, but stray bullets also killed the young boy and wounded his father and another man close by. The pub is no longer there but, when I walk past the building now, I still get that eerie feeling of what happened there in the early 1970s.

Cars also helped fine tune my Roy Boy antenna. Twice I was hit head-on when I was a kid, and on another occasion a car backed into me. I always came off second best. The most severe accidents were the head on collisions when I was eight or nine. The first happened in Chapel Street outside George Street Primary School. I came tearing out of the school playground and through an open wooden gate, which was attached to a high wooden fence. I couldn't see much of the road from the school yard. As I sprinted out of the gate and onto the road, a car came out of nowhere and ran me over. I was taken to the hospital by the driver but apart from shock, I suffered only a bruised knee. The second time a car collected me was near the corner of Kerr Street and Brunswick Street. I began running across Kerr Street but didn't reach the other side. A car crossing Brunswick Street, towards Nicholson Street, whacked into me and dragged me under the wheels for a few feet until it stopped. I have no memory of that accident other than seeing and smelling the undercarriage of the car as I was dragged along the road. Compared with what might have happened on each occasion, I was lucky. But ever since I've been very wary of crossing roads, even if I can't see a car coming from any direction. And if I'm crossing a road with someone else I check for possible escape routes for both of us, just in case.

Apart from my childhood experiences with cars, there have been other rare times over the years when I've been caught out by not listening to my antenna for incoming signals of potential danger.

More recently in 2014 my antenna failed me when I was in Greece researching some of my family history. It was a very hot day and I was returning to my hotel after visiting the Acropolis in Athens. I had to catch a train for only a couple of stops. As I boarded, I noticed a seedy-looking short fellow standing near the doorway a few feet away. The Roy Boy antenna went up automatically sending a signal – not of danger, but that he was 'not quite right'. Stupidly I ignored that signal and stood in front of him, to his right side, where I couldn't see him. Soon after, a neatly dressed fellow in front of me, bumped into me and I also felt a slight bump from behind. I didn't take too much notice at the time – until I got back to my accommodation and discovered my wallet was missing! Gone were my credit cards, money, and car licence, though luckily my passport had been in my other pocket. Just as in the old Fitzroy days, it was a case of once bitten twice shy. When I returned to Greece in 2018 for a holiday and rode the train in Athens, I made sure I sat down and kept an eye out for potential pickpockets. As an added precaution I travelled around the country with a small, zipped money bag, threaded through my belt, with the bag hanging down the inside my trousers. I made sure I only used the bag when I was out of sight of anyone nearby.

A quivery antenna for sensing potential threats has stayed with me all my life – it's part of my Roy Boy DNA.

Characters

There were many memorable characters in Fitzroy and my favourites were within a block of the fish shop.

Dot was one of them. She would come into our shop two or three times a week, park herself at the end of the counter and face the entrance. Her shopping trolley was always next to her, and there was usually a jumper or a blanket in it. She wore an old black dress, which draped her thin body, and her curly black hair was unkempt. She was about the same height as I was at the time and probably around 40 to 50 years old, though it was hard to tell her age. She was just old. Her dark complexion and black piercing eyes suggested a southern European background, possibly Italian. But when she spoke, she sounded like a dinky-di Aussie. Others who entered the shop kept their distance from her. Perhaps she looked threatening to them but to me she was just Dot and I liked her.

Whenever I saw her, I'd say, 'G'day,'

'G'day, how are ya?'

'Good.'

'How's school?'
'Ah, aw right.'
I liked her funny ways. She would order her fish, chips and potato cakes as usual, unwrap the newspaper and then ask for our small vinegar bottle so she could sprinkle vinegar over her chips. She would then spray a little bit of vinegar over the inside of her wrists, as if it was the most natural thing to do. She was the only customer I knew who would eat her fish and chips in the shop and spend at least half an hour doing so. It was as if she had nowhere to go and the shop offered her a brief refuge from the streets. She would occasionally talk to my dad and mum, but most of the time she would simply watch our customers come and go. I only saw the friendly side of her though there was another side. Sometimes people stared at her and one time a lady looked at her the wrong way. Dot jumped up, smacked the woman in the mouth and walked out.

I always thought she was a homeless person, until I found out much later that she lived in a house down the end of Argyle Street, across the road, in Nicholson Street. In the 1960s her house was compulsorily acquired by the Housing Commission of Victoria to make way for flats. It was virtually pulled down around her because she refused to move. After some years Dot stopped coming to the shop. She disappeared and I don't know what happened to her. It was as if she had never lived. But she did, and she still does in my memory of her. I can still see her at the end of the counter, eating her fish and chips and spraying drops of vinegar on her wrists.

Nick the Greek was another character I saw nearly every day. He owned one of many milk bars in Fitzroy that sold lollies, drinks, and ice-creams to kids. I shopped there almost daily. Nick was around forty or forty-five, had greying hair and worked long hours, day and night, just as my parents did. He was friendly but could become a little testy if kids like me spent too long deciding what lollies to buy.

Every time I entered the shop, I'd eye off the shelves of lollies displayed in a glass cabinet to my right. That cabinet was the El Dorado (place of riches) of my lolly world. It held most of my favourites and, if I had any money, I'd usually lash out and buy some. The process was always the same. Nick would hold a small white paper bag open and wait impatiently while I took ages to decide which lollies I wanted.

'I'll have chocolate bullets, um, ah, mmm, bananas, mmmm, ah, snakes – no black ones, hmhmmm, clinkers, sherbet, and some hundreds and thousands.'

'Is that it?'

'Yeah, oh, hang on a sec, I'll have a Freddo Frog too.'

I'd hand over the cash for my dream lollies to end the transaction.

Nick must have gone through this process with just about every kid and, when serving lollies, he seemed to be thinking 'Oh, come on, hurry up, make up your mind, Jeez.' He'd stare at me in resignation and frown.

I had a few favourite lollies, though I suppose anyone that tasted good was my favourite while scoffing it. Fags were great. They were sugary replicas of real cigarettes. But unlike real cigarettes you couldn't inhale, stain your fingers with nicotine and ruin your health like many blokes who smoked real fags. I'd hold my lolly fag in my fingers, pretend to inhale and then exhale the imaginary smoke. After a few puffs I'd eat the lolly.

Lolly Fags came in a packet of about six cigarettes, and the design on the front of the packet was enticing for a kid. A bird sat on the top left corner of a red sign which read FAGS, and below that were two children, a boy and girl, running up a yellow path towards the sign. I felt so grown up when I'd say, 'I'll have a packet of fags, please,' just like an adult would.

During the summer, a Sunny-boy was the thing to suck on to cool myself down. They were orange flavoured triangular ice blocks and I could never bite into it them because they would send shivers down my spine. I had to suck until it melted away, which was okay because it seemed to last forever.

Snakes were another favourite lolly that I could play with as well as eat – I always bought yellow and red ones, never black because they looked inedible. I would stretch one out as far as I could without breaking it because I figured the longer it became, the more I could eat. I would bite the head off first and work myself down to the tail until it disappeared. I also loved musk sticks, smarties, liquorice, wagon wheels, toffee apples, milky bar chocolate and my ultimate chocolate lolly that I still eat today, the almighty Cherry Ripe. Though it doesn't seem to taste as good now as it did in those days. And if I had bugger all to spend when my mother sent me to the milk bar to buy milk for the family, I could still stare at the lolly cabinet and dream of my next haul.

Nick's was my lolly heaven and Tony's newsagency, a couple of doors away, was my comic book heaven.

Tony was Irish with a very large gut, balding grey hair, bushy eyebrows and what seemed a permanent expression of effort. He didn't smile often but he was friendly and I liked him. He was a good egg, like all my favourite shopkeepers in that block. I liked him even more because he had all the comics in the world in his paper shop. He often delivered newspapers himself and owned a bicycle with a huge seat to support his large frame. As he sat on the bike it sank, threatening to burst a tyre or two, though it never did. I can see Tony now, on his bike outside his shop, pushing down on the upright pedal to propel himself forward. As the bike slowly moved along the footpath, the loose chain threatened to fly off and decapitate nearby pedestrians, who would wisely stick to the edge of the footpath to avoid a collision.

Tony's newsagency was dimly lit, but there was enough light to see the comics and that was all that mattered to me. It also had the same old-world feel and look about it as the museum in town. As I entered, I'd say, 'G'day Tony,' and head straight for the comic section on the left-hand side of the shop. Tony would look up and say, 'G'day,' as he stood inside his work area – a rectangle of counters in the middle of the shop. He looked like a captain on the bridge of a ship, aware of all that was going on around him including little kids like me checking out the comics.

Jeez, that comic section was a bonanza – it felt like winning first prize in a Tatts lottery every time I stood in front of it. My favourite was The Phantom, which I pronounced, 'The Pantom.' Superman and Batman were next on my list. Occasionally I'd buy a Mandrake the Magician, Green Lantern, The Flash, The Amazing Spider-Man, Fantastic Four, Archie, or Hot Stuff the Little Devil. The covers were all colourful with dramatic action heroes and villains fighting each other. The backs advertised items such as X ray specs, sea monkeys or a Charles Atlas strongman course. I couldn't afford to buy these, but I'd imagine being able to see through something, give life to a sea monkey (which was really a form of shrimp) and be as strong as Charles Atlas.

The comics were positioned upright, in wooden racks attached to the wall. A stringy elastic band was stretched over the top third of each row to secure them from drooping. I'd carefully pull the band towards me so I could easily take one out of the rack. I'd then flick through the pages and be instantly catapulted into my hero's world of action, drama and suspense. I'd browse several comics, one at a time, only long enough to avoid pissing Tony off. Though he was pretty good giving me time to indulge myself because I was a regular customer and I bought heaps of comics from him. Sometimes my Roy Boy antenna would sense Tony was getting irritated with my dilly-dallying, so I'd quickly decide whether to buy the comic or put it back saying, 'See ya,' and walk out of the shop. I wasn't stupid – getting banned from Tony's would have been the end of the world for me.

The only other place to buy a comic locally was at Nick the Greek's milk bar, which I did occasionally, but it was a poor alternative to Tony's vast collection. Nick sold surprise packets containing a comic and a lolly. But that was a pain in the arse because you could never see what comic you bought until you opened the packet. I'd hold it up to the light to see if I could see the front cover, and it used to piss Nick off if I didn't buy it. Sometimes a packet would contain a comic I already had but that didn't really matter if it was a Phantom comic. You could never own enough Phantom comics, even if it was a duplicate issue. Any other comic that I already owned was a waste of a zac.

Another good egg was Frank J Dempsey who owned a butcher's shop a few doors down from Tony's newsagency, on the corner of Brunswick Street and Kerr Street. Frank was pretty old, probably in his fifties, a true-blue Aussie with white curly hair. He wore a butcher's apron and his rolled up white sleeves revealed faded blueish tattoos on his forearms. His working arsenal consisted of various sharp, short and long knives, a cleaver, and a chopping block bench. He seemed to have been there forever and for me he was THE butcher shop while I was growing up in the fifties and sixties. There was another butcher that opened down the road, but we rarely shopped there in the early days. I can still remember Frank's shop front in Brunswick Street displaying all sorts of meat and the side window facing Kerr Street with, in capital letters, F. J. DEMPSEY and below in thicker capital letters the word, BUTCHER, followed by a five-point star. A venetian blind covered the side window.

My mum would send me to Frank's to buy various cuts of meat for our family. I'd push the swinging door open and step onto a floor covered with sawdust. To my left were the counter, scales and display window. Sometimes I'd see fresh animal carcasses hanging up on hooks across the room, which was exciting if I didn't get close to the dead meat. Frank was easy going and we'd usually have a good laugh when I was there. We developed a banter that included, 'How's the meat business going Frank?' 'Not bad, how's the fish business going?' Frank was like my mum and dad when it came to serving customers – friendly, helpful, talkative and professional. Not only was the service great but Frank's meat was good stuff, just like our fish and chips. I never fully appreciated how professional my parents were in the shop when I was a kid. But looking back now they, like Frank, were consummate professionals in their chosen trade and gave real meaning to the buzz words 'excellent customer service' used by many businesses today.

Eve's toy shop, next to Nick the Greek's milk bar, was another place I'd visit frequently. Eve wore glasses, was probably in her forties and always friendly to me. She was patient too when I took a long time to decide which I toy I wanted to buy. Whenever I walked past Eve's shop, I'd either glance in, or stop and stare through the window at all the toys on display. I was very careful with what I bought; I couldn't afford to waste my money on a toy that I sort of half liked. It had to be a you-beaut purchase that I couldn't wait to take home and play with. When I was inside, I'd ignore all the girl's stuff – prams, dolls, teddy bears, skipping ropes – that just took up space for boys' toys. The toys I loved were American Western toys such as cowboy hats, guns, holsters, pop rifles, bows and arrows, or a sheriff's badge. I also liked cap guns, toy cars, model aeroplanes and thumb sized plastic toy soldiers. Buying a brand spanking new toy was such a thrill. I'd run home clutching it in my hand, and sometimes I'd only get as far as the kitchen before ripping the wrapping paper off to play with what I had bought. If I was patient, which was very difficult for me when holding a new toy in my hand, I'd run upstairs to the living room or my bedroom before unwrapping it.

I never made any rash decisions to buy lollies, comics or toys because I usually had only a few coins in my pocket and couldn't splurge. I had to ask and beg for money from my parents – I never received a weekly allowance. Though I usually did get what I wanted if I didn't ask too many times or for a large amount. Not having much money as a kid was an invaluable experience because it has saved me from wasting money throughout my life. I'm not a tight arse with money and, on some occasions, I do lash out and spoil myself but with almost anything I buy I can hear myself saying, 'Do I need it and can I afford it?' before I go ahead.

When I was a kid I didn't work for money, but Lorna did from the age of eleven until she was fifteen. She worked at Eve's store after school for an hour, and on Saturday mornings from 9:00 am to 1:00 pm. At fifteen she left to work full-time at International Harvester in Port Melbourne. It was not uncommon in those days to leave school at fifteen and either work full-time or start a trade apprenticeship. It was probably not legal for her to work as a part-time employee before that, but she did. Eve travelled from her home in Preston to the store, and on most Saturdays Lorna would open the shop before Eve arrived. When it was quiet Eve would sit in Nick the Greek's car parked outside and knit. One day when she was sitting in the car, the driver side door suddenly opened and a stranger climbed in and said, 'What are you doing in my car?' She realised she had been sitting in a car that was identical to Nick's! Lorna enjoyed working there, and occasionally Eve would take Lorna to her beach house in Coronet Bay for a weekend. Every fortnight they would rearrange the items in the shop windows for a different look – 'It was amazing what sold when you moved things around a bit,' Lorna told me. Eve closed the store in the late 1960s and I felt a sense of loss because it was another childhood icon that had disappeared.

One of my favourite non-human characters was our grey and white cat, Fluffy, who lived in a dream world – our fish shop. He had a smorgasbord of fish scraps to choose from and was often shooed away from our shop counter and preparation areas when he was hungry. Fluffy was also keen on our blue and yellow budgies, which were kept in a cage above our kitchen door. He would stalk them by creeping towards them, jump from the table or window ledge onto the top of the half open door, while they shrieked in terror. I'd yell at him, grab him, and lower him to the ground. But he always kept an eye on the budgies planning his next attack. I reckon Fluffy earned his keep, because I never saw a rat scurrying around the shop as they did during a plague in nearby shops at one time.

Lorna giving our cat Fluffy a kiss, outside our fish shop.

Occasionally, he would sunbake on the corrugated tin roof that covered one of the work areas. I'd play with Fluffy by tapping my thigh and he'd race towards me and jump up on my lap for a pat. He'd even sprint upstairs to the living room when I called him from there.

Another character I loved was Rags the dog. He was a beautiful Collie, with a reddish, brown and white coat – a dead ringer for Lassie from the 1950s American TV series. He wasn't our dog; he was Fitzroy's. The owners would take him for a walk along Brunswick Street where kids like me would come pat him. Rags obviously enjoyed all the attention from his fans. One day I was in my living room upstairs watching television when I heard some noise in Brunswick Street and popped my head out of the window to see what was going on. I saw a crowd of people, including Frank the butcher, standing around something. I couldn't see anything else, so I went back to watching TV. But the next day I found out what had happened. The crowd had been gathering around Rags, who had been hit by a car and was lying on the ground. Frank Dempsey came over from the butcher shop to investigate and realised Rags was too far gone to save. I was told he covered Rags with a sheet and put the poor dog out of its misery using his butcher's knife.

Brunswick Street was never the same again without Rags. He was a living part of Fitzroy and just as important to me as Fluffy my cat. I would never be able to pat that gentle, beautiful dog again.

As I write this, I still get a tear in my eye. I miss Rags.

Still and Moving Pictures

I didn't just look at photos as a kid. I gazed at them until I could feel a story unfold from the picture, the expressions, postures, backgrounds, and the way people related to each other in the photo. If an image was blurred, poorly framed, or boring to look at that didn't matter – I'd still see a story, real or imagined.

Our first camera was a black Kodak Brownie C six-20 that I think my old man bought from a customer in the fish shop. It's one of the few possessions from the old days that Lorna kept, and it still brings back fond memories when I see it now. Some of the black-and-white photos I still have were taken in the 1950s and 1960s with this camera, which was manufactured in 1946. As a kid I could never figure out why it was called a Brownie when it was black. I found out later it was named after the inventor, Frank A Brownell, and released to the public in 1900 by the Eastman Kodak Company.

I loved playing with the Brownie. It was kept on a wardrobe shelf in my parent's bedroom and I would take thousands of imaginary photos without spending a penny on film. There was no film when I mucked about with it, because that was too expensive for a kid. I'd hold the camera waist high, run my fingers over the textured body and look at the two rectangular viewfinders at the top and side corners. The image in the viewfinder was upside down, so I thought perhaps if I stood upside down, I could correct the image angle – but that was too much of an effort.

When I was a teenager in the mid-1960s I bought an instamatic Kodak camera that was far smaller and easier to use than the Brownie and much later on I got my hands on a Polaroid instant self-developing camera. I loved taking the occasional snapshot and over a few decades that interest has developed into a passion for amateur photography, especially black and white street photography. Most of the early photos I have are black and white and it's a wonder they survived my active little hands as a kid. Some I tore up and others have bits ripped off. But luckily my destructive phase didn't last long, and most pictures of those early days have survived.

Though photography was great fun, I was even more passionate about watching moving pictures. My favourite movie theatre was the Regent Theatre in Johnston Street, near Brunswick Street. I remember standing in line outside the ticket box in the white marbled foyer with other excited kids on a Saturday afternoon. I'd hand over my sixpence so I could sit in the cheaper front seats, saving a few pennies because the back seats cost a shilling.

The 1940s American-made Batman serial was terrific to watch. It usually ended in a cliff-hanger, so I never knew if the baddies had successfully killed Batman and Robin. There would be a short preview enticing me to tune in next week and I always turned up again next Saturday to find out if they survived. They always did. One Saturday afternoon I arrived at the pictures halfway through the session but insisted on paying to go in and watch the Batman serial. I had to find out what had happened to Batman and Robin.

Just before the Regent Theatre closed in 1960, after thirty-one years in operation[24], I remember sneaking out of the fish shop one evening and meeting up with John to go see a movie. It was an ancient Roman sword fighting film so there was no way known I'd miss it, even though I was not allowed to go to the pictures at night. John and I both sat about halfway down the theatre, on the left. Part way through I turned my head and spotted my mum at the back of the theatre looking for us. I nudged John and we sank down into our seats so we could not be seen. I don't remember what happened afterwards on that occasion, but I assume I would have got into big trouble. Not unusual for me as I'd often sneak out if I wanted to see or do something during the day or night. Sadly, the Regent Theatre was demolished in 1984 which still pains me to this day.[25]

There were two other picture theatres I visited after the Regent Theatre closed. One was the Adelphi Theatre in Nicholson Street, just across the road from St Brigid's church. It had great sword fighting pictures as did the other, the Carlton, in

---

24 I was eight years old at the time. I can't remember now exactly how it felt when the picture theatre disappeared, but I imagine I was pretty devastated because it meant so much to me.

25 There is now an office block where the Regent once stood. Whenever I walk past the site during my regular visits to Fitzroy, I still feel a sense of loss.

Faraday Street, near Melbourne University. I remember the colourful movie posters in the foyer of the Carlton – they were often better than the movies they advertised except for the sword fighting pictures. If you disregarded the acting and plot, which I did, the movies were terrific. I still remember one scene when the hero, Victor Mature, got shot in the back with an arrow – so sad. Another reason to go to the Carlton pictures was Gordon, who I think was the owner of the theatre. He'd come out during intermission, stand on the stage, and throw out toy balls about the size of a kid's clenched fist – they had long elastic strings attached to them. Most kids, including me, would jump onto our seats and yell, 'Gordon, Gordon, over here, over here.' If I was lucky and caught a toy ball, it would make my day.

The only picture theatre that pissed me off was a makeshift one that opened up across the road from the Fitzroy footy ground. Someone hired a hall and screened movies there and I remember partially seeing *Jason and the Argonauts*, a 1963 sword fighting picture. Just as the sword fighting skeletons sprang into action the projector packed up and that was the end of the movie. What an absolute mongrel of a time. I never went back and the theatre closed shortly after.

In 1964 I was eleven years old and my life changed forever. That was the year my dad bought an Astor television set. It was a black and white set – colour TV would not be available until 1975. My dad had no interest in TV or movies; he probably bought it because Lorna and I pestered him to do so. Previously I could only catch glimpses of TV through an electrical goods shop window or watch it at my mate John's place, where Lorna and I would spend many evenings doing just that. We always knew when it was time to go home because our mum would knock on the window and yell, 'Lena, Chris.' (Lena is Lorna's true name.) We rarely came home of our own accord. I remember my excitement when my dad took me with him to help choose a TV set. Jeez, buying a set and getting a chance to choose one – it doesn't get any better than that for a kid. He took me to an electrical store near the City Baths in Swanston Street and after looking at several on display I narrowed it down to two. Dad said, 'Which one do you want?' I pointed to the Astor, my favourite, because it had four legs whereas the other TV sets had none and looked like big boxes with a screen on them. The four-legged set was like the one in *The Jetsons*, a futuristic cartoon TV series I watched at John's.

There were three commercial TV stations, HSV7, GTV 9, and ATV O, as well a government run one, ABV2, which I rarely watched because it was boring.[26] Four stations to choose from – what a bloody ripper! I could now watch my favourite programs at home

By the time our set was installed in our living room, my watching habits were well and truly ingrained from watching TV at John's place. One of my favourites was a local variety production called *Sunny Side Up*. It was filmed on a Friday night at the HSV7 Teletheatre in Johnston Street, formerly the Regent Theatre. It was hosted by Bill Collins, a horse race caller known in racing as 'The Accurate One', and featured

---

26 The second Melbourne television station was ABV-2, the second Melbourne television station to go to air. It was operated by the Australian Broadcasting Commission (later named Corporation) or ABC, and funded by the federal government. "Channel Two" opened on 19 November 1956.

Our almighty black and white Astor television set bought in 1964.

my favourite comedian Syd Heylen, who starred in comedy sketches with his straight man, 'Honest' John Gilbert. Syd used to crack me up with laughter whenever he stuck a feather duster between some one's legs from behind or when he'd raise his leg, rotate it in a vertical circle, lower his heel onto the floor in front of him and whistle. The other highlight was the Bill Collins and 'Honest' John Gilbert comedy sketch, when both dressed as mature housewives having a yarn over a back fence. Solo, duo and group singers were mixed in with dance numbers. One song I still remember is Shirlene Clancy's interpretation of, 'I'm Going to Knock on Your Door'. The show started with a group song and ended with the entire cast singing 'Sunny Side Up', which was a terrific, uplifting finale. I remember going to a live production and was almost overwhelmed with joy by the colourful costumes, TV cameras, applause, floor manager and staff racing around. It was my first experience of a television studio and the only thing that annoyed me was those bloody huge cameras that got in the way of watching the performers. It was much easier watching the show on my TV, even though that was in black and white.

I also loved the iconic Graham Kennedy's *In Melbourne Tonight*, which aired from 1957-1970. Cheeky, quick witted and full of energy, he was regarded by many as the king of television although some said he was rude and vulgar – all the more reason to watch him. Graham was famous or infamous, depending on your sensibilities, for his crow call imitation on TV many years later. He said, 'Faaaaaaaaark' which sounded like 'fuck' and the Australian Broadcasting Control Board banned him from live performances. Graham is still a legend to me – whenever I hear a crow call now, I hear 'fuck' screeched in a protracted way.

Other locally- produced shows I enjoyed watching were for children, such as *The Happy Show*, later renamed *The Tarax Show*. Happy Hammond was the host, dressed in a hat and tartan coat always singing happy songs, clicking his fingers as he danced. Other characters I liked were Joffa Boy, Professor Ratbaggy, ventriloquist Ron Blaskett and his cheeky doll, Gerry Gee. Zig and Zag were also favourites, from the Peter's Fun Fair, the first Australian children's show, broadcast in 1956. They dressed as clowns in costumes advertising Peters ice-cream. They were easily distinguished by the hats they wore: Zig's was an upturned red and white striped ice-cream bucket hat, Zag's was an ice-cream cone. My original fond memories of Zig and Zag have sadly been tainted though, as I discovered the character playing Zig was convicted of indecent assault of his granddaughter in 1994.

My favourite – and probably the only – British program I watched in the early years was *The Adventures of Robin Hood* starring Richard Greene. The theme song was great, but as with all the classic shows' theme tunes, I could never remember more than the first line or two of the lyrics – I'd just hum along. I always wished I could draw a longbow and fire an arrow like Robin did at the start of every episode. The arrow would fly through the forest and hit a tree with a thud. Whenever I tried firing my toy bow and arrow it would usually bounce off whatever I hit.

I watched just about all the American TV series across several genres.[27] Probably the show I loved most was a western called *The Adventures of Rin Tin Tin*, which aired here during the late 1950s and early 1960s. It starred a very smart German shepherd dog and Rusty, a twelve-year-old orphan who was raised by soldiers at Fort Apache. They got into all sorts of adventures, and I used to dream of running around with Rinny and my best mate Rusty, fighting Indians and crooks in the old west – a welcome break from Fitzroy.

---

27 Some other television shows that come to mind include westerns (*Wagon Train, The Cisco Kid, Bonanza*); cartoons (*Mighty Mouse, The Flintstones*); science fiction (*Star Trek, Lost in Space*); sitcoms (*Dick Van Dyke Show, Beverley Hillbillies*); dramas (*Adventures of Superman, The Fugitive, Mission Impossible*); horror/comedy (*The Munsters, The Addams Family*); war (*Combat, Rat Patrol*); for children (*The Mickey Mouse Club*); anthology (*The Magical World of Disney*)

I remember the first few days we had our TV. Lorna and I would watch it all day when we were not in school, from the test pattern in the morning to the closing programs at night. Over the next few years our TV was almost always on and occasionally a valve or two would burn out in the back of the set. When that happened, it was a bloody dead set emergency to get it fixed as soon as possible. Waiting for the repairman to arrive was absolute torture – a broken TV was just a box sitting in the corner until it came to life again. The round plastic channel selector knob also got a decent work out until it snapped off one day and became useless. We ended up using a pair of pliers to change channels, until we got a new channel selector knob.

Looking back now I reckon I was attracted to shows that had cheeky, funny, quirky, or irreverent characters and shows that were full of energy. And it's interesting to reflect that these same adjectives have been used by others to describe me, both then and now.

*1961 George Street Primary School, 3B class photo.
I'm in the back row, second student from the left.*

George Street Primary School

I loved George Street Primary School in the late 1950s and early 1960s, a two-storey building established in 1855. What I loved most was mucking about with my mates before school started, during recesses and at lunch time. The only thing I didn't like about our breaks during the day was how short they were. No sooner was I tearing around and having fun, than that bloody bell would clang to signify fun time was over and it was back to class. It wasn't fair. Why couldn't our class times be short breaks instead?

The school is now called Fitzroy Primary School, though it will always be George Street primary to me. It was about four blocks away from home. I'd usually walk up to the intersection of Brunswick Street and Johnston Street, and cross both until I reached the Post Office on the corner. I'd then duck into a bluestone cobbled laneway beside the Post Office, walk a few yards until I reached an adjacent laneway and turn left to keep walking to the end. I'd emerge in a side street and walk a couple of blocks to school. On the way home I'd leave school through the side entrance in Chapel

Street or out the back through Napier Street and head for those lanes again.

The laneways were fun for a kid walking to and from school, as were the Marshalite traffic signals at the intersection of Brunswick Street and Johnston Street. These mechanical monsters were better than any toy in Eve's toy shop and they were free. Marshalite traffic signals were created and installed by the Fitzroy firm of Charles Marshall Pty Ltd. after 1945, and were eventually replaced by electronic traffic signals in the 1960s. They had two large metal dials, about three feet in diameter, attached one-above-the-other to the top of a 15-foot pole. The dials were at right angles – one faced Johnston Street and the other faced Brunswick Street. In the middle of each dial, a white metal arrow rotated clockwise over three colours painted on the inset of the dial: a small yellow section at the top of the dial, followed by larger sections of red and green.

Just like current traffic lights, the colours indicated when traffic and pedestrians could cross the road. Stray dogs took their own chances and the smart ones waited until a human started to cross the road before scurrying over. Watching the white arrow circle clockwise was hypnotic and exciting as I was raring to go once it passed into the green zone. I had to get a hurry on once it entered yellow because it was only a very short time before it hit red. I would have stayed on the corner watching these signals for hours but had to move on so I wouldn't be late for school.

George Street Primary School was bordered by three streets: George Street with the main entrance, Chapel Street at the side of the school and Napier Street at the rear. The fourth walled border ran along the sides of a milk bar and Mr Cadman's caretaker house.

Within a short yonnie (stone) throw from the borders of the school, you could hit small factories, houses, the Salvation Army Hall and a milk bar across the road that I rarely visited, preferring the lollies in the milk bar next to the school. If you threw another yonnie with full force, you could just about hit busy Johnston Street a block away. A fellow student, Colleen Lacy, lived in the milk bar over the road and I envied her access to all those free lollies and drinks. But I suppose there were kids envious of me living in a fish shop and getting my fish and chips for free.

The school was enclosed by a wire cyclone fence, about a kid and a half high, only interrupted by a high wooden gate next to the school building in Chapel Street. There were three playground areas; two narrow strips at the front and side of the school and a large playground at the back. Rows of drinking taps and troughs were located behind the school, as were toilets, a big tree set in a small patch of dirt and two open-fronted shelter sheds side by side with bench seats – one for boys and one for girls. Our school bell was at the back of the school on the wall of the second storey. Attached to the bell was a rope threaded through the wall so it could be pulled by a student inside the building.

On the ground floor were classrooms for the bubs, grade one, grade two and grade three. Near the front door our headmaster, Mr Johnston, had his office, outside of which was a bench seat where glum naughty kids sat waiting to see him. I think I landed on that seat once or twice. Beyond the office, a main stairway led up to grade four, five and six classrooms.

A secondary stairway at the other end of the school also led up to the same classrooms.

Pupils at the school came from different backgrounds – some kids were born overseas, others, like Lorna and me, were born in Australia to migrant parents, and the remainder were Aussie kids. I'd say at least half the kids came from migrant families, mostly from South European countries such as Greece. Probably all the parents could be classified as belonging to the working class. Unlike the students, our teachers were not a culturally diverse group. The majority were white, middle-class and Australian born. Their ages ranged from early twenties to fifties or sixties and, perhaps unusually for a primary school, they were evenly split between male and female.

When I attended the school between 1958 and 1964, average class sizes were around 35 to 40 students packed into tiny classrooms. Unruly boys and mostly well-behaved girls sat in rows of single-seat wooden desks that dominated the room. Under the slightly inclined lid of a desk was a recessed area with enough room to store books, pencils and chewing gum. I remember the teacher seated behind a table at the front of the class saying, 'Take out your books and pencils.' I would lift the lid but occasionally a careless kid would drop his.

'Bang!'

'Who did that!?'

'He did, Miss.'

'You silly little boy, Be careful.'

The top of the desks had a groove where I could place my pencils, and a hole for an inkwell. I certainly wasn't a craftsman when it came to writing in ink in my textbook. The smudges and blobs looked more like a dog's breakfast than decipherable text. I found it difficult to dip the nib of my pen into the inkwell and draw enough ink to write legibly. I'd usually end with ink all over my hands, as did the ink monitors who distributed and collected the inkwells.

School assemblies were held at the back of the school every Monday morning, when lines of bored and fidgety kids sang the national anthem, 'God Save the Queen'. I never could figure out why God should save the Queen, but she must have been important enough to save because we sang this at every assembly. In a framed picture of the Queen hanging on the wall in the school, she wore a crown and a necklace, which proved she was important – to adults anyway. Assemblies did serve one important purpose for a kid – they meant less class time. But jeez, they went on forever. Standing still and listening to an adult rattle on about something I usually had no interest in was dead set boring. It was a relief when the assembly ended, though that feeling didn't last long because we had to make our way to our classrooms to learn stuff. It would be a long, long, time before the bell rang for our morning recess.

I remember one assembly in the early 1960s was a solemn occasion held in front of the school. We all stood in silence watching a hearse drive along George Street, carrying a dead kid from our school. He had been run over by a car near the corner of George Street and Johnson Street. That was probably my first experience of being somehow associated with death – the sad, heavy feeling almost overcame me as the hearse drove past. I can still clearly see the hearse heading towards the spot where he was killed.

My cheekiness at school got me into a fair bit of trouble with teachers. I liked to push the boundaries to see how far I could go for a laugh before I was in trouble. I could usually sense when to back off if my words or actions were upsetting anyone – but not always. I remember one time I pushed it a bit too far during a school outing we had at the Fitzroy Gardens in East Melbourne, near the corner of Clarendon Street and Wellington Parade. One of our supervising teachers was standing about fifteen feet away with his back to me. I had a ball in my hand and threw it gently hitting him in the back and making him swing around to look at me disapprovingly. I waited until he turned and did it again. He looked over his shoulder, and said, 'Don't do that again.' What I heard was, 'Do it again.' So, I did, and he gave me a real serve for being cheeky. I was enjoying the fun of being a smart arse but I reckon I'd really miscalculated how far I could go – I should have stopped after the second throw. I learned my lesson – until the next time.

It was great to get a laugh in class and I remember talking to Maynard, a kid who sat behind me. My teacher yelled, 'Turn around Chris!' So, I did. But not to the front. I spun around the other way, so I was facing Maynard again. Everyone cracked up laughing except the teacher. They were hard buggers to earn a smile from but occasionally I did get half a smile, which made my day. One of the rare times I was outdone for a laugh in class happened when a kid threw a paper aeroplane. It zigged and zagged across the room towards the teacher, who was sitting at his desk writing. The pointy end of the plane hit the front of his hairline and became embedded. He looked up in complete surprise. The class cracked up laughing and he yelled, 'Who did that?' No one owned up and the kid who threw it was my hero. I certainly would not have been game to do that.

Something else I enjoyed was drawing, especially a comic book character called Hot Stuff the Little Devil. He was a baby red devil dressed in a nappy, carrying a trident, and he got up to all sorts of mischief. I related to his cheekiness and drew the character repeatedly on large sheets of paper. I'd first draw a large circle for his head and then draw his white eyes, black pupils, black eyebrows and mouth. Occasionally I'd draw a bolt of fire coming out of his mouth. I'd then add two large, pointed ears and two little horns above his eyebrows. The arms, legs and body were drawn next, followed by a nappy and a trident, which he held in his hand. The comic book character was always coloured red wearing a white nappy but sometimes I'd colour him green.

I remember the teacher saying to me, when I showed him yet another drawing of the little red devil, 'Is that all you can draw?' Even that veiled criticism didn't dampen my enthusiasm and it was a long time before I lost interest and stopped drawing him.

Another activity I thoroughly enjoyed was building model aeroplanes. My favourites were World War One British and German planes. The German Fokker triplane, flown by the famous Red Baron, was terrific. And of course, I painted it in bright red. Wow. A triple winger. What a bloody beauty! I was always impatient to build the plane and it didn't really matter if the end results never quite matched the photo on the model aeroplane kit box. Constructing a plane was a delicate job with several bits and pieces that had to be carefully glued together. The easy part was putting the body together first, as there were just two long parts to glue. I used Tarzan glue and realised very quickly how it got that name when some of it stuck to my fingers. I had to be Tarzan to pry my fingers apart, but at least it held the plane together.

Whenever I opened a box and saw grey rows of plastic frames with bits attached to them, I couldn't wait to build the plane and fly it. Once I pulled all the bits off. I'd lay them out in front of me on the table and read the instructions. If I got stuck, I'd ask the teacher for help. After quite a bit of fidgeting I'd eventually construct the plane and when the glue was set, I was almost there. The next job was to paint and bring it to life with colour. There were tiny tins of coloured paint and a fine brush to paint the right colours carefully in the right places. I'd then attach the little insignias on the tail, and wings. A German insignia was a thick black cross on a white background, and a British insignia was a red dotted bullseye with white and blue circles. Finally, there it was. My plane. Ready for a test flight.

The models usually were about eight inches long, no moving or noise-making parts or electronics, so it was always hand-held pretend flying. I would never chuck it in the air because it would crash and break; I had to remind myself it was not a paper aeroplane and take care handling it. I'd hold the plane between my thumb and forefinger and wave my arm around in the air attacking and shooting down other kids' aeroplanes who were also trying to shoot mine. The engine would roar, 'mmmmmmmmmmmmm' and the machine guns on the plane would 'ehehehehehe.'

Unlike the Red Baron who was eventually shot out of the sky, I managed to stay airborne and win all my dog fights. I was the hero, the air ace until the school bell rang ending my campaign.

Punishment for misbehaving in class ranged from mild to severe, so I had to be careful. I didn't push it too far. Otherwise, I could be asked to come out to the front of the class and turn to face the backboard and that was a long and embarrassing walk from the safety of my desk. I remember one kid wet his pants while standing in front of the blackboard. Other punishments included being yelled at, hit with a ruler, pushed, grabbed by the shoulders and shaken like a rag doll, hit with a flying piece of chalk or blackboard duster, or (as happened to one kid) chucked into a bin headfirst.[28] And even good behaviour was no guarantee – a wrong answer could also get me punished.

1964 was a turning point in my life at George Street Primary School. That was the year when fun in the classroom ended. I was in grade six with Miss Williams as my teacher, a strict disciplinarian who tolerated only good behaviour and correct answers. You didn't dare muck about in her class and I made sure I always sat near the back to keep out of harm's way. Miss Williams was grey haired and rarely smiled. To us she seemed ancient but she was probably in her fifties. I didn't like her or respect her; I just tolerated her. The only thing I liked about her class was when the bell rang to end it. Every day felt like a year of misery and I was so relieved to escape. I can still remember the very slow walk up the stairs to her classroom, steeling myself for another bastard of a day. There was a caring side to her, where she set up a special couch for my mate's sister, who suffered epileptic fits. But I wasn't aware of her soft side, only her hard-nosed, no-nonsense, in-your-face attitude

---

28 I never saw a kid chucked in a bin head-first but discovered it did happen. At least two former students who had witnessed this told me about it.

that punished every infraction. She was like an army drill sergeant yelling into a recruit's face. But she went further – she physically punished us, as did some other teachers.

One memory burned into my mind was a time the class had to figure out a stupid bloody useless question on perimeters by drawing a rectangle and calculating the measurements in our exercise books. I racked my brain but couldn't work out how to calculate the numbers along the rectangle. It was a complete mystery to me, so I simply made up an answer. I knew I was going to cop it from Miss Williams. I had to walk up from the back of the classroom with my book to where she was sitting and show her what I had written. She looked at my work, and said, 'No! Do it again.' Back in my seat I knew I was doomed. I had no idea what to write and I had to come up with something quick smart. One more time I was yelled at – even more loudly. It definitely wasn't going to be third time unlucky because my life was at stake now! So, I looked around and quietly asked a kid sitting next to me for the answer. To my huge relief he told me, and I wrote it in my exercise book.

I wished I could just yell out what she wanted to know from my seat because it was safer there – at least I could dodge the chalk or duster I knew she would throw at me if I was wrong. No such luck. There was no escape and I knew this time it could be fatal. I held my breath, walked very slowly towards her and gave her my exercise book. I nervously watched her as she peered at it, expecting to get a whack, and was stunned when she said, 'Yes, that's right.' And she then even gave me a half smile. Phew, that ordeal was over until the next time we had a bloody question on perimeters.

I do remember another teacher from whom I copped a slap in the face for misbehaving. It happened outside the museum in the city during a class excursion. I was being cheeky by not lining up properly and she momentarily lost it. Though that didn't stop me from liking her because she was young, pretty, had red hair shaped in a beehive and dressed well.

That excursion to the Melbourne Museum was probably my first visit there. At the time it was in the city on the corner of Swanston Street and La Trobe Street. My least favourite parts were the art rooms, all those old boring paintings with no pictures of a little red cartoon devil, The Phantom, Mighty Mouse, or Superman. No, those were really old people's rooms and just a short cut to the good stuff. Now that I'm part of the old brigade (elderly) myself, I do enjoy looking at what I once called 'all the arty farty stuff'.

There were two entrances to the museum, the main front entrance in Swanston Street and the back one in Russell Street. Both provided a path into the old world. The steps at the rear led to the stuffed animals – well and truly stuffed in glass cages. However, they were real to me because their eyes followed me around the room, especially the huge black gorilla that towered above me. I kept my distance just in case he broke through the glass cage and grabbed me. He would have torn me to shreds, not just slapped my face like my teacher did earlier on in the day. It was a fair dinkum creature compared to the phoney ones I saw on the Jungle Jim TV series. It kept staring at me, so I kept one eye on it and the other eye on the exit, ready to sprint to safety if it broke free. I figured if the gorilla chased me into my jungle, busy Russell Street, I could use my dodging and weaving skills and get him run over by the green and yellow bus. I stood there for a while, and he hadn't moved – yet. I decided to move on in case I pushed my luck.

My favourite part of the museum was the upstairs hallway where they displayed all the war stuff, usually inside glass cabinets and on the walls. There were medieval helmets, swords, crossbows, arrows, armour, knives, old guns and rifles, a cannon and other cutting and shooting weapons that I had never seen before. You beauty. I could almost reach in to grab a weapon and imagine I was in a movie cutting, stabbing or shooting villains. What great fun, provided you were not on the wrong end of the fight. Though I suppose it didn't matter if I carked it – I could always come back to life and fight another day in my next dream.

Phar Lap, our champion racehorse of the 1920s and 1930s, was also worth seeing. His skin was preserved and moulded to material on a frame, producing a replica of the real horse. It looked beautiful inside the glass display, and it was awe inspiring when I learned he won 36 out of 41 races at various distances. The only other horses I could get that close to were the huge draught horses in the stables around the corner from our shop.

Bell duty and bin duty at school were complete opposites on the love or hate scale. Every kid in the school wanted to ring the bell. It was pure joy to pull the rope and hear the loud clanging. For a short time, I was in control of all the students and teachers because everybody paid attention to its sound. Ringing it was the only time I could tell a teacher what to do, because they had to obey the bell too. The only time I hated hearing the sound was when it rudely interrupted a game I was playing in the yard. And if I dawdled on my way back to class there was always a teacher nearby to give me a hurry up. Bloody hell, jeez.

Bin duty was an absolute pain in the arse because it cut into my playing time before school started – and anything that interfered with that was an ordeal. Fancy walking a million miles around a concrete school yard just to dump galvanised empty bins in certain spots. The hardest part of the job was starting it because I'd always be thinking how I could avoid it. But there was no escape. Bugger. I never shirked my responsibility no matter how I felt or thought at the time. Even today I go through the same process when it comes to doing housework or outdoor work. But once I get started, away I go and get the job done – usually.

Out in the school yard boys and girls lived in their own separate little worlds of play. Boys didn't play sissy games like skippy though occasionally a boy would burst through a girl's skipping rope game to ruin it. The girls would yell, 'I'm telling on you!' and the boy would laugh, though later he'd be in trouble with a teacher for interfering with the game and would settle down – for a while. I can't remember playing girls' games or girls playing boys' games. Perhaps the younger bubs or grade one kids did, but certainly not the older boys and girls. The sexes were further separated in the playground by two shelter sheds. A shed for me was just a brief stop-over to eat lunch, before dashing out to play as soon as possible. It was absolute murder when it rained so I had to take shelter in the shed to keep dry. A complete waste of playtime. I remember feeling miserable watching and hoping the rain would stop.

My favourite games at school were British Bulldog, soccer and marbles. British Bulldog was the roughest game because it involved running, dodging, twisting, turning, pushing, pulling, bumping, grabbing, lifting kids off the ground, and occasionally dumping them. I loved this game, which we played in the yard at the back of the school where there was plenty of room. The rules were simple. A group of boys would nominate one boy to be the 'bulldog'. The bulldog would go to the middle of the ground and face the other boys who had spread out across one end of the yard. The boys would then run across the playground and try and avoid being caught by the bulldog. He would then try to catch one of the others, as the whole mob raced across to the other side. If he did, he'd lift the kid up in the air, making sure both feet were off the ground, and yell, 'British Bulldog.' The captured boy would now become a fellow bulldog. This process was repeated until all but one were bulldogs and the last boy was declared a winner.

I hated being nominated the bulldog at the start of the game because it meant I had to stay in the middle of the yard for the whole time, I much preferred running and evading capture rather than chasing other kids around the yard. It was such a great feeling making it to the other side without being caught. It became increasingly difficult to evade capture as more kids were added to the middle. Then you'd be facing ten or fifteen lunatics coming right at you. It was nerve wracking and a thrill to be the last two boys left, not knowing which of us would be the main target of the pack. And when the pack jumped on you, the sun was blocked out by bodies, arms, and legs. Thankfully it was only a temporary eclipse and not a permanent one.

Some kids were mean; they'd dump you onto the asphalt yard and hurt you. But mean bulldogs had short life spans because they too would be dumped to the ground in a revenge attack. There were tactics involved to catch a runner. You'd go for the slowest and most uncoordinated kid first and leave the toughies for later when more bulldogs were available to help you. Some devious bulldogs would make a pact and target a specific runner, which made it very difficult for him to get through. But it could work the other way too because a runner would sometimes help his mate get through by pushing an attacker away.

Yelling and swearing was a big part of the game.
'Charge!'
'Argggg.'
'Gotcha.'
'Missed me, ya bastard.'
'Get orf me.'
'British Bulldog!'
'Piss weak.'
'Weak as piss.'
'Piss off.'
'Ya wacker.'
'Fucking useless.'
'Ya mug.'

The Greek and Italian kids had their own words of 'endearment' like 'malaka' or 'fongoul'.[29] One yell I rarely heard was, 'Let go, you are hurting me.' No, that was a sissy yell and real boys didn't yell that out. It was not the British

---

29 These are both rude, crude insults. A Google search produces many results for them. The Greek word "malaka" means masturbator and the Italian insult 'fongoul' comes from an original Italian phrase that literally means 'go do it in an arse' and is similar to the English phrase 'fuck you'.

Bulldog ethos. Yelling and swearing at each other was all part of the fun, but if a teacher was lurking nearby you had to be careful what you said or you'd get into trouble.

I'd sometimes come home with a torn shirt and bruises, telling my mother I fell over so she'd say, 'Be careful next time.' I didn't lie to her, I just left out the part about being dumped to the ground by a kid playing British Bulldog. I didn't want to worry her with details or be in trouble. I can't remember if the school eventually banned the game because it was too rough, but I'm certain that I would never have voluntarily stopped playing it. I loved it and so did all the other boys.

Soccer was not as rough as British Bulldog unless you were the goalkeeper. And I was usually first choice for the goalie position when kids selected their teams. I was fearless and would do just about anything to stop a goal from being scored. Even throw my body at a player's foot and risk being kicked in the head or hitting the concrete ground. I was pretty average when it came to foot skills, compared with some of the other kids in the game, so goalkeeper was the ideal position for me. There were twinkle-toed kids who were very talented, as well as the hackers who kicked at anything that moved. I preferred to face the coming onslaught of players charging at me rather than have my feet kicked from under me or be tackled from the side or behind. Our turf, or soccer field, was a space about twenty-feet wide in front of the school toilet. Our goals were the six-foot high and wide brick entrances, either side and to the front of the toilet block. One toilet entrance was for boys, the other for girls – and any kids having to go in did so at their own risk when the ball was in play. It didn't matter that both our goal areas faced in one direction towards us, compared with goals facing each other on a normal soccer field. We quickly adapted and the layout was convenient for us kids.

Each team had about five or six players, sometimes more depending on how many kids wanted to play. The game started with one team nominated as attackers and the other defenders, with kids spread out over the area. Once the ball was kicked, positional play disappeared until a goal was scored and the game restarted. Kids usually swarmed on the ball to get possession so they could score a goal. A pass to another player occurred occasionally but you didn't hold your breath waiting for that to happen. Selfish players made a pass only if they could not out dribble the whole opposition team. Sometimes the ball would disappear under a sea of bodies, which made it difficult for me because when I lost sight of it an opposition player could score a surprise goal. The game ended only when the school bell rang to end recess.

Every game I played at school was my favourite game while playing it. And the best game of all was marbles. I played virtually every day, under the big old tree that was surrounded by the only dirt patch in the school. It was a tiny area in between the toilets and the boy's shelter shed. The only time I didn't play was when it rained heavily so I was stuck in the shelter shed to keep dry – and those were miserable days. I developed a five-marble policy, whereas other kids would bring a heap of them to play with. I figured if I had bugger all to start with, I had to really concentrate to win, or I'd quickly lose all of them and not be able to play. That rarely happened. If by some fluke I did lose my small stash, I'd borrow some from other kids and always pay them back when I won. That mindset is still with me – always pay back what you owe. I was a good player and usually won. How could I not win when I had my almighty red and white bloodsucker? Other multi coloured or see-through marbles were expendable, but a blood sucker was the top of the range weapon for a fair dinkum player. I don't think most of the other kids valued the power of the blood sucker like I did, but that was their loss. And if I won a blood sucker they owned, I was completely rapt because you could never have enough of those.

At home I kept my marbles in a two-gallon tin container, which was usually full. I rarely bought packets of marbles because I usually won enough to stock up. I loved holding the tin up in the air to feel the weight of them all in my hands. The heavier it felt the happier I was, and I enjoyed putting my hand in the container to sift through my collection.

The games we played involved drawing a small triangle in the dirt with a stick, after which each player would place a marble in it. To start a game, every player stood behind a line drawn in the dirt five feet away. From behind the line a player would shoot towards the triangle, and if he knocked a marble out he would claim that as a prize. He would have another go from where his marble landed until he missed. Then it was the turn of the next player to do the same. The game ended when all were knocked out, after which each player would place another marble in the triangle to start a new game. This particular game I remember vividly but can't remember if we played a similar game with a circle drawn in the dirt instead.

Shooting a round object was an art form and after many experiments I came up with a technique that worked for me. First, I'd fold all my right-hand fingers except my forefinger so the tips would rest in my palm. Next, I'd fold my thumb inward and slightly under a bent forefinger. I'd place a marble on my thumbnail and hold it in position with my forefinger. The thumb was always in a horizontal position, never vertical. I'd then flick my thumb out to launch it. The only moving parts were my thumb and forefinger because the fewer moving parts there were, the more control I had. Plus, it improved accuracy. If I was firing a marble from behind the line, I'd place my right foot forward, bend my knees and place my left palm over my right thigh. Then I would rest my shooting hand over the back of my left hand to keep it steady. I always looked for a bridge to support my firing hand, even when shooting from ground level. Shooting from behind the line was the only time I was in an upright position. Every other time I was on my knees and my hand was close to the ground, because every player knew the closer to the ground you were, the better chance you had of knocking a marble out of the triangle. After a day's play my thumb and thumbnail would be sore, but that was a very small price to pay when it came to winning.

Another game I played was cricket, though not until I was in grade five and six because little kids were not invited to play. I had to wait to become a big kid. Little kids like me played French cricket until it was our time to step up to the big league. This involved just two players, a batsman and a bowler. The batsman held the bat in front of his legs with the blade of the bat facing out. The bowler would stand about three to five feet away and throw the ball, underarm, at the bat. The batsman would try and strike the ball and the bowler would try to catch it to get him out. French cricket was easy to play because only a small amount of space and two players were required.

Eventually it happened. I became a big kid and could now play fair dinkum schoolyard cricket. All those years of waiting and watching and dreaming of playing cricket in the front yard were over. Jeez, it was a bloody long wait, but I got there.

The game was played during summer in the narrow yard in front of the school. There was a permanent wicket painted on the wall of the milk bar and I don't think we ever played it as a team game. The objective was to bat and stay in for as long as you could. Other kids spread out in fielding positions ready to get the batsman out. The bat was passed to whoever bowled a batsman and/or caused a LBW (leg before wicket) or caught the ball in full flight. Whacking the ball over the school fence also was penalised with an out because it meant it would bounce on to busy George Street and teachers would stop the game if that happened too often. Occasionally a kid would accidentally or intentionally belt the crap out of the ball and it would sail over the fence.

The only decision that was always contested was LBW.

'LBW!'

'Not it wasn't!'

'Yes, it was. You're out.'

'Bullshit, it was nowhere near it.'

I loved batting, tolerated bowling, disliked fielding and hated getting out. Batting was my motivation for playing cricket because it was a thrill and a challenge to compete against everyone else who all wanted desperately to get me out so they could have a turn. It was bloody tough to get a chance to bat because of the lack of time to do so. The next best thing to hitting the ball was bowling or catching someone out – pure bliss. When that happened, I'd shout, 'You're out,' sprint to the crease, grab the bat and tap it on the ground a few times, ready to smash the next ball.

Ironically, I never enjoyed watching cricket live or on TV because it bored me. But place a cricket bat in my hand and I would become a swashbuckler, winning a test series by belting the ball for a six on the last ball of the game.

British Bulldog, soccer, marbles and cricket were not the only games we played at primary school.

Brandy was another popular game with the boys. This involved a kid with a tennis ball chasing a group of others, trying to hit one with the ball. If, you were hit with the ball you were 'branded' and out of the game. The game continued until everyone was branded. I enjoyed all aspects of the game, chasing kids and hitting them with the ball or trying to avoid being branded myself. Both these endeavours required skill, which made the game even more fun. This was one of the few games where you could hit someone with a ball deliberately and not be in trouble. The best part was not hitting just any kid, it was branding your mate – pure joy. When you hit your mate out you would stir him up, 'Gotcha', ha ha, ha.' The only problem with branding your mate was that he'd look for revenge and try to brand you next time he had the ball. There was always a price to be paid for being cheeky. We never aimed for heads, only bodies. But once in a while someone would get hit in the head with a stray ball, scream in pain and curse. Pain and cursing went hand-in-hand when it came to playing rough games.

Tiggy, chasey and hide-and-seek were gentle running games compared with brandy. Tiggy involved chasing kids and touching or tagging one with a hand. The kid tagged would become 'he' and it was then his turn to try and tag somebody else. Chasey was simply a game where you ran after someone to try and catch him, after which it'd be his turn to chase you. Hide-and-seek was more of a little kids' game. The seeker would usually stand behind the tree in the dirt patch, cover his eyes with his hands, count to certain number and then try finding all the kids who had run off to hide.

We also played poison ball which was fun. Two kids, one with a ball, stood either side of a group of others. The two outside kids would, in turn, throw the ball trying to hit someone who was usually running and dodging to avoid being hit. If anyone was touched by the ball, they were out and the winner was the last child left. Two other rules made the game exciting. If someone in the middle caught the ball without it hitting the ground, he gained 'a life' and could use it to remain in the game if he was hit the next time. And if one of the two outsiders caught the ball on the full, he or she would yell, 'freeze' and everyone in the middle had to stand still. It was bloody nerve wracking to stand like a statue waiting to be hit.

I also remember playing tunnel ball during school sports. Two or more teams would line up, facing ahead in the same direction, about an arm length apart. They all stood with legs apart, thereby creating a tunnel. The kid at the head of the line would push the ball between his legs backwards, and the other players would also tap it backwards until it reached the last one in line. He would grab the ball and run to the head of the line to begin the process again. The game would end when the first player who tapped the ball backwards reached the head of the line once more. The winning team was the one that completed this process first.

Stacks on the mill was probably the shortest game we played. A kid would be tossed to the ground and someone would yell out, 'Stacks on the mill.' Then others would rush in, one at a time and jump on top of the poor soul. The game ended when there were no more jumpers to add to the existing pyramid of squirming bodies. Jeez, that was fun for everybody, except the first kid on the ground.

We also made use of the metal troughs of drinking taps not only to quench our thirst but also to squirt water over others standing nearby. I'd place my thumb partially over the round headed tap hole so the water would squirt to the side and drench someone. With practice I could squirt a target from a distance of four taps away. If I was sprung by a teacher I would be in trouble. So, I had to be careful to make sure no teacher was hovering around if I wanted to have a decent water fight.

Just about all the games I played involved others. The only game I can remember playing by myself was chucking a tennis ball at a painted target on the side of the school wall. But that was just a brief respite from the fun games we played with each other.

I have other fragmented memories of my time at George Street Primary School. I remember crates of small milk bottles delivered to the school for kids to drink. I didn't mind drinking fresh milk but sometimes the crates would sit outside for a few hours, so on warm days the milk would go off. We still had to drink it regardless, which was absolutely yuck. At some stage we were given or bought our own flavoured straws – chocolate or strawberry – which greatly added to the flavour and made milk drinking almost tolerable. But not even flavoured straws could completely rescue milk that had soured in the sun.

I also remember a yo-yo demonstration at the school one day. After watching the skill of the presenters, I became hooked. I had an orange Fanta and a red Coca-Cola yo-yo – and these were fair dinkum, unlike the little tinny toy packet ones you could buy from a milk bar. They were solid and had decent strings attached, which allowed me to work them into a variety of tricks. I learned how to walk the dog, go around the world and keep the yo-yo spinning after the string unravelled, but I could never master that bloody rock the baby trick. For that I'd have to somehow spin the yo-yo, grab the sting about midway to form a triangle with it and then get the yo-yo to rock in and out of the triangle. One danger was if the string broke, which it did occasionally a yo-yo could fly off in any direction and hit somebody. Another risk was hitting myself in the head.

One primary school experience that has stayed with me, not just in memory, is when I injured my left knee because to this day it's weaker than my right. I was arseing about, swinging on a chrome-plated handrail on a stairway landing just outside in front of the school. I had my left leg hooked around the top of the rail and was rotating my body round and round. I mistimed one rotation and fell off hitting the concrete landing with the inside of my left knee. It left me with a knee that has given way occasionally ever since. Fortunately, after several years of Tai Chi practice, it has strengthened, and I hardly notice it.

The primary school was a relatively safe area to play in and around though one of my classmates, who was playing in a warehouse behind the school one day, discovered bloodied plastic bags containing various body parts. He ran home and told his mother who then informed the police. A few days later a newspaper reported a lady had murdered her husband, cut him into pieces and deposited them in various locations around the suburb.

My seven years of primary school ended in December of 1964, and the following year I was bound for the tough and scary secondary school of Collingwood Tech.

Dressed in my Collingwood Technical School uniform. About 1965. I think it was my first day at tech.

The Big School

My life as a knockabout and carefree school kid came to an end in February of 1965, on a hot summer's day when I enrolled at Collingwood Technical School.

Aged twelve, I was about to become a little kid in a big school again. It was both exciting and a little scary because I heard rumours first-formers were initiated by either having their heads held under a running tap or pushed down into a toilet bowl, which was then flushed. I crossed my fingers and hoped I'd only get the tap treatment.

Collingwood Tech was a secondary school in Johnston Street, a few blocks up the road from George Street Primary School. There were five forms (levels), and between 620 and 770 students. In 1965, forty percent of the junior school came from migrant backgrounds. The school provided a pathway for students who wanted to learn a trade as well as those who wanted to go on to higher education. I enrolled at tech because it was close to home and some of my mates were going there. I had no interest in learning a trade and I didn't know what higher education meant at that time.

I remember the first time I walked down the hill in Johnston Street, past the front of the three-storey school to the student entrance, a concrete tunnel driveway. The 30-foot-long tunnel felt like a vacuum between the free world and one where time would usually stand still for six hours a day for the next five years. You could only escape through the tunnel at the end of the day – or at lunchtime if you had a pass.

When I stepped out of that tunnel into the large concrete quadrangle for the first time and looked around, it felt like a monster of a place compared with George Street Primary School. Little kids and big kids were scattered around the yard standing, walking, and nattering away to each other.

There were three ways of getting to and from tech and the route I chose depended on how lazy I felt on the day. If I slept in or felt slack, I'd catch the Johnston Street bus and travel two stops to Smith Street before walking down the hill to tech. If I wanted to save money on bus fare and felt energetic, which was more usual, I'd walk both to and from school. A year or so later when my parents bought me a second-hand bicycle – they couldn't afford a Malvern Star, the top-notch bicycle in those days – I'd cycle to school and had to be vigilant when I turned right into the tunnel entrance, as Johnston Street was always busy with traffic. The cycling was a quick and enjoyable way of traveling to school, but riding home up the hill from the entrance to Smith Street, about half a block, was a pain in the arse. I'd usually walk on the footpath pushing my bike along and, when I reached Smith Street, hop on and cruise the rest of the way home on a relatively flat street.

My first few days at tech were nerve wracking as I waited for my turn to be initiated. It was something I couldn't avoid.

The Big School

So, it was such a relief when I discovered a kid I knew and he gently stuck my head under a running tap to complete the initiation. It always pays to know someone on the inside. Once my head was wet it was over and done with. I was fortunate to avoid the dreaded toilet treatment, unlike one or two students who I heard copped it.

There were a few adjustments I had to make and tolerate as a new kid. One of those was wearing the school uniform of a black blazer with a school logo on the pocket – the letters CTS encircled by an open calliper and set square – a grey jumper with black, white and yellow trimmings around the collar and sleeves, a white shirt, grey pants, black shoes and a black tie with yellow stripes. Back in primary school I could wear whatever I liked but wearing the uniform was compulsory at tech.

There was only one part of it I detested and that was the tie. The bloody thing was uncomfortable, so I'd usually wear it loose and hear a 'do up your tie!' from a teacher. Dressed in my Collingwood Tech uniform I did look half decent, but I preferred the scruffy look because that felt more natural and was much easier to maintain.

My school bag was full of new textbooks, pens, pencils, a compass and other bits needed for various school subjects. It was heavy, so during recess I'd usually place it against a wall in the yard while I played. One day I left it just outside the metal shop for a few minutes and when I returned it was gone. I panicked at first but then thought I must have put it somewhere else. As I searched everywhere in vain, I got a sinking feeling that some thieving bastard had knocked it off. When I finally realised it must have been pinched, I reported the theft to the teachers but there was nothing they could do. The rest of the day was crap because I eventually had to go home and tell my parents what had happened. They were working class people who struggled to pay the next bill, so having to lash out for another school kit would cost them a fortune. They were certainly angry with me for my carelessness, but they did buy me a new bag and books and I made sure I would never be caught out again. From then on, the bag was stored in my number 29 locker during lunch time and, whenever I did place it on the ground in the school yard, it never left my sight. No bastard tea leaf was going to knock it off again. Losing my bag was such a shock that I learned a major lesson, which has stayed with me ever since. Even today I'm always careful when in public with a bag. If I sit down, I make sure it's touching my legs so I can feel it, or I place it close by where it's in sight.

I loved the look and feel of a well-designed textbook with diagrams and pictures, such as my chemistry book, even though I may have hated the contents. Chemistry was a subject I could never get my head around; I usually ended up with low marks when I sat for tests. I was inspired to read books by my third form social studies teacher, Mr Lees, who was one of my favourite teachers. He guided me beyond school textbooks into a world where I enjoyed reading. I read fifty novels that year and it never felt like schoolwork. Once I finished one novel I couldn't wait to I start reading the next. In comparison, school textbooks were boring and would usually suck the life out of me when I tried to decipher them.

Mr Lees had a gentle and patient manner that encouraged students, very unlike some of the raving teachers who yelled and carried on like pork chops. He was also a wonderful teacher who helped us learn through questions and discussions. I remember the time he walked into class carrying a stack of thick books, which he placed on a table, and I thought, 'Oh no, this is going to be bloody boring.' So I decided to distract him from the books by asking questions and it worked. For the entire lesson he didn't touch the books. I was so pleased with myself because I had outsmarted him. What I later understood was that he'd used those books as a prop while craftily guiding the lesson by asking questions that led to discussion on the theme he was teaching.

Other memories of teachers include Mr Syovitch, my physical education teacher, who had the habit of rocking on his heels and toes while saying, in a thick accent, 'Two lines please.' Ted Potter was another physical education teacher, a friendly bloke who played for the Collingwood Football Club. Mr Jones, our mathematics teacher, who often wore a dust coat, had a friendly smile, which was a rarity for teachers in those days. I liked him too, even though once in a while he'd give me the strap for misbehaving. I remember Mr Morrin, our physics teacher, whose back seized up one day; he tried to continue with the lesson but eventually had to be helped out of the room. Mr Williams was our bearded English teacher who sprung me in class holding a book up to hide my face while I made a funny face at another student. He took me out into the corridor and gave me a good talking to – he may have even strapped me although I don't really remember because I got strapped by so many teachers it's all a blur now. Our solid geometry teacher was Mr Clarke and I remember we once had a test that none of us could figure out, so eventually he drew the answer on the board and left the room. I don't know if he did this because he was frustrated by our lack of response or was just doing a good turn. That was an easy test to pass. Chemistry was taught by Mr Boyd. He was a strict teacher and I don't think there was good chemistry between us, but I don't blame him for the fact I failed the subject. Social studies was probably the only subject I enjoyed. I didn't mind art and physical education because they were pleasant distractions. Religious instruction was okay because the teacher, Reverend Mountford, was a good bloke, although I had no interest in religion. I remember him taking one class on sex education, keeping a straight face while a few kids sniggered all the way through the lesson. It was all sex, sex, sex, though using descriptions different from the street language with which we were familiar. So, I suppose for most of us sex education at school was a bit of a let-down.

There were a number of subjects I couldn't understand, had no interest in, barely tolerated or just hated. I couldn't understand chemistry. Maths was full of boring formulas and numbers. Physics was difficult – learning about vectors was confusing. English was mind numbing because it was taught the traditional way. Music was dull. Technical drawing and solid geometry were a waste of time and effort – drawing lines or shapes neatly on large pieces of white paper and interpreting schematic diagrams drove me crazy. I didn't have the patience, talent, or desire.

Trade subjects – turning and fitting, woodwork, sheet metal, and electrical fitting – were a refreshing break. I could do something active instead of just sitting and listening to a teacher rattle on about stuff in which I had no interest. When it came to metal, wood and wiring projects, I managed to assemble and sometimes destroy class projects. But I passed all my trade subjects; not with any real talent, just with good-old perseverance. Sometimes that perseverance didn't pay off. I remember in a woodwork class making a two-pattern fruit bowl with legs. I used a jack plane to smooth out the base of the legs and kept going until I realised the legs had virtually disappeared because I'd shaved off too much. I had to start again with a new set of legs to finish the job properly. I took the completed fruit bowl home and proudly showed it to my parents, though I never told them about the first lot of disappearing legs.

The turning-and-fitting room was a huge area with all sorts of tools, from small ones to large heavy machinery. There were lathes, milling machines, drill stands, drill bits, files, vices, micrometers, metal rulers, curled metal shavings, protective glasses, rags, chuck keys, oil and brushes. If you wanted to turn raw metal of any size or shape into something that was functional, then the turning-and-fitting room was the place to be. It smelt like a machine shop with the smell of oil and other lubricants wafting across the room, so at times it was a bit hard on the nose.

Safety in operating machinery was always emphasised by our teachers because of the danger involved. One of the instructions I heard over and over again was, 'Make sure you take the chuck key out of the chuck before you turn the lathe on!' The chuck was a circular device attached to a lathe at about waist height; it had jaws that would hold a piece of metal so it could be shaved, knurled or cut. You could tighten and loosen the jaws by using a T-shaped metal chuck key.

Once in a while a student would forget to take the chuck key out before turning the lathe on and the key would shoot up in the air threatening to knock anyone close by for a six if they got hit. Flying chuck keys were quickly followed by a student yelling, 'You fucking idiot.' I admit I once made this mistake. After the chuck key flew out, I realised this was one time teachers knew what they were talking about. It had just missed me.

My favourite tool was the bastard file. Not because it did anything other than shave bits of metal but because of its name. I loved going to the store in the turning-and-fitting room and asking for a bastard file. It was the only time I could swear in front of a teacher and not be in trouble. It was apparent even from the early days at tech that I wouldn't end up a tradesman.

The music room was the domain of Mr Holmes, a tough old bastard who yelled and strapped kids a lot. He once chased a misbehaving kid right around the classroom. I didn't muck around in his class though it was difficult to hold my tongue. Even if I had what I thought was a witty one-liner, I kept my mouth shut because I wasn't stupid. Holmesy was unpredictable so I stayed clear of him as much as possible. All I can remember from those classes were the notes E.G.B.D.F memorised as 'every good boy deserves fruit' and F.A.C.E. memorised as 'face'. All of the notes sat on or between lines drawn on a blackboard, which meant very little to me until I started playing a cornet. Then they came bouncing off a sheet of music and into my cornet where my pursed lips blew a half decent note.

The most exciting day of my five years at Collingwood Tech happened in the music room. Holmesy was teaching but had

The Big School

*Collingwood Technical School class photo, form 3C. 1967.
A scruffy looking me, middle row, second student from the left.
Tie as usual, hanging loose.*

to leave urgently for some reason, warning us all to behave as he closed the door behind him. His warning was soon ignored when a kid sitting near the windows spotted something across the road that got him excited, 'Ooh, have a look at that.' We all drifted across the room to the window so we could see what he was carrying on about. I had to jostle my way through the crowd to get a stickybeak and there it was. A vision of splendour. My fourteen-year-old eyes saw a semi-naked woman walking around in the upstairs room of a two-storey house across the road. Wow. This was a fair dinkum woman in the raw and not just a picture you'd see on page three of *The*

Truth newspaper. It was hard to get a decent perve because kids were shoving each other out of the way so they could perve too. So I think occasional snatched glimpses were all any of us really saw, but it was exciting, nevertheless. Live breasts certainly beat pictures. All too soon we heard three words that caused us to race back to our seats, the only three words that could do so: 'Here comes Holmsey!' As soon he entered the room, we were all seated so he saw twenty well-behaved kids. He probably knew this was bullshit, because no class behaved if a teacher left a classroom at tech. After that, it was very difficult to focus on music theory because all I and everyone else could think about were breasts. I couldn't wait for our next music class so I could see the breast lady again. Sadly, she never re-appeared, though in my dreams she was always there.

   I was bored by most classes but that was not going to stop me from having fun. The first two years at tech I mucked around in class by talking or throwing in what I thought was a witty one-liner to get a laugh. That usually cracked up my classmates but unfortunately not my teachers. Once in a while I'd be in trouble for other reasons. I remember in one of our art classes I was trying to mould damp bits of clay into some recognisable shape and the teacher had to leave the room. Without adult supervision the fun began. On the wall were posters of semi-naked women and the temptation was impossible to ignore. All of us started to throw bits of clay at the posters where the targets were the breasts of course. The scene resembled a group of monkeys going crazy at a zoo. Jeez that was fun, until I turned my head as I was about to throw another bit of clay. In the doorway stood the principal, Mr Barberis, watching me. I was led to his office where I got the cuts. I still remember his short, thick, black strap coming down on my open palm. It bloody hurt. Most teachers had straps of various sizes, widths and thickness to punish students. Mr Barberis's strap looked like it wouldn't hurt a fly until it hit your hand. Even though I was punished by him, I still liked him because he was a quiet sort of chap who occasionally wandered around the school to see how things were going. On this day it didn't go well for me – that was the price I paid for having fun, but it was worth it.

Corporal punishment was normal in those days and you'd get the cuts for misbehaving. If you really pissed a teacher off, you'd get 'six of the best' across the palm of your hand. And if you dared to pull your hand away from the strap you'd be told, 'Hold your hand still!' and be hit even harder. Each teacher had his own style of strapping a kid and there were a few teachers who put their whole body into the exercise. These psychos were to be avoided, but sometimes I got caught out and had to experience the excruciating pain. As a kid you had to take it like a man when you were strapped, and you never cried. That was being a sook, so everybody acted like it didn't hurt even though it did. Getting the strap was no fun but bragging about getting it was. Once in a while a teacher would really lose it. I remember hearing about how a teacher grabbed a student and threw him to the floor, pinning him down by placing a knee across his chest. I also heard another teacher had punched a student in the mouth because the kid was going crazy in the playground. That particular teacher got into trouble with the school authorities, though he continued to teach. They were not the only ones who sometimes went off the deep end. I heard of one kid who punched a teacher and was expelled.

There was hardly a day that would go by in my first two years at tech when I didn't get the strap. My half-year report book would usually read, 'If Chris could apply himself, he would do better,' but for me having fun was more important than results. I'd do the minimum of work and get average results, which didn't bother me until I finished second form and missed out on a scholarship. In that year, the first fifty boys were eligible, and I came in about fifty-sixth. The scholarship was worth £39 over four years[30] – a significant amount in those days. I was good enough to receive one but had missed out because I mucked about. That was a turning point, a boot up the arse, and I realised I had to knuckle down and stop messing about. I still threw in the occasional witty remark to relieve the boredom but paced myself so I'd avoid the strap. For the remaining three years I settled down and eventually obtained my fifth-form Leaving Certificate.

---

30 £39 was worth $1069 in 2021 – calculated using the Retail Price Indicator, developed by the Australian Bureau of Statistics. https://www.thomblake.com.au/secondary/hisdata/calculate.php

Good Blokes, Ratbags and Toughs

Collingwood Tech had its fair share of good blokes, ratbags and toughs among both the students and teachers. I remember one day I yelled out something I thought was clever, but it didn't go down too well with a kid sitting at the back of the class. I could see with my peripheral vision I'd upset him, so I quickly said, 'I didn't mean you.' I thought that was the end of it, but during the next recess when I was playing wall ball, I suddenly copped a whack in the side of the head. I turned around and there was the kid I had upset, with his mates around him.

I yelled, 'What was that for?'

'That was for what you said in class.'

'But I didn't mean you.'

However, it was too late for an explanation and everybody was watching me to see how I'd react. I wasn't a fighter so said nothing and very luckily for me the kid and his mates walked away. That experience didn't stop me from chucking in one-liners during class, but it did make me more careful I didn't offend a classmate.

Another head shot I received happened near the concrete ramp that led to the small yard at the side of the school. I was mucking about when, all of a sudden, I felt this almighty whack on the side of my forehead. I doubled over in pain holding my head. An argument had erupted between two kids nearby and one of them had thrown an iron bar at the other kid but missed him, hitting me instead. It was one of the few times I got caught out at tech because my Roy Boy antenna had an off day. It failed to work and I was left with a scar that's still visible today.

I remember a few other students at tech. One was Chooka, who got his nick name from his fantastic chook impressions. He used to break me up with laughter when he'd hunch over, flap his elbows and cackle like a chook. He was in popular demand for these imitations and I'd often say to him, 'Come on, do another one.' I could never get enough chook impressions from him because it was a guaranteed laugh. Another, Joe Nesci, was in my third form class and one I day I noticed something different about him. He was walking down the stairs towards me wearing a plastic Beatles wig, which was popular in those days. I'm not sure if he would have passed as the fifth Beatle in the band, or how long that wig lasted on his head, but he sure had guts to wear it during school. It's something I would never do because I wouldn't leave myself open to stirs from other kids. There was also Frank Bianco, a talented youth boxer whose pugilistic skills couldn't save him one day from an argument with a heavy-set kid in the corridor. It got pretty heated but before a punch was thrown, Frank was kneed in the balls, which ended the fight. There were no Queensberry rules at tech. The only rule was survival and a knee in the balls always trumped a smack in the mouth – if you got in first that is.

In the Collingwood Tech gene pool of intelligence, we had some students who were Einsteins and others who probably should have been in the wader's pool. One of the waders was a kid who decided to blow up our science teacher, Mr Kott, a slightly stooped fellow in his forties, who had a moustache, smoked a pipe and usually wore a frown. The kid's motivation for scheming to get rid of our teacher was probably due to Mr Kott's habit of reacting to a dumb answer or question by staring at you and holding his nose with his thumb and forefinger as if something smelled. He would then hold his other hand above his head and imitate pulling a toilet chain down to flush away the toilet bowl contents. Everybody copped a Mr Kott response; he had no favourites in his class. Anyway, this kid decided to leave his bunsen burner on at the end of class, hoping that the next day when Mr Kott entered the room and lit his pipe, it would ignite the gas and blow Mr Kott to smithereens. The kid hadn't thought it through because the gas escaped under the doors, just leaving a room smelling of gas. Mr Kott survived this assassination attempt, although he almost didn't survive another day when he fell down the concrete steps. But that was an accident – I think.

Another kid from the same wading pool of intelligence thought up of a way of looking up a female librarian's dress without being caught. He polished his shoes, which was probably a first for him, and positioned himself close enough so he could see up her dress by looking at the reflection in his shoes. I'm not sure if it worked, but I certainly wasn't going to polish my shoes to get a sexual thrill. I had a better way, which involved reading a book called *A Bunch of Ratbags* by William Dick. It tells the story of the author's experience growing up as a teenager in a rough western suburb of Melbourne. And it has some sexy bits, which made it worthwhile reading for a young teenager like me. I did read the entire book, but every so often I'd take it from the library shelf again and read only pages 114 and 115. They were the best pages, where the author describes his first sexual experience. That page had more thumb marks than any other book in the library, and I don't think they were all mine. I've read it again recently, for research purposes of course, and pages 114 and 115 are very mild compared with today's standards. But back then it was full on for a fourteen-year-old like me.

Tony Popovitch was a short, stocky student with a cast iron stomach. He'd invite us to punch him in the guts as hard as we could and we'd line up to have a go. He stood there smiling, with his arms apart, as each one of us in turn whacked his stomach. He didn't flinch. I had a go and almost broke my hand. Then a big kid had a go and I thought that would be the end of Tony. The other kid was huge, weighed a ton and threw everything into his punch as he whacked Tony in the gut. Nothing happened. He threw two more punches – still nothing. He stood there looking at Tony in disbelief, shook his head and smiled. I liked the big kid who was overweight, tall, simple minded and friendly. The only student who could rile him was Neville the Devil, a cheeky red-head. Neville used to tease the big kid, who would then chase him, although Neville was usually faster. One day Neville's luck ran out, as it always does if you push things too far. The big kid lost it and ran at him. This was serious and Neville knew it, as he ran for his life. The big kid caught Neville, grabbed him in a bear hug and almost squeezed the life out of him. Eventually let go, Neville collapsed and whimpered off. Neville had never learned rule number-one about being cheeky like I did. If you were to survive tech and have fun, you never gave cheek to the tough kids. You'd always keep them on side by laughing with them, not at them.

Greg was a nasty bastard and a bully. He was tall – tall for a little first former like me – and for some reason he hated me. I can still see him staring at me from the end of the corridor. I avoided him as much as possible. He would sometimes make a smart-arse remark to get me going, but I would never answer back because I knew I'd come off second best if I fought him. I remember one day he knocked some books out of my hands and they dropped to the ground. I didn't say anything, simply bent down to pick them up. A kid beside me knelt down and I thought he was going to have a go at me too, so I lightly tapped him in the guts saying, 'Leave me alone'. He said, 'I was only trying to help you pick the books up.' I looked up and saw it was Con, a kid who had been at primary school with me, so I apologised. Greg stood there sneering at me as I grabbed my books and scurried away. There was no point in complaining to the teachers about Greg because I'd be labelled a dobber and probably get even worse treatment from him. I don't remember Greg ever hitting me, it was intimidation more than anything else. Then one day he disappeared and so did the bullying. I'd outlasted the bastard and the problem was solved.

I don't remember getting into any physical fights that lasted more than one punch to my head. I avoided fights with fast talk, humour and listening to my Roy Boy antenna. Besides, I couldn't fight, nor did I have the desire to do so. It was dangerous to win a fight at tech because there was the possibility the loser's mates would get you. I remember a kid in my class, who was friendly and had a solid build, once got into a fight and won. A few days later, the loser kid and his mates gave him a hiding.

There were very few angels at Collingwood Tech; all the students broke or bent the rules if they could. And for some kids, getting away with it was the only rule they followed. I wasn't a ratbag, but I bent the rules too. I remember playing a gambling game with pennies, which were about the size of a two-bob piece. You weren't allowed to gamble at school. We played the penny game up against the side wall of the bike shed, which was down the back of the school and far enough away from teachers' prying eyes.

We'd stand about six feet away from the wall and the object of the game was to throw your penny as close to it as possible. The student whose penny was closest to the wall won the game and all the other pennies on the ground. With about six kids playing you could win a fortune in just one game. Jeez, fancy winning six pennies in just one go. The only problem with winning was you'd end up with a pocketful of pennies and the weight would threaten to pull your pants down for the rest of the day. Unlike marbles at primary school, I didn't win many games, but it was fun to play while it lasted. I much preferred to play marbles, but we didn't play that game at tech because it was considered a kids' game. I missed my marble playing days, one of the many changes I had to adjust to in my first year at tech.

I had my own style of playing pennies. I'd lean as far forward as possible over the line to reduce the distance, hold the penny between my thumb and forefinger and then move my arm forwards and backwards about three times to get the feel of the throw. When it felt right, I'd throw the penny and hope for the best. I had to be careful not to throw it too hard or it would bounce off the wall and come back towards me. Too soft a throw and it would come up short, though once in a while a soft throw could cause the penny to hit the ground and roll on its side towards the wall. But that was too much of an arsey thing to rely on. No, soft throws were to be avoided. It had to be the right throw to have a chance of winning. One day a teacher was lurking nearby, and we were sprung so that was the end of our penny game. Bloody teachers, they always spoiled our fun.

The Choir, Band and Cadets

The choir at tech consisted of 55 form one and two boys, and it was one of those 'volunteer' activities you were expected to join if you made a half decent sound when auditioning. To my surprise I did. I vividly remember the day we were auditioning for the choir in the school hall. I was in a line across the stage with other students. To my left was Holmsey, playing piano as we sang. He became annoyed, stopped playing, yelled something to us and resumed playing. A few moments later he did the same thing and I could see he was getting really pissed off. It happened a third time but this time he stormed over to the end of the line and yelled, 'Sing!' I was getting nervous because I couldn't really sing, and it was only a matter of time before I was caught out and punished. We sang when Holmsey walked along the line, stopping briefly in front of each kid, leaning in and listening. I was sweating as he approached me and to my huge relief he kept going. I was lucky to survive but the next kid didn't. Holmsey grabbed him by the shirt front, yelled, 'Get out!' and threw him off the two-foot-high stage. He then walked back to the piano as if nothing had happened. He played, we sang, and no other student flew off the stage for the rest of the session.

Another 'voluntary' effort was auditioning for the brass band. The audition was held in the music room. I remember Holmsey lining up all the students, shoulder to shoulder. Mr Shea, the band master, got each student to blow into an instrument to see if he had any talent. He gave me a cornet. I blew an acceptable note and that was it. I was in the band of 27 players, including six drummers and one cymbal player. We practised three times a week: twice before school started and once during lunch time. I managed to advance from third cornet to second cornet. I could never get to first, because Sandro Donati was just too good a player to lose the top spot – but that didn't stop me from trying. I practised in our living room and had to be careful not to play too loudly because customers in our fish shop would hear me. Eventually I decided to get private lessons at a music shop in Johnston Street, next door to the HSV7 Teletheatre.

My favourite pieces were 'Men of Harlech', 'Halls of Montezuma' and 'Wairoa', but practicing bloody scales was dead-set boring. We played 'God Save the Queen' at school assemblies once a week, even on the hottest of days. One day was too hot for me; after standing out in sun I felt wobbly and fainted. I was taken to a nearby shaded spot, seated on a bench seat and told to bend my head towards my knees. You'd reckon teachers would have had more sense than to force a band to stand in 100-degree heat instead of finding a shaded area to play. But no, there was a band spot just behind the assembly of students and that's where we played, regardless of the weather conditions.

I'm posing with my cornet at the back of the fish shop. 1966

Mr Shea, the band leader, was a grumpy old bugger who didn't like loud drums. I'd often hear him say, 'No, no, no', when someone played out of tune. He was at us all the time to get it right and play better. Occasionally, I'd say to myself, 'Oh, for fuck's sake, give it a rest.' But he never did – he was after perfection and he never let up. Highly regarded, he was band master for several school bands as well as Collingwood Tech. Once he took us to hear the Footscray Hyde Street band play, a top-rated band at that time, and after the session I was stunned and inspired by the quality of the sound. His experience and drive certainly improved my cornet playing and the band's sound. At the time I don't think I fully appreciated what he was doing for us. He was just Mr Shea, the band leader who yelled a lot and rarely smiled.

I also joined the school army cadet band and was soon outfitted with an army uniform of a green beret, shirt, jumper, pants, white webbed belt with a brass buckle, gaiters and black boots. We had to keep the uniform spotless – brass buckles polished with Brasso, belt and gaiters lacquered with whitening paste and boots that shone. For a kid who was careless about clothing it required a lot of effort to keep all that gear clean. But I had no choice if I wanted to avoid having a cadet sergeant or officer yelling in my face for being untidy.

The only time a telling off upset me was once when we were practising marching drills in the school quadrangle. My mate John was the drum major leading our unit when he suddenly yelled at me, 'Goulopoulos, get in line!' I felt like saying, 'Oh, get fucked', but you can only say that to your mate and not a drum major.

We had the same activities as all the other cadets, with the addition of learning to march while playing our instruments. The band side of cadets was boring but the activities at camps were terrific. I remember one of the camps at Puckapunyal (Pucka), an Australian army training base, about six miles from Seymour in central Victoria. We had band practice in an old dusty hall out in the scrubs, marched around and played our instruments. I couldn't wait until that was over so I could join the other cadets in far more enjoyable activities.

The only happy memory of my time in the cadet band was when Holmsey organised us to play some tunes for regular army officers. They were in one tent and we were in another. He said to us, 'Just pretend you're playing,' picked up a record of a professional band, placed it on a turntable and switched it on. We cracked up laughing and wildly pretended to play our instruments. He told us afterwards that the officers were highly impressed with our playing. This was one of the few times I saw Holmsey smile and act like a human being. Within a couple of days his demeanour changed back to the old Holmsey and I copped it big time, though I thoroughly deserved the verbal spray he gave me.

We were on patrol with our .303 rifles, loaded with blanks, walking very carefully on an open bush track alongside a hill. Suddenly, a couple of smoke grenades came rolling down the hill and out popped Holmsey from under cover yelling, 'You're all dead!' It was an ambush. But I didn't consider myself dead. For some reason I rushed up the hill towards Holmsey and fired two blanks from my .303 over his head. And jeez, did he go off the deep end.

'You, fucking idiot Goulopoulos, I said you were all dead.'

He threw more obscenities at me, but it felt really good because I had got one over Holmsey.

When we first arrived at Pucka, we saw rows of tents with wooden floors and sleeping stretchers inside each one – a five-star hotel compared with our temporary Scrub Hill camp, 90 miles away. There we had to put up our own tents, dig trenches around them to stop the rain coming in and sleep on ground sheets. We'd spend a couple of days there to rough it and do manoeuvres. One night we camped near tank tracks, on orders from the regular army. In the middle of the night, we were woken up by the noise of tanks. We were ordered to pull the tents down quickly and move to a safer area. The next day I saw Holmsey tear strips off two regular army soldiers in a jeep for placing us in a dangerous position.

Once settled into our main camp, we soon became bored. One bright spark came up with the idea of holding a kangaroo court, so we organised a judge, jury, prosecutor, defence lawyer and an accused. It was hilarious and we all laughed ourselves silly with this nonsense game. Of course, the accused was eventually convicted of murder but fortunately avoided execution. He was sentenced to twenty push-ups.

Another game we played during our free time was splits with a pocketknife. Two cadets faced each other, about five feet apart, one stood at attention and the other held a knife. It was thrown into a wooden floor, landing a few inches to the outside side of the other cadet's boot. He'd then move his foot outside the knife. This process was repeated until he could no longer hold a split. We were lucky we wore army boots for protection, otherwise there would have been a few wounds from poorly aimed throws.

I'm on the far right, dressed in my cadet uniform, looking neat and tidy for a change. Far left is John, and Joyce is in the middle wearing her Fitzroy Girls Secondary School uniform. 1965.

It wasn't all fun and games at camp. Once there was a major diarrhoea outbreak, with most cadets affected. I was lucky I didn't get it, but John did. It was the day we were leaving camp. We were on parade when he collapsed and ended up in hospital. Earlier, from my tent, I watched the poor buggers who copped it race across the parade ground to the toilets. Some made it in time, others didn't. Another mishap occurred one night when, after a meal in a hall, we were told, 'Don't run across the parade ground, there's barbed wire.' As soon as we were dismissed a few kids forgot the warning and ran straight into the wire. I was one of the few cadets smart enough to obey orders, walking past kids cursing and untangling themselves.

One of my favourite activities at camp was the lantern stalk. It was held at night and involved two teams: attackers and defenders. A lantern was hung in a tree in an open area. The attackers had to capture the lantern and the defenders, who were spread out hiding in bushes nearby, had to defend it. The rules of combat were simple. If a cadet was tagged with an open hand by a defender or attacker, then he was considered dead and no longer part of the game.

I remember crawling through the bushes to get to the lantern and being confronted by a defender. We both tried to be the first to tag each other and we both yelled as we made contact.

'You're dead.'

'No, you're dead.'

'No, you're dead.'

Somehow, I managed to remain 'alive' and continued on, although I didn't make it to the lantern. It was impossible to go unnoticed and not be tagged when I scrambled from the bushes into an open area.

I also remember having fun on the rifle range, firing .303's and a Bren gun. The Bren gun was a machine gun holding 30 bullets inside a curved magazine mounted on a small tripod positioned near the front of the barrel. We were very carefully supervised by our officers as we lay on the ground, firing at targets attached to boards in the distance. They didn't muck about when it came to safety. Before one night manoeuvre, we had a weapons inspection of our .303 rifles, which were loaded with blanks. Each cadet, in turn, presented his rifle to an officer. One kid did not have his safety lock on; he was bawled out, had his rifle taken and was told, 'You're not going out tonight.'

The best marksmanship I saw was Holmsey firing a self-loading rifle at a small wooden target wedged into the ground. He hit the target, which flew up in the air, then he fired again, hitting it while it was in mid-air. Jeez, he was good. I heard much later on that he had been in the Special Air Service of the British Army, so he had plenty of experience firing weapons accurately.

After two years in the school band and army cadet band I'd had enough. I wanted to leave, though it took me a while to work up the courage to tell Holmsey. I remember talking to him just outside the music room expecting him to yell, carry on and force me to stay. But he surprised me. He was calm, polite and asked me questions about why I wanted to leave. He accepted my request to leave, which was a huge relief. I was finally free. That meeting with Holmsey was the second time he came across as a human being. He was a tough bastard of a teacher, but I also discovered he was a good bloke.

Organised Sport

Collingwood Tech had regular school sports on a Wednesday afternoon at Yarra Bend Park, near Fairlea women's prison. I remember walking to the park along Johnston Street and then cutting through the back streets to walk past the Collingwood football ground, enemy territory if you were an opposition supporter. The area was usually dead as a morgue, but on a Saturday afternoon when Collingwood played at home, it would erupt into a frenzy of one-eyed feral Magpie supporters egging their team on and abusing the umpire. Once I had passed the footy ground, I'd walk a few more streets towards the footbridge over Merri Creek to reach our sports ground.

We played footy during the winter. I was a fairly average football player. The games were chaotic with most players swarming on the ball like frenzied bees in the hope of getting a kick and scoring a goal. Positional play disappeared as soon as the ball was bounced and players moved towards the ball regardless of where it was. I remember in one game I stayed in my position at centre and it was bloody lonely. Nobody was within cooee of me as I stood watching all the other players up the ground running around like chooks with their heads cut off. All I could do was wish the ball would come towards me, which it eventually did. In a flash, I had the ball, turned and gave it a huge kick. With no one in front of me I chased the ball to give it another belt towards the goals. As I was just about to kick it again, I heard some kid yell, 'You're going the wrong way!' No wonder there was no one in front of me. I kicked the ball back up the centre towards the spot where I had started my brilliant run – but this time headed in the right direction. Jeez, fancy scoring a goal for the opposition. Of course, I was stirred for going the wrong way – I never lived that down.

In another match I was in the thick of things on the forward line and somehow managed to burrow my way into a pack, grab the ball and kick it. The ball flew off my boot, hit my mate George in the head and sailed through the big sticks for a goal. The goal umpire pointed his two forefingers forward and grabbed two white flags to wave an official goal to the scorekeeper. George went bananas. He yelled, 'It hit me in the head, it hit me in the head!' I was rapt. I had scored a goal that should have been only a point because it was touched by bouncing off George's head. It was probably the only goal I ever scored in an official football match. I was on cloud nine that day.

Such feelings were rare for me playing school footy. In one game I came down to earth with a dull thud. I turned up at the best field in the park with my brand-new footy boots and was not selected to a team. I was a bench player, the worst position to be on a footy ground. It was a long and slow walk to the bench after the teams were selected and I can still feel the disappointment. Sitting on a bench waiting for a chance to play was slow torture because in those days you could only get on to play by replacing an injured player. I sat there for the whole game and, when the final siren sounded, I sighed with my shoulders slumped, almost crying with disappointment and a sinking feeling that stayed with me for some time.

I only experienced that feeling one other time. It was during a physical education class when our teacher organised a soccer game on the small asphalt playground at school. For some reason I told the teacher I had a slightly crook knee although I could still play. To my horror he insisted I couldn't play, so I had to stand on the bench seat watching what I was missing out on – two teams of kids running, chasing, kicking a ball, yelling, waving arms, and occasionally lunging at a shin. I was pissed off and disappointed. He could have at least put me in as goalkeeper, which required little running and less danger of injuring my knees. I was, after all, a former star primary school goalkeeper. But unfortunately, he didn't know that and I wasn't going to big note myself by telling him. The irony was that soccer was not my favourite sport at tech – I just loved playing any sport. Being on the bench was open solitary confinement.

In summer we played cricket at Yarra Bend Park and it was fun if I batted. I was a plodder as a batsman, usually blocking the ball rather than risking being bowled out by trying to belt it for a six. Also, the fear of being hit by a real cricket ball probably added to my cautious batting. Sometimes a bowler or fieldsman would shout out in frustration, 'Hit the bloody thing!' Bowling was a pleasant distraction because it was active, though I hated fielding because I'd stand in the outer field like a mushroom to wait until a ball was hit in my direction, forcing me to run after it. This was a big effort because the grassy field was a huge area compared with laneway and primary school cricket. Like with footy, I was an average player even though I always played to win.

I looked forward to our yearly swimming carnival at the Fitzroy baths. It was exciting to get away from boring classrooms and spend a day at my favourite swimming pool. I remember lining up at the edge of the deep end with other kids, leaning forward, arms behind, ready to dive in to start a race. Occasionally a kid would nervously stumble or dive before the starting signal and we'd have to restart. I don't remember winning any event, but I do remember watching my classmate Joe Alagona swim. For a thrasher he did well to swim halfway down the pool. He looked like a fish who had forgotten how to swim. Suddenly Joe's straight-line path turned into a hook and teachers and students all yelled, 'You're going the wrong way!' Joe did not place in that race but at least he'd had a go.

We also had a yearly athletics day, usually held at the Collingwood Harriers Athletic Club ground, near the Clifton Hill overpass. I did not have the talent, technique, stamina or the desire to compete in athletic races so I just tolerated the day because it was compulsory. Though I was pretty good at dodging and weaving when kids chased me over short distances, I hated running in school sporting events. I remember one school athletic day when I had no choice but to compete in a distance race. Students belonged to four 'houses' at the school, Perry, Johnston, Wellington and Smith. I was in

Perry house, and this day there was no-one to represent them in a distance race. I was pressured by others to compete.

'Ah, come on Chris.'

'Naagh, I don't want to.'

'We need you, there's no-one else.'

'I can't run, jeez.'

'You'll be okay. Just have a go, will ya?'

I finally accepted and lined up, feeling nervous because I didn't think I could manage running several laps. A starting signal sounded. Too late to back out. We were off. I began running with a bunch of other kids who very soon started to drift ahead of me. I was breathing heavily trying to catch up but no matter how fast I ran I fell further behind. The gap widened to half a lap and I was struggling to keep going. A running official nearby tried to help me by yelling advice, 'Keep your elbows down.' I tried to do so but I was still stuffed and eventually all the other runners overlapped me to the finish line, where a grandstand full of cheering kids waved their arms. The race was over for my competitors but not for me because I still had a lap to complete. I was out of breath and on the verge of collapsing, but all I could think about was, 'Don't give up, keep going.' Somehow, I managed to stumble towards the home stretch and I could hardly hear the jeering from the crowd in the grandstand. I was too tired to be embarrassed or fire back at the stirrers, as I lay on the ground gasping for air.

The next day in Mr Morrin's physics class, I was sitting minding my own business when he opened up and let the class have it. 'You should all be ashamed of yourselves for carrying on. At least Chris had the guts to finish.' I sat there feeling uncomfortable and embarrassed when I realised he was talking about my effort in finishing last at athletics the day before. No one said a word, although I got the odd look from students in the class. I sensed thereafter I'd gained a bit more respect from them.

Coming last in that race is one of my most successful moments in the fifty years I've been involved in playing and coaching sport. It certainly wasn't my favourite moment when I was experiencing it, but the loss helped shape my character and attitude – giving up is the absolutely last resort. With wisdom that attitude has been tempered by the knowledge that sometimes you need to give up or walk away to move on to the next phase of life, no matter how painful that is. Although I still strive to run that last lap when I want to be successful in my endeavours, I usually pace myself to avoid dropping over the line exhausted.

Relentless

'I smell fish and chips.' I heard that bloody comment just about every day during my first two or three years at Collingwood Tech and it pissed me off. I'd mentally prepare myself to cope with the inevitable stirs by saying to myself, 'Okay, it's going to happen, be ready,' and, when it did, I'd fire off a witty put-down to the smart arse having a go at me. That took the sting out of the remark until the next time. In primary school it had never really bothered me, I'd just laugh it off. I suppose I grew into a sensitive teenager who did not deal well with perceived negative personal remarks.

There was nothing I could do to mask the smell though I did try. I remember once coming up with the idea that if I avoided walking downstairs past the friers I could avoid the smell. I decided to climb out of my parents' bedroom window, lower myself onto the roof that covered the work area, step carefully to the end of it, lower myself again into the backyard, climb another roof and ease myself into a back lane that led to Kerr Street. I tried this long detour a few times, but it never worked. I was stuck with the fish and chip smell. I grew to hate living in the fish shop and couldn't wait to be old enough to leave.

Stirrers I could deal with, but friendly advice on how to get rid of the odour was difficult to handle. One kid pulled me aside after school and suggested I put on some perfume after I told him I was going to a private cornet lesson that night. I was fuming inside but knew he meant well so I said, 'Yeah, no worries,' just to end the conversation. The last thing I wanted was advice I hadn't asked for. Now I was not only nervous about going to my first private cornet lesson, but also worried about the teacher's reaction to the smell of fish and chips. When I entered the small music studio, near the HSV7 Teletheatre in Johnston Street, I focused only on the lesson and not on his possible reaction to my odour. He was a patient teacher and I had several lessons with him. I don't remember any mention of the fish and chip smell, which was a huge relief for me. Maybe he did smell it but was too polite to mention it.

Max Deliopoulos, a fellow student in form two, was the only kid who stuck up for me when someone said, 'I smell fish and chips.' We were standing in line about to head into class when the other kid said those five words and before I could fire off a reply Max said, 'Don't worry about it, his old man probably works digging ditches somewhere.' We both smiled and that silenced the stirrer. I shared this story with Max in 2014 and told him how much I appreciated what he had said almost fifty years earlier. An act of kindness can last a lifetime.

In my later years at school the stirring eased up a fair bit with the help of a liberal lathering of Brut after-shave lotion, but those first two or three years were relentless.

It was not just at tech where I copped the remark. It occurred in a few social situations as well. I usually tolerated it because it wasn't said in a mean-spirited way. Though I do remember going to a pre-recording of a TV pop show at the HSV7 Teletheatre, when I scrambled into one of the rows of bench seats that faced the camera. You beauty! I was going to be on TV. I managed to squeeze in between two female teenagers before the camera rolled – and then it happened. One of them said, 'I smell fish and chips.' I was devastated. Even when I was having fun I couldn't get away from that remark. I kept quiet, focusing only on the camera to distract myself from the hurt welling up inside me. Distraction was a technique I honed to the nth degree when someone I didn't know said those five words. It was a way of dampening the hurt and is something I still use to this day when faced with difficult situations.

The irony is that I could never smell it on myself because I was so used to it.

Even going to the bank to deposit the shop's takings of coins would usually cause a reaction from a bank teller. Though the reaction wasn't a comment, it was usually an upturned nose that spoke just as loudly as words. I'd take the small bags of money to the bank and place them on the counter. The teller would then empty the bags, pick up the coins and weigh them. While doing this he felt some of the grease on the coins and the friendly expression on his face changed. It was always embarrassing for me to take the shop's takings to the bank because I knew I'd cop that look from a teller and I couldn't get out of the bank quickly enough. I think Lorna and my mother also experienced the same reaction when they did the banking. After a few of those reactions from the bank teller we eventually decided to wash each coin before it was bagged, which ended the problem.

Looking back now, all the 'I smell fish and chips' comments ultimately had a positive effect because over the years it developed my resilience in coping with negative situations and people. After an upset, I focus on getting through the day, having a good night's sleep, and looking forward to a fresh start the next day.

Girls

Geoff Hampson was in my form two class at tech and I was jealous of him. A confident lover boy who attracted girls with ease, he was handsome, blond haired, and wore black dress boots. Apart from the black boots I could not match his other attributes. I remember going to the Westgarth picture theatre with him on a Saturday afternoon and as we made our way down to the middle seats, I could see many girls turn to stare at him. I had the same sexual desires as all other boys my age but lacked both the confidence to attract a girl and the knowledge of what to do with her if by some miracle I did.

Unlike Geoff, a natural born chick magnet, it was all trial and error for me as a young lustful teenager and each experience with a girl got me closer to sex – from distant infatuation almost to the promised land.

One of my earliest memories is my infatuation with a girl who lived about a block-and-a-half away from the fish shop in Kerr Street, just past Fitzroy Street, in a house with a veranda and a picket fence. She was blonde, pretty and I think her name was Sandra. I fell in love with her the first time I saw her on my way home from tech one day. I'm not sure if it was love at first sight or just lust. Either way, I wanted to get to know her, but I never had the courage to talk to her. I think she showed interest and smiled at me early on as we passed each other on the street, but I'd avoid eye contact to disguise my emotions, even though I wanted desperately to talk to her. My feigned lack of interest was self-defeating because it put a stop to any chance I had. I always looked forward to our chance encounters after school and tried as hard as I could to say something to start a conversation, but nothing would come out of my mouth. My mind raced with thoughts, but I couldn't say anything. I always looked forward to seeing Sandra as I crossed Kerr Street, but one day she was gone and I never saw her again. Even today when I walk past the house where she once lived, I am reminded of Sandra and what might have been.

Maxine was different. One night I was standing near the ANZ bank on the corner of Brunswick Street and Johnston Street when I spotted Maxine with her head out of the second-storey window of the Provincial Hotel across the road. Somehow, we started a conversation, and I sat down on a doorstep next to the bank. Occasionally a tram would stop in front of me, passengers would alight, and the tram would whizz off, interrupting our conversation. Once the iron beast had disappeared, we'd start gasbagging again. We had several more conversations at different times. One night we were interrupted by my mum who – most unusually – was checking up on me. She walked towards me asking 'Shorpraysh?' (What are you doing?). Embarrassed, I said, 'Nishtor' (nothing). She went back to the fish shop and I resumed talking to Maxine. I

Girls

only ever saw the top half of Maxine and wondered what the rest of her looked like. The closest I ever got to her was from across the road, which was probably a good thing because it felt easier talking to a girl from a distance rather than up close.

All my mates were having sex, or at least that's what they told me, and I believed them when they boasted about their conquests. Looking back now I reckon the only sex they had as young teenagers occurred in their imaginations and their right hands. Though a few would have been left handers among that lot. I reckon the only exception to that crowd of wannabe sex maniacs would have been Geoff Hampson, because he attracted so many girls, he had to have reached the promised land sometimes.

I had as much chance of getting sex as winning first prize with a Tatts ticket. But you've got to be in it to win it, and one day I had a chance with a girl in the red telephone booth on the corner of Westgarth Street and Brunswick Street. She was someone I knew and I had chatted her up. By then I was becoming more confident with girls and could open my mouth to say something half intelligent. She had a little girl with her, probably her sister or niece, which was awkward. But I was on a mission and determined to overcome any obstacle. She opened the door and invited me in. I didn't hesitate because she was a girl with breasts and that's all the motivation I needed. It was a narrow space, so I was close to her, and I thought here's my chance to kiss her or go even further. I was aroused, moved my head forward and was about to give her a peck on the cheek when the little kid wet her pants. That was the end of my romantic interlude. Jeez, I was so close yet so far away.

Faye, a red-head, was my first girlfriend. She lived close by in the four-storey flats across Nicholson Street in Carlton. I don't remember how we met, but I know I was attracted to her the first time I saw her and managed to strike up a conversation. We developed a friendship and I'd often visit her to have a yarn outside the quadrangle of flats where she lived. One momentous day I invited her to the Carlton picture theatre and she accepted, which was pretty exciting. As we walked into the theatre, I guided her towards the back row seats, a spot I never sat in whenever I was at the theatre by myself. I chose this because there would be fewer people behind us and I'd be less conscious of prying eyes when I carried out my plan to put my arm around her shoulders and kiss her.

I have no idea what the movie was about because all I thought about was how to slide my arm around her. I was nervous and not sure how she would react. I breathed in her perfume, and it was wonderful, adding to the pressure I felt on a fair dinkum first date. I didn't look at her, but kept my head pointed towards the screen and, after what seemed like days, I finally lifted my left arm and gently placed it around her shoulders. She didn't resist, I felt terrific. I could have left my arm there for an eternity even though it was getting a bit sore. I had never kissed a girl before and was very nervous I would stuff it up. I had prepared beforehand by practising kissing my forearm and trying to work out how far apart my lips should be, how soft or hard I should press and how long I should hold the kiss once I made contact with her lips. Well, the pressure eased a little bit when I decided I'd better not push things and risk buggering up my first full-on-the-mouth kiss, so would sneak a quick peck on her cheek instead. I quickly kissed her on the cheek before turning my head back to the front to avoid eye contact. She smiled and seemed to like it, so I was rapt. I had taken a girl out on a date, put my arm around her and kissed her, and she had liked it. I thought, wow, it doesn't get any better than that for a kid like me.

The only other memory I have of Faye was the time I visited her outside her flat in the quadrangle, when her sister and her sister's boyfriend were there as well. I didn't know the guy, but I do remember mucking about on the swings and wrestling with him. He pinned me down to put an arm bar-hold on me and held it for a long time. It was painful and I thought he would never let go. I tried to pretend it didn't hurt because I didn't want to look like a wimp in front of Faye.

I don't remember how long I dated Faye, but I do remember it was the best time in my fourteen-year-old life. I was getting closer to sex with a girl, but I still had a long way to go before I reached my destination.

One day after school sports had finished at Yarra Bend Park, I had another chance to further my sex education. I was heading home with a mate of mine when we bumped into two other students we knew, who had two girls with them. We were near the riverbank and stayed there for a while talking until someone said, 'Let's have a dare.' It involved the two girls lying on the ground not moving. The boys then had to get them to flinch by hovering a finger over their bodies. The girls lay down on their backs and the other boys had a go at the game. When it was my turn, I hovered my finger over her head, neck, breasts, stomach and jeans. When I somehow managed to lightly touch a breast, she hit my hand away and laughed. I apologised but that didn't get me another go at the game for some reason. After the dare the two other boys whisked the girls away and they all disappeared into the bushes. I don't know what happened, but I could guess. Lucky buggers. Well, at least I had my first touch of a breast and that made it the best sports day I ever attended.

Gemma had the biggest breasts I ever saw, and they looked even bigger when she wore a bikini at the Fitzroy baths. She was also blonde, attractive and very popular with the boys. She got a lot of annoying attention because of her looks. I remember watching her dive into the pool and half a dozen yahoos dived in, surrounding her and splashing water at her with their hands. I knew her through a friend and remember swimming with her near the shallow end of the pool when she let me place my hands around her waist from behind. I let my hand slide down into her bikini and she did not resist. I lowered my hand further to touch her pubes, but she grabbed my hand to push it away. I'm not sure what startled her, my hand or the stiffy I had pressed against her; but I knew it was time to withdraw and swam away. Though I did stay in the pool for a long time waiting for my erection to go down.

Stiffies were a curse when I was sunbaking on the concrete ground watching girls swimming and walking past. I couldn't just get up if I cracked a fat because it was too embarrassing. Sometimes I had to wait for ages for the little fella to go down before I got up. It was always safe to lie on my stomach when I sun baked because if I lay on my back and got a rise everyone could see.

Two other relationships with girls involved letters only. On one occasion my mates convinced me to write on their behalf to girls they met at a school camp. The guys' writing skills were average and they knew I could write reasonably well with a dash of humour – just what they needed to impress the girls. I crafted several letters for the boys and for a while the relationships flourished, with each letter keenly awaited. Then one day it all changed. My Greek mate George decided to add small sperm drawings at the top of the letter.

I said, 'You can't do that.'

'Why not, it's funny.'

'Maybe to you but not to the girls.'

'Nah, it's okay.'

That letter was the last one I wrote for them because they never received another reply from the girls.

Darlene was another girl I had a long-distance relationship with for a brief time. She was my pen pal. I can't remember how I heard about pen pals but the idea of exchanging letters with a girl from America was exciting and something I really enjoyed while it lasted. I was rapt when she accepted my request to become her pal and I would quickly snatch her letters off the shelf above the bench in the fish shop. All letters received by the postie were placed there. Usually, I'd leave other letters there for a couple of days before reading them. This used to drive my mother and Lorna nuts, as their curiosity would get the better of them and they'd say, 'Aren't you going to open it?' My response would be, 'When I'm ready.' I figured whatever it was could wait, especially if it was bad news. It was also kind of fun teasing them by leaving the letters there.

But Darlene's letters were different. I'd read them within seconds of receiving them. I'd take the letter from the ledge to the kitchen, lie on the bed and read it several times. Then I would start to craft a response in my mind before writing it. I didn't waste any time. I'd write her a reply within a couple of days. We eventually exchanged photos, which was a bit scary because I was self-conscious about the way I looked. I thought she may have thought I was ugly rather than good looking or handsome.

She wrote back after receiving my photo and said something polite like, 'I was alright,' and that was a relief. When I looked at her photo, I thought she was beautiful, though now I can't remember what she looked like. I'd gaze at her photo when writing a letter because it felt like she was physically in the room with me. I remember she enjoyed my quirky sense of humour. In one letter I wrote that her name reminded me of Charles Boyer, a romantic lead in a Hollywood 1937 movie, *Algiers*. In the trailer for the film, he said to his co-star, Heddy Lamarr, 'Darling, come to the Casbah.' His heavy European pronunciation of the word darling sounded like Darlene. I'm not sure if she understood my attempt at humour on that occasion, but usually what I considered was funny worked. After a while her letters arrived less frequently until they trickled to a stop and I no longer had a girlfriend, a pen pal. I don't know why she stopped writing to me but while it lasted it was terrific. For a short-time I had an American pen pal, and she was a girl!

Wow. What an experience for a teenage boy from Fitzroy who never got to the promised land.

Feeling Unsafe

As a kid I felt completely safe running around the streets of Fitzroy during the day and at night, even though it was considered a rough area. I rarely got into strife with ratbags or gangs of other teenagers.

However, I do remember one day when Lorna and I were in Alexandra Parade, near the Fitzroy baths. It started to rain so we headed towards a shelter shed nearby to stay dry. Out of nowhere some teenagers appeared and started to mouth off at us. We were trapped and scared. They came closer and I thought they were going to bash us up, but they eventually stopped tormenting us and let us go. As they soon as they left, we darted out of the shed into the rain and ran home.

There were gangs of teenagers occasionally roaming around the streets in Fitzroy, usually at night: the Bodgies and Widgies in the 1950s and the Sharpies in the 1960s. I saw them once in a while and numbers varied between a few mates knocking about to the largest gathering I ever saw of about thirty teenagers walking along Johnston Street, just past the HSV7 Teletheatre.

I was never beaten up by a gang, but I did cop a belt in the mouth from louts on one occasion, and a punch in the guts on another. One night I was walking past a cafe in Brunswick Street. A teenager was standing outside and I could sense there was going to be trouble. I was right – he belted me in the mouth without provocation and I took off up the street. I didn't wait to hang round in case his mates inside the cafe decided to join him. I avoided walking past that cafe at night for a long time afterwards and would go down a nearby laneway to avoid him and any other louts in area. It was much safer. I'd also sprint down the laneway, rather than walk, to avoid any other ratbag that may have been lurking around. On another occasion I was walking along Bourke Street in town, near the Southern Cross Hotel, and a group of teenagers spotted me from across the road. One of them ran across towards me and yelled, 'Ah, Goulopoulos,' and belted me in the guts, making me double over. He was a Collingwood Tech kid and for some mysterious reason had a go at me. Again, there was no provocation. It was just another example of being in the wrong place at the wrong time.

Paying attention to my Roy Boy antenna helped me avoid fights in the streets. If a group of gathered teenagers looked sus, I'd automatically look for escape routes in case something happened. The potential for something happening when a group of youths were roaming the Fitzroy streets at night was high, because often they were looking for trouble.

I remember coming home by tram from town after a night out. I alighted on the corner of Brunswick Street and Johnston Street because it was well lit compared with the next stop outside Sims Supermarket known as SSW (Self Service

Wholesalers), two blocks away. I was about to cross at the lights when I spotted a group of teenagers walking up Brunswick Street towards me about a block and a half away. They looked suss in the dark, so I turned left and walked several blocks out of my way to avoid them. It was a relief when I reached my front door, unlocked it and went inside. I always had my key in my hand a few doors from home, because I figured the less time I spent fumbling for it in my pocket the less chance I had of being attacked.

I also remember walking with John along a footpath in the main street of Frankston when a few toughs appeared, heading towards us. It didn't look good, so I quickly manoeuvred John into a milk bar nearby. I thought we were safe until a couple of them came into the milk bar and one said to us, 'Where are yous blokes from?' I said, 'Fitzroy.' He said, 'Oh that's okay.' My heart restarted and I felt such a relief when they ambled out the door. We had dodged a bashing.

Walking or running away from potential trouble was not the only strategy I used to avoid getting another smack in the mouth. Some of the local toughs were customers at the fish shop and I'd say g'day to keep on the right side of them. It was handy to drop a toughie's name if you were challenged in the street. Though I almost got caught out with Tony, who I knew from Cubs and George Street Primary School. I hadn't seen him for a while when I bumped into him at a carnival in a park in Carlton. He had a shitty look about him and didn't recognise me. I sensed that I was about to be hit and said, 'G'day Tony, how's it going?' This stopped him in his tracks and he looked confused. He obviously didn't recognise me but said, 'Ah, pretty good, how you going?' I reckon my fast talk saved me, but I also reckon some other poor kid got a smack in the mouth that night because Tony was definitely looking for trouble.

Apart from these few scrapes, I saw very little violence in Fitzroy. The only fight I can recall seeing happened in Brunswick Street, near David Street. Our family had attended a Maco dance at Cathedral Hall and, when it finished, we all started to stroll home down Brunswick Street. I said to my father, 'Let's catch a tram home,' as I didn't feel it was safe. My father said, 'No, we'll walk.' That made me nervous, so I kept my eyes peeled for possible danger. Halfway home, we saw a fight across the road between an elderly drunk and a young bloke. Well, it was more like an uncoordinated dance with light punches thrown about, some even landing. The young bloke seemed more concerned about keeping enough distance to avoid being hit, and the drunk did well to protect himself. They swore at each other and continued to fight. We just kept walking.

Another time I remember hearing loud bangs coming from the street as I was watching television upstairs in our living room. I stuck my head out the window to see what all the noise was about. I saw two men in suits in front of a knock shop, one of them swinging a sledgehammer trying to smash the door down. I sort of knew they weren't anxious customers trying to get in for a quickie; I guessed they were coppers or Dees raiding the place. After a few more whacks with the sledgehammer, the door gave way and they entered the premises. I suppose it was a sort of foreclosure because the knock shop was soon out of business and disappeared. Another knock shop appeared later a few doors down from the fish shop, but that disappeared before the red bulb light out the front needed changing.

When it came to violence or the threat of violence, Fitzroy had its moments just like any other working-class suburb in Melbourne.

It's such a hard life. Here I am at Port Melbourne pier, fishing.

Hobbies

As a teenager, one of my favourite hobbies was collecting pennies. The fish shop had plenty of them available to build a collection. My target was to collect one for every year they were distributed, from 1911 to 1964. My favourite pennies had the head of a crowned King George V of Britain, surrounded by some Latin words, which I could never figure out. On the reverse side were the words 'Commonwealth of Australia' with the year on the outer circle. The inner circle had the words 'One Penny' in capital letters. This penny was issued between 1911 and 1938. Soon after that the reverse side featured a leaping kangaroo. There were three more redesigns; King George VI (no crown) from 1938 to 1952 and Queen Elizabeth II (wearing a wreath) from 1952 to 1964. No pennies were minted after 1964 and decimal currency was introduced in 1966.

Even though I had access every day to the shop drawer full of pennies, I never found that bloody 1930 one. So few were minted that they remained extremely rare. Recently, one of the proof (highest quality) 1930 pennies sold for $1.15 million dollars! Every now and again I'd remove all my pennies from the plastic bag in which I kept them, spread them out on the kitchen table in several rows in yearly order and smile at my treasure of coins. And of course, there would always be a gap between 1929 and 1931, which made me more determined to find one and complete my collection. I lived in hope that one day I'd go to the cash drawer and discover the 1930 penny waiting for me, but it never happened.

Another hobby I loved when I was very young was riding a tricycle in the narrow space of my backyard, pedalling furiously to avoid boxes and other obstacles in the way. It had no brakes so to slow down or stop I'd reverse pedal. It was such fun to have my own set of wheels and just play.

In my early teenage years, I graduated to a you-beaut two-wheeler by pestering my parents to buy me a bicycle because 'everyone else has one.' Eventually they relented. Jeez, my own bike. It turned my world upside down for the better. It was fantastic. I now had my own set of wheels and could go anywhere rather than walk or catch public transport. I don't remember where I bought it, but it may have been at the bike shop near the corner of Fitzroy Street and Johnston Street. I'd often walked past this shop on the way to the Exhibition Gardens and dream of owning one.

It was a fixed-gear bike, which meant the pedals kept turning while it was in motion. I remember it had a curved handlebar facing down, just like the racing bikes on the *World of Sport* TV program. There was no way I was going to ride with the curved handle facing upwards, the standard position, because I would have looked like a sissy. Fancy sitting upright like a girl – no, I had to lean over and look like a fair dinkum racer, though the upright handles bars would have been easier on my back muscles.

It was a no-frills bike without mud guards or extra gears. I replaced the plastic seat with a blue and white spring seat, which was much more comfortable. My bum muscles would seize up after riding on the plastic seat for a while, so it had to go. I had a white pump attached to a crossbar and I eventually bought a headlight, which was powered by a dynamo. It caused a bit of a drag when attached to the front tyre, which slowed me down, but I had to use the headlight to see where I was going because many of the side streets were poorly lit at night, as they are today,

There were three ways of braking – use the standard hand brake on the left side of the handlebar, reverse pedal or use the heel of my right runner by placing it on top of the rear wheel until the bike stopped. The heel option was a backup in case my hand brake failed, though if I did this too many times the heel of my shoe would eventually be ruined. Sometimes I'd brake this way to show off because it looked dramatic.

I loved racing around the side streets going as fast as I could then taking my feet off the pedals to cruise along. Another fun trick was to brake suddenly at high speed, causing the rear wheel to swerve, before sticking my leg out to balance the bike until it stopped. I'd also let go of the handlebar while in motion to see how far I could go without crashing. This was a challenge on bumpy paths or roads, so I did this only on flat stretches of road. One trick I never tried was to jump off the bike backwards and grab the seat of the bike to stop it. I saw another kid do that, but I was afraid I'd de-knacker myself if I tried it.

Sometimes I'd dink my mate John and he would do the same for me to get around. One of us would sit on either the handlebar or crossbar, while the other would pedal furiously. Once John was dinking me along Argyle Street on the way to play a pinball machine at an espresso bar in Smith Street. He spotted a ten-shilling note on the road, jumped off the bike, and I went arse over head off the handlebars into the road.

'Fucking hell, what are you doing!'
'I had to stop.'
'Why?'
'To get the note.'
'Ah, Jeez, be careful next time.'

I was bruised, but it was worth the fall because we both were able to spend money on a pinball machine.

Sometimes dogs would go berserk, barking and attacking my leg as I cycled past. I remember riding my bike at Yarra Bend Park when a German Shepherd attacked me, biting my calf muscle and drawing blood. I tried raising my leg to avoid getting bitten, but I was too slow on this occasion. Usually if a dog attacked and was persistent, I'd jab at it with the sole of my foot without hitting it, to shoo it away.

Another danger was falling off or crashing my bike, which happened once in a while when I mucked about or rode carelessly at high speeds. I remember speeding down a steep winding path near the Studley Park Boathouse when the front wheel clipped the edge of the path and I flew off and hit the footpath.

One way of drawing attention to myself and the bike was to attach a playing card to the front wheel so the edge of it was between two spokes. As the wheel rotated, the spokes struck the card causing a loud, 'tat, tat, tat,' just like the sound of a machine gun being fired.

I could handle some maintenance and repair jobs like punctures, replacing brake pads, adjusting or replacing the chain, tightening and loosening nuts, bolts and washers. If there was anything more complicated that needed fixing, I'd get John's help as he was pretty cluey about mechanical stuff. I never took my bike to the bike shop for maintenance or repairs because I couldn't afford it.

The only sour memory I have of my bike days was when a local ratbag talked me into letting him borrow my bike. When he returned it, he had replaced my front wheel with an inferior one. The bastard had knocked off my good wheel. What a prick. I had a verbal go at him but that was where it ended. I never got my good front wheel back again.

My bike also helped with my first part-time job delivering morning newspapers each weekday. I tried to get a job at Tony's newsagency just up the road, but he wasn't hiring so I eventually got a paper round at a newsagency in Smith Street, across the road from the post office, several blocks away. The first few mornings were a struggle to get out of bed, hop on my bike in the dark and ride to the newsagency. I thought, 'What the fuck am I doing?' and I had to focus on the money I'd make to stop myself from turning back and heading home to my warm bed. On my way to work, the streets were quiet, but when I arrived that silence was shattered with the bustling activity of newsboys reporting in before collecting and stacking their newspapers into each half of a small, open, hessian saddlebag. I'd drape my newspaper-filled bag over the horizontal bar of my bike, wheel it out of the shop and ride off into the dark to begin my delivery round. The bag was a bloody nuisance because every time I turned it would clip my front wheel. I soon discovered I needed a smaller version of a carpenter's wooden horse attached to the horizontal bar to sling the bag over. This would raise the bag high enough to avoid contact with the wheel when I turned. I built a simple structure, nailing a couple of two-foot planks on either end of a main plank to serve as legs. It worked like a charm and I was now able to cycle freely, without cursing, around the back streets of Fitzroy to deliver my papers.

During my rounds I'd check to see if there was a newspaper rack attached to a letter box and I'd place the rolled-up newspaper there. If there was no rack, I'd chuck it over the yard so it would land near the front door of the house. I rarely got off my bike to deliver newspapers as that would have wasted time. When it rained, I pedalled quickly and swore silently, which made the run go faster. The best part of the job was the ride home, and of course the money I earned. After a few weeks I quit because I preferred to stay in a warm bed than work when most people slept. The cold wet mornings and coming home like a drowned rat killed my desire to continue working. By then I reckoned I'd made enough money anyway.

I was a skinny teenager and became self-conscious about the way I looked, so I decided to build up my virtually non-existent muscles to attract girls and feel good about myself. I stumbled across a Charles Atlas ad on the back of a comic, which I thought would solve my problem. Charles Atlas really was Angelo Siciliano, an Italian American body builder who sold an exercise program on how to build muscles. The cartoon ad featured a skinny kid on a beach being insulted by a muscle-bound bully in front of his girlfriend. He doesn't fight back, is embarrassed, discovers the Charles Atlas ad, and buys the program to build his physique, determined to be able to defend himself. After he builds his muscles, he goes back to the beach with his girlfriend and is confronted by the bully – but this time successfully defends himself. He walks away, arm-in-arm with his admiring girlfriend.

Well, I wasn't interested in confronting bullies or going to the beach, I just wanted to look good. I couldn't afford to pay for the course, so my muscle building efforts were put on hold until I discovered the bullworker, an isometric exercise device. I bought it and it soon began working on it almost daily. The bullworker was about three feet in length, tubular shaped and was metal with plastic hand grips on either end. I gripped the handles and pushed inwards to get an isometric workout. It also had two thick plastic-coated cables on either side of the tubular shape, and I'd pull the cables outwards, like pulling a bow to shoot an arrow, for a different isometric workout. I held it at different angles, compressing and pulling the cables, which worked various muscles. Despite my efforts over a long period of time I only managed to build strength and not muscles like Charles Atlas. I was still a skinny kid so for the time being had to avoid bullies on beaches.

I was also fascinated by a crystal set, which was a basic pocket radio receiver. I decided to build a kit though, like my earlier projects, was interested in the result rather than the construction. The set was a beauty. Unlike my small transistor radio, it didn't require batteries or an external power source because it was powered by the antenna. It was easy to build, even for me. The only store I could find that sold them was near Brunswick. This meant a tram ride of several blocks away from home and a long walk along Scotchmer Street to get to Nicholson Street. The first time I arrived at the store I was excited until I found out they were out of stock. The second time it was still out of stock. Jeez, what a wasted effort. Finally, on my third trip after waiting several weeks, they were available. I was rapt. I took it home, quickly unwrapped the kit and started to build the crystal set. The bloody instructions were confusing, which made reading the manual an irritating but necessary evil for an impatient teenager.

Collecting stamps was fun. I used to save all the international stamps from letters my mother received from Greece, as well as stamps from letters I received from my USA pen pal. I hit the jackpot when I discovered an ad on the back of comic book where you could buy over a hundred stamps for about twenty-five cents. I got onto that quick smart and bought a batch of international stamps. I remember opening the packet when they arrived by mail. I spread them across the table and just gazed at them. My stamp book became full of various international stamps, and I loved flicking through the pages wondering what it would be like to travel to a stamp's country of origin. My stamp album took me around the world in one sitting.

I was always into something as a kid. If I got bored with a hobby or activity, I replaced it with something else that fascinated me. I still do.

Favourite Hangouts

In my early teenage years, I used to haunt Alex's fish shop after school to play the pinball machine. The shop was in Johnston Street near the corner of Smith Street. Alex was a fellow Maco who knew my family and we got on pretty well, though occasionally I did test his patience by spending up to two hours playing pinball, winning game after game. I remember him saying, 'Why are you wasting your time?' I'd just shrug my shoulders and continue playing because I loved that game. It was almost as good as playing the penny chewing gum machine we'd had in our fish shop years before. Playing pinball was also a welcome break between school and home. The excitement of winning, the flashing lights, pressing my fingers on the flipper buttons to strike the steel ball into various scoring structures and crevices inside the glass cover, sounds of points racking up towards a free game – these all sent me into pinball heaven and kept me there until early evening. My favourite moment was when I heard a loud click signalling I had won a free game. Sometimes I'd hear clicking two or three times in a row. Pure bliss. Every free game meant I'd save a shilling for the next game, and when that had happened several times, I'd get a frown from Alex. I was tying up the machine, preventing customers in the shop from playing and spending their money, which was income for him. I'd push my luck and stay as long as I could, leaving only when I felt I was in danger of being chucked out – just like I did as a kid at Tony's newsagency when I hovered around the comic section for a length of time.

Playing the machine was an art form and I spent several hundred hours perfecting my skills to become a fair dinkum pinball artist. There were two ways of winning a game. One required skill and the other pure arse. If you scored a certain number of points, you'd win one or several games in a row. The arsey way of winning was to match the last two numbers of your score with the machine's random two numbers that flashed on when the game ended. I wasn't proud, I didn't care how I won. As long as I did win I was a happy little vegemite. I discovered through trial and error I needed to master five skills to win games: basic stance, relaxation, focus, flipper control and the nudge.

I'd bend my knees, feet apart and slightly crouch forward to psyche the steel ball into doing what I wanted it to do. My palm and thumb rested on the top of the machine while my fore fingers gently rested on the flipper buttons on either side of the machine, ready to spring into action once the ball came within striking distance. Sometimes I'd press the buttons early just to let the ball know it was going to be hit as it rolled downed the slanted table. I then made sure I relaxed my body so I could react quickly because I knew if I tensed up I'd lose control of the ball and the game. Only amateurs tensed up and they usually lost games. Once my body was relaxed and the ball was in play I had to focus on where it was, the direction it would roll in, and at the right moment to strike so it would hit a point-scoring area. Focusing while the ball was in play was difficult because I could be distracted by the sounds, flashing lights and the score line of the machine. But with practice I could do it for an entire game and ignore the distractions. Flipper control was crucial to keep it in play to score enough points to win a game. Sometimes I'd keep my finger on the button as the ball rolled down the inside chute towards me. It would stay in a horizontal position causing the ball to stop. This would give me time to consider which direction I could send it once I let go of the button. When it was released, I'd let it roll down the flipper and quickly press the button again to strike it.

There were two ways of losing the ball, which pissed me off every time they happened. If it rolled into the outside chutes, near the sides of the table, it would disappear into the cavern of the machine. The inside chute was where I wanted it to roll because that led to the flipper. The worst way to lose a ball was when it travelled straight down the guts of the machine without being hit at all. For an amateur that was typical but for an experienced pinball artist like me that was bullshit. Occasionally I could save it if it travelled towards the gap between my flippers by pressing the flipper buttons in a quick one-two sequence. If I was lucky, I could hit the edge of the ball onto the other flipper and keep it in play. This was a very difficult skill, as it involved timing and luck to achieve this miracle save. When this happened, I was absolutely rapt because it meant a higher score and possibly a free game. One thing that comforted me when I lost a ball, no matter how long I kept it in play, was to swear at it when it disappeared out of sight. 'You bloody bastard,' was my usual refrain before I composed myself for the next play. I didn't allow my mind to dwell on the bastard one that disappeared, or I'd lose my focus.

The nudge was also important and a difficult skill to master. It had to be applied correctly – otherwise you'd tilt the machine and the game would automatically be over. And that was worse than losing a ball, because once the game was over it was over and you'd stand there like a stale bottle of piss. Not very pleasant. It had to be a soft, co-ordinated nudge to work, and it involved your palms, bum and hips, and the timing had to be spot on. There were usually about three or four mushroom shaped structures near each other at the top of the table. When one was struck, I'd scored points and then the ball would continue travelling downwards unless it hit something else to change its direction across or up the table. Once it hit a mushroom, I would automatically nudge the machine by wriggling my bum, turning my hips slightly and pushing the machine with my palms in a twisting motion. This would help keep the ball in play between the mushrooms, scoring more points. Sometimes I'd do two or three nudges in a row to give it a bit more oomph.

My infatuation with pinball machines lasted for a year or two. The next time I had a real go at playing a game was about fifty years later, when I visited a friend who had about six machines. My skills were very rusty, though I could still do the essentials. But after a few games I found myself getting tired of playing. That would never have happened in my heyday. The modern machines have more bells and whistles and are flashier, but they are no match for the nuts-and-bolts ones I played in the 1960s. My mate's machines didn't have the same feel, were more complicated and I was playing for free. And somehow there's no comparison between playing a free machine or a paying machine. I'm sure if Alex's pinball machine had been free, I'd have lost interest very quickly. There was nothing like losing my last shilling to a pinball machine – the thought of losing money galvanized me and motivated me to beat it.

During the footy season I'd usually hang out at the Fitzroy footy ground and watch Fitzroy play their home games on a Saturday afternoon. Fitzroy was part of the twelve team Victorian Football League as it was then, and their ground was in North Fitzroy next to the Edinburgh Gardens. The club was founded in 1883 and over time was nicknamed The Maroons, The Gorillas and finally the Lions. It merged with the Brisbane Bears for financial reasons to become the Brisbane Lions in 1996. I wasn't a fanatical Fitzroy supporter, but I was a follower so, when my old team folded, I was sad that a part of the history of my youth had also folded. Some supporters never got over it and refused to follow the league again. Though in spirit it still exists in a way, in the form of the Fitzroy Football Club that plays in Victorian Amateur Football Association lower grade competition. The current club players wear basically the same jerseys and play the same theme song they did in the 1960s. And that's enough for me to travel back into the past when I visit the Fitzroy footy ground.

There was always a big media build up to Victorian Football League games throughout Melbourne before the game, and post-mortems after the game on Saturday night and Sunday.

Newspapers, like *The Herald*, *The Sun*, and *The Sporting Globe*, covered every aspect of the game, as did radio shows and television panel and sport shows. The TV panel shows were on Thursday, Friday and Saturday nights with *World of Sport* on Sundays, which ran from 1959 to 1987 hosted by Ron Casey. My favourite footy show was *League Teams* late on a Thursday night with Lou Richards, Bob Davis and Jack Dyer. They were all previous footy champions turned TV commentators. Lou Richards was known as the kiss of the death for his failed predictions on matches. To say there was saturation cover of football by the media is an understatement. During the footy season there was no escape from VFL football. It was in your face virtually every day and for some die-hard supporters even that was not enough.

I'd usually get to a footy game just before the main game started at 2:30 pm but there were always a few supporters who were there beforehand, supporting the under 19s and reserve games. They'd be rugged up in their woollen beanies, scarves, jumpers and overcoats on a cold winter's day, and would be carrying their thermos flasks to keep themselves going for the day. My favourite player was Kevin Murray, known as Bulldog. He was a tattooed, tough player who stood out for his determination and the skills he displayed during a game. And of course, he was a Fitzroy player. One of our own. I loved the way he marked and burst out of the packs with the ball before kicking it down field. Sometimes I'd stand in the outer if the bench seats were full, among boozy men yelling, 'Carn the Roys!' (come on Fitzroy) and swearing at the umpire, 'You fucking white maggot. You fucking gotta be joking' and other obscene phrases. There were a few elderly ladies who could put the men to shame with their swearing, but they were not part of the outer. Men ruled the outer as it was 'no place for ladies.'

Some men wore Fitzroy-coloured beanies, scarves, footy jumpers, ate Four 'N Twenty pies and drank a never-ending supply of Foster's beer out of cans. At quarter time breaks there would be a mass migration so the blokes could go to the toilets to piss all the beer away, come back revitalised, and start the same process again. Mixed in with this macho environment was the occasional fight, the threat of violence and a fair bit of humour. Empty beer cans littered the outer and they came in very handy to stand on so I could see over the row of men in front of me. I'd also collect the empty cans to sell and earn a few pennies. Once in a rare while I'd sneak into the grandstand where I could sit down in comfort on the bench seats to watch the footy. It was a civilisation away from the prehistoric outer and had a better view of the play. Other times I'd position myself behind the goal posts near the railway yard end of the ground, opposite the Brunswick Street end. It was a spot where you could touch the Sherrin football after it sailed past the goal posts or point posts. I'd grab the ball if I could and either hand pass or kick it to the goal umpires so it could be returned to play. If the footy sailed over our heads and the fence behind us it would be lost forever as kids used to wait outside the ground to nick a football.

I didn't have the patience to stand outside a footy ground waiting for the rare time a footy magically appeared over the wall – even if it was a Sherrin football, the best money could buy. No, I wanted to be part of roaring crowd. So playing with paper and plastic footballs would have to do instead of pinching the almighty stray Sherrin footy.

After a home game, the crowd mood would depend on whether Fitzroy won or lost. A shitty or elated result would still see the pubs full, where scores of supporters would drown their sorrows and blame that mongrel umpire for the loss, or celebrate another fantastic, rare Fitzroy win. Pubs were not the only winners, the fish shop across the road and ours got a fair amount of trade from customers after a footy match.

Footy was a tough game in the 1960s with players colliding, grabbing or belting each other, and occasionally you'd see the aftermath of a king hit. A player would be hit from behind and lie unconscious on the ground. Sometimes the weirdest king hit happened up the other end of ground from where the ball was in play, somewhere in the back line. One moment there would be two players beside each other and in a blink of an eye one player would be lying unconscious on the ground, while another stood with his hands on his hips looking up the ground.

When the footy season was over it felt like living in a huge vacuum, only partly replaced by the upcoming cricket and tennis seasons. Footy was the heart and soul of most suburbs and for many rabid supporters it was a matter of life and death.

Another place I used to haunt was the Fitzroy Library in Napier Street. The library was part of the Town Hall. Walking up the several concrete steps and past the huge pillars near the entrance, I felt like a victorious ancient Roman general about to be received by Caesar. The entrance to the library was guarded by two huge wooden doors about 20 feet high and, once I walked past one of the open doors, I left Fitzroy and entered a sanctuary. The atmosphere inside the library was similar to the museum in town – old world. And it stayed that way for a long time until they refurbished the room and added a large chandelier. Then it became a modern library.

I loved reading books and as a kid would read them in bed at night until it was past our bedtime, when my mum would tell me to turn the light off and go to sleep. If it was a good book, I'd turn the light off and shine a torch to read it under my blanket. When I was small, my favourite books were the children's Little Golden Books. I can't remember any of the titles, but I do remember on each of the front covers was a golden floral vertical strip on the left-hand side. I also remember reading the orange-covered John and Betty books at primary school. I didn't have much of a collection as a teenager because most of the books I read were borrowed from the library. I loved going to the library. When a huge number of books were waiting to be read, selecting one was almost overwhelming. I'd walk around the library studying the various shelves of books until I found one that might be interesting. Or I'd go to the wooden catalogue drawers in middle of the room, slide one out and flick through the cards in search of a title that appealed to me. If I found a book and wanted to borrow it, I'd take it to the librarian, show my card to verify I was a member of the library and he or she would stamp the date it was due back on a slip of paper attached to the inside of the back cover. For a couple of weeks, I had free books to read that I could never afford to buy. Sometimes I'd pick up an old book that had lived in shelves almost untouched for what seemed centuries, just to feel it. It didn't really matter what the book was about or even if was interesting to read. I didn't have to open the book and read it to connect with the author; just holding it in my hands to read the title and the author's name was enough. The old books were written by old people who were long gone, but their words lived on patiently waiting for a new generation to read them.

Silence in the library was enforced with a loud 'shoosh' by the librarian. Or if someone was very noisy the librarian would have 'a word or two' with the culprit. The library was probably the quietest place in Fitzroy back then. Unlike today where libraries are usually the noisiest spots on earth and if you want a bit of shoosh you need to wear ear plugs. My time in the library was like a never-ending Fitzroy Sunday – quiet and otherwise only occupied by the occasional stranger or friend.

I used to catch up with Dennis, a mate of mine from Collingwood Tech, and we'd hang out together on the corner of Fitzroy and Westgarth Streets, across the road from the milk bar. We'd sit on a ledge outside a factory and have a yarn.

I remember one time a tow truck raced up Fitzroy Street past us, ignoring a stop sign – the driver trying to be first on the scene of a car crash, a few blocks away. Dennis and I sat there staring at each other in disbelief as this kamikaze driver sped away.

Another time I happened to be at the scene of a car accident and two trucks arrived within seconds of each other. The towies jumped out and ran towards the driver of the car to get his signature so the car could be towed away. An argument broke out between the towies about who got there first, but one managed to prevail and get a signature and later a commission. The other cursed and drove off. You could make some money if you were quick enough to telephone a tow truck company to report an accident and they were successful in towing a car away. Jays 24-Hour Towing Services paid three pounds for one car or six pounds for two cars towed away.

My other hang outs were picture theatres. Until I was about twelve or thirteen, I went to local ones, The Regent, The Adelphi and Carlton. Then I frequented city theatres, where my favourite was the Athenaeum in Collins Street, next to the Town Hall. I'd hop on a tram at the stop near Johnston Street to get there. Occasionally I'd accidentally catch the wrong numbered tram and end up in Latrobe Street, which made it a long bloody walk across town to the Athenaeum. Even now when I catch a tram, on the occasions I visit Fitzroy to go into town, I always check to see if I'm on the right one. Even if it is, I still get antsy until I feel that left turn into Collins Street. Then I can relax.

My favourite movie was the *The Longest Day* in 1963, set during World War Two and featuring many of my favourite American, British, European stars and character actors. The list included John Wayne, Henry Fonda, Sean Connery (pre-James Bond films), Kenneth More, Jeffrey Hunter, Edmond O'Brien, Gert Frobe, Curt Jurgens and many more. Just about every scene had an actor I recognised, which was one of the major reasons I saw this film five times in its run at the Athenaeum. It was still as exciting lining up for a ticket for a fifth time as it had been for the first and I'd always sit in the front stalls, about mid-way down the centre, in the middle seat. I couldn't afford the balcony seats but that didn't matter because the spot where I sat felt like I was part of the movie. I loved the dramatic sound of 'da, da, da, dum' belting across the theatre at the start of the movie. The huge wide screen lifted the atmosphere of the film and, even though there were several indoor scenes that I appreciate now as an adult, as a kid

I was more interested in the outdoor action.

I'd always stay and watch the end credits to see who else was in the film – as I still do today when I go to the pictures. I never leave until the credits roll by, the music stops and the screen fades to black. It pissed me off if people left before it really ended because they'd usually distract me from reading the credits and enjoying the music. I used to think, 'Jeez, will you just bloody well sit there until it's over'. I have *The Longest Day* on DVD and have watched it several times. It's still good but nothing can match the Athenaeum experience where I watched it as a teenager.

Another theatre I remember was The Plaza, across the road from the Athenaeum. I saw a three-hour 1962 movie, *How the West was Won*, on a huge screen and I almost strained my neck turning my head from side to side to follow the action. The Star theatre in Elizabeth Street played the same movie all day. When I went to see *The Gorgon* and arrived halfway through the show, I stayed after it ended to watch the first half of the next screening.

When I was about nine or ten, I loved hanging out at the Brotherhood of St Laurence youth club in Brunswick Street, near the rough-as-guts Champion and Rob Roy pubs. It could get rowdy outside the pubs but I felt safe walking to and from the club on a weeknight with my mate John, even though I was aware of the possible danger. We'd go there at least once a week, and my favourite night was movie night. Gee, free pictures, what a beauty. I remember the projector at the back of the room shooting out a beam of light towards a screen and highlighting dust particles in its path. Sometimes the dust particles were more interesting to watch than the B grade westerns shown.

Other activities at the youth club included woodwork, playing basketball on the rooftop, games and drawing. I remember winning a prize for drawing – a white western cowboy wagon with red wheels. I treasured that wagon and whenever I played with it I always thought of my drawing that had won this fantastic prize. It was always fun to be there. When club night was over and we walked out of the door, I was back in the real world of Fitzroy, and I couldn't wait to come back next week.

A couple of years later a friend suggested I check out a youth club in Collingwood, run by a bloke called Skipper. I remember going on outings with a fellow group of excited teenagers. We all went to see a movie called *Viva Las Vegas* starring Elvis Presley at the Regent Theatre in town. The movie burst on the screen with colour, music and the bright lights of Las Vegas, a very welcome relief from the colourless suburbs of Fitzroy and Collingwood. On another occasion we saw a movie called *Summer Holiday* starring the British pop star Cliff Richard, also at the Regent in town. And I still can't get that bloody *Summer Holiday* tune from the movie out of my head.

I was at the Collingwood youth club for a short while. I don't think John joined me though we still kicked around a fair bit together as we always did.

I wasn't aware of it, but our relationship was about to change.

Farewell Mate

In our early teens John and I would still go to the Fitzroy baths to swim as well as to various places along the Yarra River – a brown river that some wag once said, 'Floated upside down.'

Our favourite spot was Kanes Bridge, a pedestrian suspension bridge in Studley Park, Kew, near the boat shed, where people could hire rowboats and canoes for a leisurely paddle. There were few rules about behaviour while swimming in the river and rarely anyone there to enforce a rule, such as no jumping or diving off the bridge. I jumped but never dived because it was a humongous height from the bridge to the water and I didn't have the guts to do it. There were a few brave souls who dived and even resurfaced from the water. Jumping was less terrifying and safer because I'd drop straight down feet first, not headfirst where my body could accidentally arc too far forwards or backwards increasing the chance of injury by hitting the water at the wrong angle. I remember climbing over the side of the bridge, standing on a jutting beam and preparing myself to jump. It took a while, but I'd finally do it, making sure my feet pointed downward to avoid hurting my soles when I hit the water. I'd plummet down and disappear into the brown river before quickly swimming to the surface in case something grabbed my ankles and dragged me to the bottom. I'd get four thrills for the price of one; the rush of falling from a great height, hitting the surface of water, plunging down below the surface and swimming back up to the land of the living. And it was all for free.

Sometimes jumpers would time it so they could bomb a passing rowboat, which usually contained families or a pair of lovers. Rowers had little chance of avoiding being splashed because they rowed with their backs to the bridge and wouldn't see a falling body until too late. Very few rowers had the experience or skill to manoeuvre their boat out of range of these bombs. The boatload of people had to sit there and cop a splashing. However, I never tried to bomb a rowboat, afraid I'd hit it and wipe myself out.

Away from the bridge, around the corner of the boathouse on the same side of the river, was a place we called Black Rock. It was a huge rock about twenty feet high, with jagged edges from which we jumped into the river. A little further down on the other side of the river was a large rope attached to a tree, from which we swung and did our bombs. It was a thrill grabbing the rope, taking a running jump and sailing through the air to let go and fall into the river. I remember scurrying up the narrow, muddy bank to get out of the water, half expecting to get stuck in the mud or attacked by some creepy, crawly, slithering creature. There was also another large rope attached to a tree close to Kanes Bridge where I'd swing and bomb any rowboat that came close enough – it was safer

John Burke and me in front of the fish shop, about 1965-1966.

for me than doing it from the bridge. It was so much more fun doing these bombs into the river compared with the Fitzroy baths – there you'd get thrown out for doing more than one.

It was sometimes dangerous swimming in the Yarra. One day I dived off Black Rock, surfaced and saw a bloody snake swimming towards me with its head above the water. I almost shat myself. We both turned in the opposite direction and swam like buggery towards safety. I kept out of the water for the rest of the day just in case it came back. Another time I was walking across a shallow stretch of the river, about a foot deep, and looked down to see a snake swim past. I almost stepped on it. Again, I took off in the other direction at the speed of light.

Pipe Bridge was another swimming area in Fairfield, and it also had a boat shed. Nearby was a popular cleared hilly bank that was an ideal spot for families to picnic and get some relief from the hot summer days. From the boat shed I'd hire a tractor tyre tube, pumped with air, to float around the river. The tube was a huge bugger and I had fun climbing onto it, swimming around and up into the middle of it. It was cheaper to hire a tube than a rowboat or canoe so that was the attraction of swimming there. Though this spot did not have ropes to swing from or a bridge I could jump from, it was an enjoyable alternative.

Dights Falls in Abbotsford was another part of the Yarra River where we mucked about. I loved the contrast between the calm river and the falls where water noisily descended, about six feet, creating rapids that swept over large visible rocks on the riverbed. There was no place to swim safely; the attraction was the adventure of exploring and walking on slippery rocks under the falls near the embankment. One day I slipped and fell into the water but managed to grip a large rock. Thinking I would be swept away and drowned, I yelled out to John for help. He ignored me because he was preoccupied with something else and had his back towards me. I finally struggled out of the water on my own, but the shock of falling made me feel I was in a life-and-death situation and all I could think about was John had not come to help me. The feeling of being abandoned by a mate in a tight situation stayed with me for a while, even though we'd been through a lot of scrapes together and looked out for each other.

Another adventure we shared that had an element of danger was a yonnie (small stone) fight with a couple of ratbags from tech. It was after school and we were both on top of the garage roof next door to John's place when the ratbags spotted us from the street. A few choice words were tossed back and forth. One of the buggers picked up a yonnie and tossed it at us. Then it was on for young and old, and we were soon in a fair dinkum fight. They had the advantage because there was plenty of ammunition on the footpath to chuck at us and bugger all up on the roof. I remember the last yonnie that was thrown because it hit me fair and square in the head. A lucky shot because we'd managed to dodge all the others that flew at us. My head started to bleed and I cursed the ratbag that hit me, 'You wait until school, I'll get you.' It was an empty threat, but it felt good – and it also felt safe, threatening him from the top of the garage roof. That was a serious yonnie fight as we didn't hold back, but other times they were fun. John and I often tossed them at each other although never with the intention of hurting. We aimed for the body, not the head.

Yonnies had plenty of other uses besides chucking them at ratbags or a mate. I'd throw one for the pleasure of throwing it, to see how far it would go, or to try hitting a stationary target. There was a skill in throwing a yonnie that was developed after years of practice. First, I had to find the right one, not too big or too small. I'd then pick it up and move it between my fingers and thumb pads to get a feel for it, although in a real fight there was no time to do this because I had to focus on the attacker. The correct arm and body action were important for power, accuracy and distance. After a million throws, all this became natural and I developed techniques that worked for me. Of course, a successful throw would usually be followed with a silent or loud exclamation, 'You fucking beauty!' or 'Gee, look at that.' There were plenty of yonnies lying around and there was always the temptation to pick one up to throw it. I never threw them in Brunswick Street because it was too busy with people and traffic. The safest places were down lane ways, side streets, parks, or over and into ponds.

Yonnies were also used as a toy to play a game called jacks. You'd place three or four on the back of your hand, throw them in the air and try to catch as many as you could on their way down. They were also a substitute for chalk because you could scratch out a line, letter, word or picture on the ground or on a wall. This was usually done in a laneway or side street, not in a main street.

Fighting and playing with yonnies were fair dinkum games. But John and I did some other silly things for a laugh. One of the dumb ones was our shirt ripping escapade. We decided to rip each other's shirt in turn. I can't remember whose bright idea it was, but it resembled an episode of a Keystone Cops slapstick comedy. Facing him I grabbed his shirt and ripped it. He stood there for a moment and smiled before doing the same to me. Then it was on and we continued this stupidity until both our shirts were ripped to shreds. We looked like we had been hit by a bomb. It's not easy ripping your mate's shirt to shreds with your hands and fingers but it was fun watching the buttons fly off in all directions after an almighty rip. There were lots of shouts of 'oh, yeah!' after each rip and the game got a bit willing[31] towards the end. Eventually we just stood there, breathing heavily and laughing at each other. I realised I'd better go home to change shirts as I looked a right proper dickhead. It was easier for John to change because we were near his place when we started this game. I had to walk a whole block to get home. I kept to the laneway to avoid prying eyes before slipping into the back of my place. I also made sure I avoided my parents before I changed into another shirt and threw the shredded one into the bin.

Another game we got into was sword fighting with homemade wooden swords. We slashed, whacked and stabbed each other until we were either too bruised or exhausted to continue. Even if one of us delivered what could be considered a lethal blow, we refused to 'die' because we were invincible, just like our sword fighting heroes on TV. My sword fighting days took another turn when I convinced my parents to let me join an after-school fencing class. Now I was in the big league, graduating from a home-made wooden broad sword to a steel French foil. I remember holding the foil for the first

---

31 To be 'a bit willing' describes things that are getting a bit out of hand – for example too physical, aggressive, or serious.

time in a shop in town. I gripped the curved cloth-covered handle, touched the circular metal guard and admired the thin rectangular blade, the end of which had a flat piece moulded into it for safety reasons. A real French foil with a pointy end was too dangerous to use for practice or competition. The salesman wrapped it in plain brown wrapping paper that didn't disguise its shape.

I got some odd looks on my way home on the tram as it did look like a concealed weapon. I carried it by the handle, with the blade close to my body. I didn't want to look like a sword-wielding lunatic and it was also easier carrying it that way when I was in the tram. As soon as I arrived home, I went to my room, ripped the wrapping off and in a few uncoordinated moves imitated what I'd seen on TV and in movies. I can still remember the hand positions and footwork from class. I only went to a few classes before leaving because the discipline and training killed my romantic notion of being a sword-fighting hero. Twenty years later I learned a Tai Chi sword form – by that stage I'd developed the required discipline needed to practise each week, which I still do now as part of my Tai Chi training.

Fencing was certainly easier than having a friendly boxing match. I remember when I showed John a pair of toy yellow boxing gloves I had just bought. We were in his living room with his father and a few of his old man's mates. They'd been drinking beer and were a bit sloshed yelling out, 'Have a go.' I had no choice but to box with John as their yells and encouragement got louder and louder. I'm not sure how enthusiastic they would have been if they had copped a few belts around the head. I suppose the booze they had guzzled would have cushioned the pain. I got hit in the mouth, jaw and head. I felt groggy and spent most of my time covering up, throwing very few punches. The ones I did hardly landed on target.

After my short-lived career as a boxer with a 0-1 score card, I could now appreciate the courage of the professional boxers on *Ringside Boxing* on Monday evenings. I could feel every punch that landed but it was much easier and safer being an armchair boxer watching the fair dinkum stuff on TV. The only local boxer I knew who fought on TV ringside was Leo Young, a talented boxer who won many fights. I knew him only to say hello when he came into the fish shop as a customer or when I saw him swimming at the Fitzroy baths. We both acknowledged each other by nodding our heads, but I never had a longer conversation with him.

John and I had our squabbles as kids do and we usually made up afterwards. There was only one time when it got serious and I received a smack in the mouth. I'm not sure who started the argument but one evening, in Nick the Greek's milk bar, there were a few choice words exchanged before he suddenly punched me. It stopped me dead in my tracks. It hurt like bloody hell and I was shocked that my mate had hit me. It had never happened before. Nick tried to settle things down, but I stormed out of the milk bar cursing John. As I walked past Frank Dempsey's butcher shop, a block away, I saw John leaving the milk bar. I yelled and cursed him again. Somehow, we did manage to patch things up and continue our friendship for a time.

However, one day a kid named Clarence appeared with John – and from that time on our relationship changed. Clarence wasn't a mate of mine, he was John's mate, but now when John and I mucked around together Clarence was always there. He was a nuggety type of kid, the same age as John. He had crew cut hair and usually walked with fingers tucked into the pockets of his faded jeans. He was friendly and often cracked sarcastic jokes in that old Aussie way. There were now three of us and I started to feel left out of my mateship with John. It used to be just John and me and now it was very different.

The three of us would go to Walter Lindrum's pool hall in town on a Friday or Saturday night to play billiards. We'd walk into town in the early evening, to save money on tram or taxi fares, which was okay. What I hated was the walk back late at night because, when we reached the dimly lit back streets of Fitzroy, I was always concerned we'd get jumped by louts waiting in the shadows. John and his mate didn't worry, but I was on the alert and it was such a relief to reach home safely. I'd suggest we travel by public transport, but the response was always, 'Nah, we'll walk and save our money.' I stopped asking after a while and simply had to brace myself for the worst part of the evening – the walk home.

I didn't dislike Clarence and got on okay with him until he pulled a smart-arse stunt that pissed me right off. He suggested we go to the pictures in town on a Saturday night and meet outside the Plaza Theatre in Collins Street. So, I dressed up for the occasion – brown suit, yellow shirt, a wide yellow-spotted brown tie and black shoes. I arrived at the theatre about thirty minutes early and waited until John and his mate eventually arrived dressed in their street clothes. Clarence said to me, 'What are you all dressed up for?' I said, 'We're going to the pictures, aren't we?' 'Nah, we're going to Lindrums.' He laughed and both he and John started to walk to Lindrums, while I stood there and fumed. I think they expected me to follow them, but I turned around and walked downstairs into the theatre. After that episode I just tolerated Clarence when we were all together.

One Sunday afternoon the three of us were hanging around a tram shelter near the corner of Alexandra Parade and Smith Street. We stood around talking and either John or Clarence did some chin ups on the roof of the shelter to stretch out a bit. A few minutes later a police divvy van pulled over and a cop got out and accused us of mucking about on the tram shelter. We were bundled into the back of the divvy van and driven to the Fitzroy police station at the back of the Town Hall about half a mile away. It was a very long half mile, riding in a cop van with wire guards on the windows. Because I'd been in trouble with coppers before, even though it was years ago, I was scared of what would happen once we got inside the cop shop.

Shortly after we walked into the police station I was taken to a separate room and this big bastard of a copper hovered over me yelling in my face. I was shaking like a leaf and kept my eyes on the floor. He shouted, 'Look at me.' I didn't have to be told twice so I looked up. I didn't want to get belted. He accused us of being vandals and interrogated me for what seemed like hours, though it was probably only a few minutes. Finally, he told me to get out and go home, and I left the police station holding my breath. I thought that was the end of it but a few minutes later a cop car pulled up beside me and that same copper opened the passenger side door. 'Where do you live?' I told him and he said, 'Get in.' I climbed into the car not knowing what to expect, but he simply drove me home. Not a word was spoken on the way. Looking back now I think we were probably dobbed in by someone who lived near the tram shelter and thought we were louts. I also think the copper who intimidated me may have had a guilty conscience about the way he treated me, which is why he gave me a ride home.

Later I found out that Clarence had the worst of the interrogation, because he was whacked across the head with a telephone book. The copper asked him how many brothers he had and he would have answered, 'One.' The copper then belted him over the head with a telephone book and said, 'That's for your brother.' I don't know for sure but I imagine his brother must have been in trouble with the cops before. I felt sorry for Clarence when I found out what had happened to him. For a long time after that experience, I was wary of coppers and felt they were best avoided.

However, the detectives who investigated what we thought was a robbery at the fish shop were good blokes. My dad discovered cash that he'd hidden away to be banked had disappeared and he called the cops. Two detectives arrived and they were friendly with my dad, asking questions about the money. I was surprised because of my previous experiences with uniformed coppers. Later my dad realised he had misplaced the cash and it wasn't stolen after all. He didn't report it because he thought he'd get into trouble. There was also no way known I was going to contact the coppers. We figured it was best for everyone concerned just to forget about it.

In my teen years I remember going to John's place to help him work on his go-kart, which he stored in his backyard. My intention was to help but all I really did was stand around and watch John and Clarence work on it. I was never mechanically inclined or interested in the mechanics of a go-kart. My interest was the end result – a go-kart that didn't fall apart while I was driving it. I suppose I could have developed an interest, but I rarely had a chance to do so because it was quicker for John to do the work. All the same, I felt left out.

Once the go-kart was ready to go, John would tow it behind his bicycle all the way to a concreted area beside the start of the Tullamarine Freeway in Flemington, about three miles away. All up that was about six miles of towing there and back. A bloody huge effort for John, though not for me as I don't remember ever towing it. Racing the go-kart on the concrete expanse was ideal because it allowed us to travel a decent distance without any obstacles. We'd each have a turn at driving the go-kart flat out and it was terrific. The engine noise, the speed and the open area felt like we were on a racetrack.

However, we had to be careful of the open drainage areas scattered around because the walls had a drop of about four to six feet. I remember seeing another go-kart in the distance, travelling away from us at high speed, when it suddenly disappeared. The driver had failed to stop when he reached an open drainage area and plummeted into it. Apparently, he didn't know the area well enough and paid the penalty. It was deceptive when you looked across the concrete landscape because you couldn't clearly see a drainage area until you were close up to it. We knew the area and knew when to stop, so we were able to avoid the same fate as that kamikaze driver.

My relationship with John had been slowly changing from best mates, when we hung out together just about every day, to occasional hangouts, often including Clarence. Then one day it happened. We stopped seeing each other, even though we lived only a couple of blocks away from one another and at one stage he worked for two days a week at Penders cake factory next door to the fish shop. There was no falling out or dramatic moment to end our relationship as mates. It just evolved to a point where he had different interests and responsibilities.

One or two years later I bumped into him outside the Evelyn Hotel in Kerr Street and we said, 'G'day, how ya going,' and had a brief yarn. Curiously a copper walked by as we were talking and said, 'What are you doing here, Burke?' I didn't know what that was about and didn't ask.

The next time I saw John was in 2014, about 45 years later, when I interviewed him for this memoir at his home in Hampton Park. It felt like old times, and we had a good yarn about the past as mates do. He hadn't changed much, and he said the same about me. Though he had far more hair than I did at that point. I was saddened to hear he tragically lost four family members over just a few weeks in 2002. His father, mother, eldest sister Helen, and a brother-in-law had all died.

This reaffirmed my view of the importance of family, relationships and the limited time we all have on this earth. I'm much closer now to the end of my life than the beginning and, as each day passes, I'm aware of the need to make every moment count.

Duelling Identities

Before John disappeared from my life I remember he'd occasionally tease me about my surname, 'Goulop-alop-alos' which annoyed me. I never worried about my surname as a kid but in my teen years I was very sensitive about it.

I was also teased at Collingwood Tech about having a Greek surname as were all the other kids who had a foreign name. Aussie kids would sometimes taunt migrant kids with derogatory words and phrases such as 'bloody dago, Itie, wog, go back to your own country'. Migrant kids would fire back with 'skips or skippy, convicts, you came here with a ball and chain'. Both sides often peppered their insults with the common language of 'get stuffed, go fuck yourself', or 'fuck off.' I don't remember copping many insults about my surname, but I do remember occasionally being stirred about it. Other kids whose names ended in 'opoulos', which means 'son of' in Greek, were not sensitive and it wasn't an issue for them. But it was for me.

I identified myself as a fair dinkum Aussie who lived in two worlds – an Aussie world and the Maco world. And as soon as my surname was mentioned it instantly identified me as Greek which I grew to dislike. In my late teens when I started playing basketball, I unofficially used the name Bozen for a short time as my surname. Bozen was a derivation of Bozinis (Greek) or Borsher (Maco), my grandfather's first name and uncle's middle name. Bozen to me sounded much better and had fewer syllables than Goulopoulos. My father also used the surname of Bozen when he signed bills for the fish shop because it was easier and more convenient than signing Goulopoulos. However, that was the only time he used this as his surname.

I tolerated my surname until 1974, when I decided to change it officially to a more common Anglo-Saxon name. One day I picked up a telephone book and scrolled though names until I discovered 'Bennett'. I thought, 'Ah, that's it, a good old Aussie name that won't draw attention to my migrant background.' I engaged my solicitor cousin, Andrew Goulopoulos, to change my surname by deed poll to Bennett. At the same time, I changed my first name from Chris to Christopher because I liked the sound of it – although everybody calls me Chris and I introduce myself as Chris. So, it's only on official documents I'm known as Christopher.

For the next four decades I never volunteered to reveal my original surname of Goulopoulos to anyone. Only my family, relatives, very close friends or officials who needed proof of my name knew my former name. One irony is that I had to use Goulopoulos to identify myself to relatives whom I'd not seen or spoken to for many years, when I contacted them for this memoir. As a Bennett, I'd sometimes be picked up on the way I pronounced a word, and someone would enquire about my background. I'd always deflect the question with, 'I was born here.' If pressed for an answer, I'd use humour to avoid answering the question.

Other relatives also changed their surnames for different reasons. One of my relatives applied for a job in the late 1950s and was told by a boss's secretary that if his name was Australian, he would have got the job. He applied for many jobs and received a similar response, but he persevered and eventually landed a job where he stayed for over twenty years. Another cousin changed his name because he felt his migrant surname would affect his career prospects in the public service. A third relative told me his father decided to change their surname to an Australian name because of the prejudice against foreigners. They were called 'bloody dagos' by some Aussies. So, when he was at high school in the 1950s, his father changed the family surname. Later his best mates discovered he had a Greek background and wouldn't talk to him although he said they 'gradually came around'.

Some of my other relatives anglicised a surname by shortening it because it was too long and difficult for some Australians to pronounce. Goulopoulos became Gould and I thought of doing this too, but for some reason never did. Other relatives changed or anglicised their surnames because they felt they were here in Australia and they might as well become Aussies.

On the other hand, there were some relatives who were proud of their surname and the Greek heritage it represented. They kept their Greek surname because everybody knew them by that name and they felt if they changed it no one would know who they were.

Duelling Identities

Although my birth certificate states my surname as Goulopoulos, that is not my father's original surname. In the early twentieth century, Greek authorities forcibly Hellenised non-Greek first names, surnames and place names. This caused huge resentment from many of those affected and added to the Macedonian/Greek identity controversy that still exists today, both in Greece and here in Australia.

The forced name and place name changes were part of the major repressive steps the Greek government took to stop what they thought was the influence of neighbouring countries interfering in Greek affairs and making claims on what was then Greek territory, such as the northern region of Macedonia. Another major step was to ban the speaking of Maco in the Lerin area and elsewhere. Ironically, throughout history, anti-Greek sentiment in neighbouring countries also included repressive measures such as forced name changes and banned language for Greeks as well. Repression and prejudice have no ethnic boundaries.

All my family and relatives who were born in Greece were affected by the forced name changes, and the spelling and pronunciation of names varied in both Greek and Maco. My father's original name of Kosta Gulefsi was changed to Konstantinos (Kostas for short) Goulopoulos and my mother's original name, Menka Stamkov (or Stamkoff), was changed to Melpomeni Stamkos. However, on her 1949 Greek passport and 1950 marriage certificate her surname was spelt Stamkou which is the feminine version of Stamkos. My maternal grandfather's first name was changed from Tarnus to Athanasios. He was also known as Arthur here in Australia. I never heard my father complain of the name changes, nor did

I ask him when he was alive what he thought of it. To Aussies he was known as Kon. However, my mother was resentful of the forced name change. She continued to use and was known by her original name of Menka in our migrant community. Here in Australia one customer in the fish shop called her Mary, a name that stuck in the Aussie community. It was a name she didn't like and I'd often correct it on her behalf when someone called her Mary. She'd never correct the person herself as she didn't want to make a fuss. Lorna's Greek name was Eleni, but her Maco name was Lena, which was what my parents called her. Her Australian name came about when a teacher in kindergarten misheard the pronunciation of Lena calling her Lorna by mistake, and that name has stuck.

Village names were also changed. My father's village Bitusha was changed to Parori and my mother's village name was changed from Armensko to Alona. The township nearby had its name changed from Lerin to Florina. Even though people and place names were Hellenised, the original names were still used privately. I remember the original names spoken in Maco at home and at functions as a child and adult.

I had heard Gulefsi mentioned when I was young – and if I'd been fully aware it was our original family name, I may have changed my own name to Gulefsi years later. Now, when I am asked about my migrant family name, I say it was originally Gulefsi but Hellenised to Goulopoulos. That covers all bases. The name Gulefsi resonates with me as it is my original family name and part of my migrant identity. But I feel it's too late to make another name change and I'm comfortable with Bennett.

One name or term that has had an impact on my identity is the word 'Macedonian'. It has also impacted my family, relatives and many others who were either born in Greece or its neighbouring countries in the Balkans area. It also had an effect on the many children who were born in Australia and whose parents or grandparents were born in the Balkans. Depending on who uses it or in what context, the terms Macedonia and Macedonian can either generate a sense of pride and nationalistic fervour or hostility and conflict. The controversy over the use of these words is over a century old – and to a lesser extent still exists today.

The controversial Greek/Macedonian major identity issue started to gather momentum probably around 1912, when the Greek authorities forcibly Hellenised people's names and place names and punished anyone who spoke Maco in public.

Macedonia was originally called Macedon, an ancient kingdom founded in 808 BC. The area was much larger than its current size and covered parts of other countries that were created over the centuries.

In 1913, after the second Balkan war – when Bulgaria fought Greece, the Ottomans, Serbia and Romania – the Treaty of Bucharest partitioned the Greek region, Macedonia. Greece held onto the southern part of Macedonia and Serbia and Bulgaria claimed the other part. Partitioning created new borders and split apart families from nearby villages. My cousin told me an uncle's wife had to get permission from customs to visit her parents in a nearby village because of the new border. People who had previously lived in the Macedonia region of Greece were now part of another country.

The current Republic of North Macedonia was previously part of The Former Yugoslav Republic of Macedonia, which formed in 1991 after breaking away from the now defunct country of Yugoslavia – which itself has had four name changes, three including the word Yugoslavia. When it existed, Yugoslavia was comprised of six republics: Bosnia and Herzegovnia, Croatia, Macedonia, Serbia, Slovenia, and Montenegro – now all countries of their own after the break-up of Yugoslavia in 1992.

Greece always objected to any country using the word Macedonia to describe a state or territory other than its own. Greece's view was that the northern region of Greece, Macedonia, was the only legitimate Macedonia. This changed in 2019 when Greece compromised and agreed with the Former Yugoslav Republic of Macedonia (FYROM) to recognise the renaming of FYROM to the Republic of North Macedonia. Currently there is a northern region in Greece called Macedonia and bordering this region is a country called Republic of North Macedonia.

There are those who regard themselves as Macedonians and speak what they call Macedonian or what others called 'po narshi'. Research suggests po narshi is a South Slav language that is completely different from the Greek language. Though there are also claims po narshi is Macedonian and was the original language spoken in Greece in ancient times. There are also those who believe the Macedonian region is part of Greece, its citizens are Greek and there is no such identity as Macedonian unless you consider the recently formed new country of the Republic of North Macedonia. And even then, many view these people as Southern Slavs who simply live in a country called the Republic of North Macedonia.

It was never an issue within my family, though I heard my father was sympathetic to the Greek view and I knew my mother was sympathetic to the Macedonian view. When I interviewed various relatives for this memoir there were some who said they were Macedonian, some who said they were Greek, and both were proud of their different identities. In the part of Greece where my parents grew up, some villages were considered more Macedonian while others were more Greek. Even in these villages, there were families divided by this issue.

One of my relatives has a small sign near the entrance of his house, positioned at eye level, that says he refuses to discuss politics – meaning the Greek/Macedonian controversy. He put it there because of his frustration with debating this topic, which usually ended in an argument.

I remember as a teenager visiting a Greek mate of mine in North Fitzroy and being introduced to his mother. It was a pleasant interaction until she asked me, 'What's your background?' I said, 'Macedonian.' She exploded in anger and said, 'There's no such thing and you're a Greek!' A similar scenario happened to some of my relatives when they described themselves as Macedonian to someone of Greek descent. This still happens today because beliefs are so entrenched on both sides, sometimes provoking a very emotional response. Because of my experiences as a teenager, I've always been wary when describing my background. I say, 'My parents were born in Greece,' and leave it at that. Sometimes the less said the better.

Within this Greek/Maco identity controversy, there's also an issue with language. I speak Maco, the language I spoke at home and within our Maco community when I was young. I still speak it with some of my relatives whose English skills are poor, though one of them described the Maco we speak as village Maco and 'not educated Maco'. Children were verbally or physically punished if they spoke Maco in public in my mother's day. She remembers her cousin chasing her in the playground yelling out, 'Menka, wait for me' in Maco. The teachers heard this and her cousin was punished the next day; she was whacked with a stick across an open hand by a teacher. Even if a teacher was out of hearing range, students could still be dobbed in for speaking Maco by a fellow student monitor who could either report it to a teacher or place a nail next the guilty child's chair. Adults were also punished. A man cursing his donkey in Maco got into trouble with the authorities. A woman and daughter walking along a street in Lerin while speaking Maco were overheard by another woman from her second storey window, and she tipped dirty dish water over them. The police were involved and said, 'What's this language you spoke?'

I remember when I visited Lerin for the first time in 1996 with my mother and sister – my mother's first visit since she left in 1949. We arrived at the train station and took a taxi to her relatives' home and were met by Magda, a cousin she'd not seen for 47 years. They embraced and we all went inside to meet Magda's son, daughter-in-law and their two children who were about eight and twelve years old. Three languages flew across the room – English, Greek and Maco – as we all spoke excitedly. The children's father spoke only Greek, and my mother would translate for me into Maco what he had said. I spoke Maco to Magda and her daughter-in-law, but English to the children, who spoke it with an American accent.

During our stay in Lerin, I rarely heard Maco spoken in the streets or the shops. I was conscious of possible conflict if I spoke it in public, just as my mother had experienced decades ago, so I only spoke it if the other person indicated they did as well. In reality there wouldn't have been as much trouble as there had been in my mother's time. On subsequent trips to Greece in 2014 and 2018 I did hear the language spoken in a supermarket and market but only by older adults and rarely by young people.

I was advised by my cousin in Australia not to say I spoke Macedonian if asked in Greece, but to say I spoke po narshi. I took his advice in case I caused offense to a Greek-speaking person.

On my last trip to Greece, Magda's son and daughter-in-law, both aged in their forties, took my partner and me for a day trip to Bitola in North Republic of Macedonia. I was astonished and delighted to hear Maco spoken in the streets and cafes as we wandered around. I could just about understand every word, unlike the Maco I hear on our ethnic radio and TV here in Australia where I only understand the odd word or two. Whenever I speak Maco nowadays, which is rare because both my parents have passed away and I don't mix with our Maco community as I once did as a child, I feel completely at home. It's in my bones and it forms a strong sense of my identity.

My Maco is basic and occasionally I throw in an English word, though I can be understood by other Maco speakers in Greece and here in Australia. When I spoke Maco in Greece I had to really focus on what I said because some of my slang Maco words, with the odd English word chucked in, did confuse the listener. I had to be more precise to be understood clearly. When I was introduced to someone in Greece who spoke Maco I always would start the conversation, 'Snay-em, po mull-lor,' (I know a little).

I remember a couple of amusing encounters speaking and overhearing Maco. In my visit to Lerin a few years ago, I was at a cafe ordering a meal in English from a child waitress. She couldn't understand what I was saying and brought her mother, the owner, over to see what I wanted. Somehow a Maco word slipped in and in a friendly, exasperated manner the mother said, 'Why didn't you tell me you spoke Maco!' On another occasion I was shopping at the supermarket trying to pay the cashier and had difficulty giving her the right amount of Greek coins. Someone in line behind me saw what was happening and said, 'Ee-vor ill-oof,' (he's stupid). I ignored the comment because I didn't want to make a scene.

I had some wonderful conversations with strangers in Lerin. There was an old man in the village square, the cleaner in my hotel and a young fellow I met at a restaurant. While there I enjoyed wandering around the market listening to the Maco spoken by elderly people, both stall holders and shoppers. It was one of the highlights of the trip because I felt at home more than 9,460 miles from where I lived, had been born and grew up.

What it means to be Greek, Macedonian or Greek-Macedonian remains a political and hotly debated issue for many. As for me, I have no fixed opinions and no interest in pursuing it. It's an endless argument that has no conclusion.

So, who am I?

I'm an Australian with a Maco background. For me the word Maco describes the culture and language of the Lerin area and our local migrant community here in Australia. A culture and language that shaped a large part of my identity when I was growing up and is still part of me today.

A Final Reflection

It's certainly been quite a journey – not only growing up in Fitzroy as a kid, but writing about it now as an adult when I decided to explore that early part of my life. There's more to my story of course and, for the curious, here is a brief snapshot of the 'what happened next' part.

1969 was my last year at Collingwood Tech. After five grinding years of boredom, interspersed with a lot of mucking around, I was about to be released from another institution. I was almost seventeen and eagerly awaited my exam results at the end of the year. I'd planned to go to college but, to my horror, discovered I was six marks below the pass rate. My bloody low mark for chemistry dragged down my total score. I was devastated and didn't know what to do. Luckily, the school relented and gave me the six marks I needed – so I was awarded my form-five Leaving Certificate and my ticket to freedom. I was rapt and on my way to the next phase of my life.

That same year I was introduced to basketball, which played a significant role in my life for several years.

A Final Reflection

I finally left Fitzroy in 1974 because I'd had enough of living in the fish shop and wanted to be closer to where I was working at the time.

In the following decades I dropped in and out of various colleges, eventually completing a Bachelor of Arts degree. I worked in some brain-dead jobs, before starting a small business in 1994 teaching Tai Chi because it was – and still is – my passion.

But all of that is another story, which I might also get around to telling one day – and perhaps in doing so I'll learn as much about life and myself as I have in writing this one.

When I started this memoir in 2011, I had no intention of including any details of my migrant background. Those were personal and I didn't want to share them with the public. However, when I told my partner, Sue, about what I planned she said, 'You can't do that.' I asked, 'Why not? It's my memoir.' She replied, 'Because your migrant background is essentially part of who you are.' It took some time for her to convince me and I'm very thankful she did. Otherwise, I would have written a 'doughnut memoir'. One that was thick on the outside but nothing in the middle – all surface no depth.

When I began, I felt uncomfortable writing about my migrant background – but my determination to complete the project overcame my embarrassment about revealing it to the public. But that's a characteristic of mine. When I decide to plunge into a project, I do everything I can to complete it, I give it a 'red hot go' regardless of real or imagined barriers.

As I kept writing, a major transformation took place that surprised me. I started to feel comfortable talking about my background to those who asked. Previously, over several decades, I would never volunteer any information about it and, if pressed, would deflect the question with humour. I must admit I still have the odd twinge sometimes when discussing my background, but it quickly disappears and away I go. Old habits are hard to break.

I had to confront my discomfort in a big way after meeting Sue in 2005. After several months together I had told her nothing of my name change or migrant background, though I knew eventually I'd have to do so. I kept it to myself – that is until she told me her current neighbours, who had previously lived across the road from my mother in Boronia, told her they had seen me at my mother's place. Right then I knew I was done for. I decided to tell her and arranged for her to meet my mother for tea in Boronia.

Now there was no way out. I was nervous and said nothing all day. Finally, just five minutes before we had to leave for my mother's place at 5:00 pm I said, 'I have something to tell you.' She listened, simply said, 'Okay' and that was it. I feel like a bit of a dill now, but back then it was a huge step for me to take. We often joke about that moment and call it the 'five to five', which has become our catch phrase for any last-minute arrangements or decisions.

I suppose the longer I kept my 'secrets' in a box, hidden from view, the more they became an issue for me but, as I discovered, not for anybody else. Since then, I've learned imaginary demons tend to disappear once they're out in the open and have nowhere to hide. Compartmentalising issues was a way I always coped, and even today I still tend to do the same thing when I'm dealing with any major issue. I put things in a box to deal with them when the time is right. The

A Final Reflection

only difference now is that I don't wait decades to wipe the dust off the box and open the lid.

The major influences that shaped my personality I now appreciate and can draw strength from them when I need to. At the time some were traumatic, but I survived them, and I've never felt like a victim of my past. I don't like using the word victim because I don't feel it's appropriate or healthy to categorise myself as one. If anything, I see myself as a kid who 'got through' difficult times over which I either had no control or did have control and stuffed up.

There are other aspects of my personality that have remained consistent since I was a kid. I still get excited about new things. I'm resilient, full of ideas, adventurous, always looking for new challenges, cheeky and enjoy a good laugh. Not bad for a seventy-year-old.

I sound like a saint, don't I? Not really. I can also be stubborn, take on too much, become impatient with those who don't try, and sometimes dismiss negative things too quickly just to get on with the here and now. I sometimes think too much about people's actions and reactions and I tend to hold back and observe people before engaging in conversation. That's probably my Roy Boy antenna kicking in to suss people out. I don't trust people easily until they prove they are trustworthy. Once I trust a person, I'm loyal.

One of the things that hasn't carried over from my childhood to adulthood is mateship. Until my mid-teens I had mates with whom I knocked around on a regular basis. We'd muck about together and I would visit their homes whenever I felt like it. However, since those days my friendships with others have relied on being part of various clubs. Many of those later friendships lasted from a short time to several years – but only while I was in a club. When I left, the friendships withered away. Once in a rare while I'd catch up with friends, but it is never the same as my childhood and teenage years.

My experience of being bullied at Collingwood Tech as a first-former and picked on over the years because of the smell of fish and chips led to a passion in me to support the underdog. If I see someone bullied, I tend to speak up in support. Another form of bullying I hate is discrimination. Some of my family and relatives were discriminated against because they were migrants, though I didn't cop any because I sounded and looked like an Aussie. But, as it was then and still is now, if you speak another language in public and/or have a different skin colour you can cop a serve from an ignorant person.

Everybody wants a 'fair go' and those who get more of a fair go are usually well off, white and Anglo Saxon. But if you are poor, from a different ethnic background or black, you often must wait in line for a fair go. And many in that line miss out. I have never understood why a rational person can be prejudiced against another person because of skin colour or ethnic background. It's not logical and probably is a learned behaviour handed down through the generations. I suppose I am prejudiced against prejudiced people, and I have very little time for them. This is awkward sometimes when I am in a social situation and have to listen to drivel. I simply switch off because I know I can't have a rational discussion with them.

From my Turana days I have developed a passion for social justice, though I'm not active in that area. When I think about that time, I wonder what happened to the kids who got into trouble like I did. Did they have a family support system

A Final Reflection

like me, or were they discarded and at the mercy of a justice system that put young kids into an institution and left them to fend for themselves? I was lucky I got out of Turana after three weeks and in one piece, thanks to the intervention of my family and relatives. Some Turana kids experienced physical, sexual, and psychological abuse. And some kids served far longer sentences than I did, ending up in a life of 'vice and crime' eventually serving time in Pentridge prison.

Before I started writing this memoir over eleven years ago, I never thought about my past as much as I have now. I've reflected, researched and analysed my history in minute detail – and I'm still curious about it. I thought I'd get sick of it after a while but the more I've learned the more I have wanted to learn. However, it will be good to finish this memoir and get a life again.

The process of writing this has also allowed me the opportunity to catch up and have a yarn with friends and relatives I'd not seen in years or even decades. Three of those relatives passed away not long after I interviewed them. Interviews gave me the chance to cross reference stories for accuracy as well as learn much more about my family and relatives and their early experience in Greece and Australia, covering the early 1900s into the 1950s.[32] Some of the surprising things I've learned

---

[32] Some of my early research was limited because official records of families were generally kept only after the Balkans wars of 1912–13. Many of those records were destroyed by the Partisans during the Greek Civil War 1944–49. Researching graves for names and dates in Greece was also difficult. At different times in the past, graves had been dug up with existing bones washed and reburied with someone else who had died, with no record of names and dates.

have given me a much deeper appreciation of what they endured, along with many other migrants of that era.

I've also found myself reflecting on the importance of relationships. As a kid I never thought much about this, but writing this memoir has emphasised to me that life is about relationships not personal achievements. In some ways this is not just about a period of my life but also a tribute to my family, telling their stories and acknowledging how much they meant to me – and still do. One of the rituals I have, to acknowledge those of my family and relatives who have passed away, is my annual pilgrimage to where they are buried. I visit the Fawkner and Springvale cemeteries, stay at each grave site for a short time to reflect, lay some flowers on the grave and say, 'G'day.'

I've also travelled to Greece for research and walked the streets of Lerin and my parents' villages to get a feel of what it was like in the old days. While there, I talked to relatives and strangers about their experiences of the past, gaining an insight into the things that influenced and affected my parents.

The memoir has also re-ignited my interest in learning Greek. As a child I had the opportunity to learn Greek when my parents encouraged me to attend a Greek school held at the Fitzroy Town Hall on a Saturday morning. I lasted one lesson because there was no way I was going to give up any more Saturday mornings when I could be roaming around the streets of Fitzroy having fun. I've tried a couple of times recently but haven't succeeded due to lack of time. I want to learn Greek to get a flavour of what my parents and relatives also spoke in Greece and here in Australia. I'd be very happy to be able hold a basic conversation with anyone in Greece

A Final Reflection

the next time I visit there. Just as I did in basic Maco, which I spoke with native Maco speakers.

My migrant, working class background and my childhood escapades certainly shaped the person I am now. As did my family, relatives, friends, a few ratbags and a bunch of other characters.

Other influences that have shaped me include my experiences in the streets of Fitzroy and its major iconic places, such as our fish shop, Fitzroy baths, the library, the cop shop, Fitzroy footy ground, George Street Primary School, Collingwood Tech, the Maco club, The Regent picture theatre, The Brotherhood of St Laurence – and of course Turana and Toolamba farm.

To share my story, I extensively researched Fitzroy's history. I've learned more about the suburb as well as refreshing and confirming memories I have about growing up there. And that's been deeply satisfying.

When I wander the streets of Fitzroy today, I can still see the ghosts, hear the sounds, and smell the odours of old Fitzroy.

After all these years, I'm still a Roy Boy.

Acknowledgements

A special thank you to Sue James who inspired and challenged me to write a fair dinkum memoir and not a doughnut memoir – one with an empty core. Her efforts in providing honest and insightful feedback over several years is very much appreciated.

I'm forever grateful for the stories my mother told me when I was growing up and the several interviews we did for this memoir. She shared her feelings and experiences growing up in Greece as a child and young woman. Reminiscences of her early life in Australia as an immigrant gave me a deeper appreciation of the achievements, difficulties and sacrifices she experienced, as did many migrants of her era.

I'm thankful to my sister, Lorna, who was always available to answer my many questions about our childhood. She verified, challenged, and triggered many of my memories of events, which has greatly added to this memoir. I'm also grateful for the cappuccinos she shouted me at the local cafe when we caught up several times for a yarn about 'the good old days'.

I was fortunate to interview several of my relatives face to face and record memories of their experiences in Greece, Australia and with my parents as far back as the 1920s. The Stamkos branch included Velika Mitchell, John Mitchell, Fania Mitchell, Magda and Tom Missios. The Goulopoulos branch included Marie, Andrew, Sophie, Sam, Angelo and Nick Gould. I was able to discover new information about my family and extended family, which intrigued, delighted,

Acknowledgements

and saddened me. It gave me rich material I could draw from, which added to the memoir, and I'm indebted to all who were interviewed. And thanks to the friends of my relatives and the strangers I talked to about their experiences when I was in Greece in 2014.

My childhood friends, John, Joyce, and Denise Burke were extremely helpful in sharing stories about our experiences in Fitzroy during the 1950s and 1960s. It was a delight to catch up after several decades apart. Sharon, John's wife, was also helpful in providing additional information during my interview with him.

Thanks to Max Deliopoulos, a mate from my primary and early secondary school days. We had a good yarn, and I was pleasantly surprised when he showed me his Collingwood Tech blazer, still in good condition. Mine disappeared soon after I left tech.

I appreciated the helpful telephone interviews with Vicky and Sheryl Scott. I learned more about their family and experiences of living in Fitzroy.

Several Facebook groups were a valuable source of information and verification of people and events. My thanks to all those group members who assisted me.

Jim Setcos from one of the groups was very helpful in providing information about my father during the 1960s. Also, thanks to Facebook contact Jim Bakker who gave me information about Toolamba Primary School.

Staff at the State, Fitzroy, and Collingwood libraries were very helpful in assisting me in my research. They saved me many hours of fumbling on my own through the huge number of records, newspapers, and other resources.

My appreciation also goes to all those who helped me by sharing their personal photographs of family, friends and places.

It was a bit nerve wracking sharing my secrets with my 'beta' readers. But I needn't have worried. Thank you, Kathryn Lyons, David Lyons, Mike Long, Sharon Beavis, Natalie King and Peter Woods for your support in reading my final draft. Your feedback, encouragement and reviews were invaluable.

Finally, this memoir would not have come up to scratch without the expert assistance and advice from Lu Sexton and Lorna Hendry. As copy editor, Lu's attention to detail, suggestions and corrections were very impressive and added a far more polished end result. And Lorna's friendly, professional support was beyond my expectations. Not only did she create a great cover design and layout, but without her guidance I would have really struggled to navigate the publishing maze.

Aussie Slang

Absolute dill – complete idiot
Ants in my pants – restless
Antsy – concerned
Arseing about – fooling around
A word or two – serious talk

Bee's knees – excellent, the best
Bloke – man
Bloody dagos – a racial slur for migrants, usually Italians and Greeks
Bloody hell – an exclamation showing anger or annoyance
Bludger – a lazy person
Bottle-O – a dealer in empty bottles
Brand spanking new – very new
Bright spark – sarcastic phrase to describe a clever person
Bugger all – none
Buggering up – ruin
Built like a brick shithouse – strongly built
Busier than Bourke Street – very busy
Buzzed around like a blue arsed fly – raced about or did something very quickly. Usually said ironically

Carked it – died
Carry on like a pork chop – make a silly fuss, complain loudly or rant
Carry on like a sook – be a cry baby, a complainer or whinger

Chewie on your boot – said to distract or wish an opponent bad luck when kicking for goal
Chick magnet – a man who attracts women the way a magnet attracts iron shavings
Chiko roll – a fried take away snack with vegetables (and sometimes meat), wrapped in pastry
Clobber – hit
Cloud nine – state of bliss
Copped – received
Cop shop – police station
Cop that – take that
Crack each other up with laughter – to make each other laugh heartily
Cracked a fat – erection of a penis
Cracked the shits – sudden attack of anger
Crook – unwell

Dag – fool-like
Dead quiet – silent
Deenas – nick name for an Australian coin – shilling
Dees – detectives
De-knacker – castrate
Dink- doubling on a pushbike
Dinky-di-Aussie – genuine Australian
Divvy van – police van
Dobbed myself in – confessed

Earn a crust – to earn a living
Excuse my French – a phrase used to apologise for swearing

Fag – cigarette
Fair bit – considerable amount
Fair dinkum – genuine
Fair go – ask someone to be reasonable or fair

Garbos – garbage collector
Gas bagging – make a lot of empty talk
Get a sticky beak – to take a good look
Get stuffed – tell someone rudely to go away, usually when you are angry
Getting belted – being hit hard
Goings-on – things that are happening
Gone off my head – acting crazy
Good egg – a good person
Good talking to – a serious talk
G'day – good day
Grouse – very good
Gutsed – ate too much, was greedy

Had a blue – fought
Hang on a sec – wait for a short time
Hanging out – spending time with someone
Ha'pennies – Australian coin – a half of a penny = half a cent
Happy little vegemite – cheerful person, came from a vegemite advertising jingle in 1964
Have a yarn – have a chat
Hit you for a six – to shock you or devastate you (e.g. from really bad news)

I'll knock you for a six – threaten to hit a person causing him or her to land far away

Jeez – an exclamation of surprise, disappointment, frustration, annoyance or exasperation
Jeezus – exclamation, longer form of 'jeez'

Kangaroo court – a mock court
Kick-to-kick footy – kicked the football to each other
Knock around with – to spend a lot of time with someone
Knock things off – stealing
Knock shop – brothel

Larrikin – a boisterous person, rowdy and cheeky, but good hearted
Little buggers – any person or thing, can be used affectionately or when annoyed
Little fella – penis

Mark – catching a football
Mind their Ps and Qs – mind their manners
Mind your language – don't swear
Mouth off – to talk in a loud, unpleasant, or rude way
Mucking about – to spend time having fun

Nicked – stole

Ocker – someone who is the stereotyped Australian, with a broad Aussie accent, usually working class and very down to earth – can be both affectionate and derogatory
Once in a blue moon – vary rarely
On for young and old – a happening for people of all ages
Other side of the black stump – very remote location
Outdoor dunny – outside toilet

Pack up – stop
Penny – Australian coin – one cent
Pinched – stole/stolen
Piss me off – annoy me
Pom – English person
Pretty cluey – smart
Pure arse – succeeding by luck

Quick smart – very quickly

Rabbits caught in a headlight – to be so frightened or surprised that you cannot move or think
Rare as hens' teeth – very rare
Ratbags – a stupid, eccentric or very annoying person
Real serve – severe criticism
Red hot go – give something a good try
Rolled his own tobacco – used loose tobacco to roll his cigarettes
Run like our arses were on fire – run as fast as we can

Scrubs – Australian bush
Seventh heaven – in a state of complete happiness
Shilling – Australian coin – equivalent to 10 cents
Shithouse – toilet
Shocker – something that shocks or horrifies
Shoosh – ask someone to be quiet
Shouted – to treat someone to something
Skips or skippy – an Australian born person, comes from the 1960s TV series, *Skippy the bush kangaroo*
Sixpence – Australian coin – five cents
Slowpoke – a person who takes their time and/or moves slowly
Sly grog – liquor sold without a licence
Smart arse – a person who is clever or funny but at the same time disrespectful or rude
Smoke – cigarette
Speccy – a spectacular mark of the football
Sprung – caught
Spuds – potatoes
Standing there like a stale bottle of piss – useless
Stiffy – erection of a penis
Stir – tease
Stuffed – exhausted
Sus – suspicious

Tatts ticket – lottery ticket
Tearing around – to move around fast and recklessly
Tea leaf – thief
Thongs – flip-flops or rubber sandals
Top notch – of a very high standard or quality

Towies – tow truck or breakdown truck drivers
Thruppence – Australian coin, three pennies
True-blue Aussie – genuine Australian
Truly stuffed – doomed
Two bob piece – nick name for an Australian coin worth two shillings, equivalent to 20 cents

Up yours – angry, rude response when someone has annoyed you

Verbal to-ing and fro-ing – same arguments repeated many times

Wag – someone who makes jokes
Wagged – absent from school without a parent's permission
What a bloody ripper – fantastic
Within cooee – within hailing distance

Ya bloody beauty – terrific
Yahoos – uncouth louts
Ya mug – stupid person
Ya wacker – you stupid person
Yonnie – small stone
You beauty – exclamation of joy
Yous – you

Zac – nickname for an Australian sixpenny coin (sixpence)

Family Trees

Both family trees are incomplete but contain all the information I had available at time of publication. Maco, Hellenic and English names are provided where known.

Gulefsi family tree

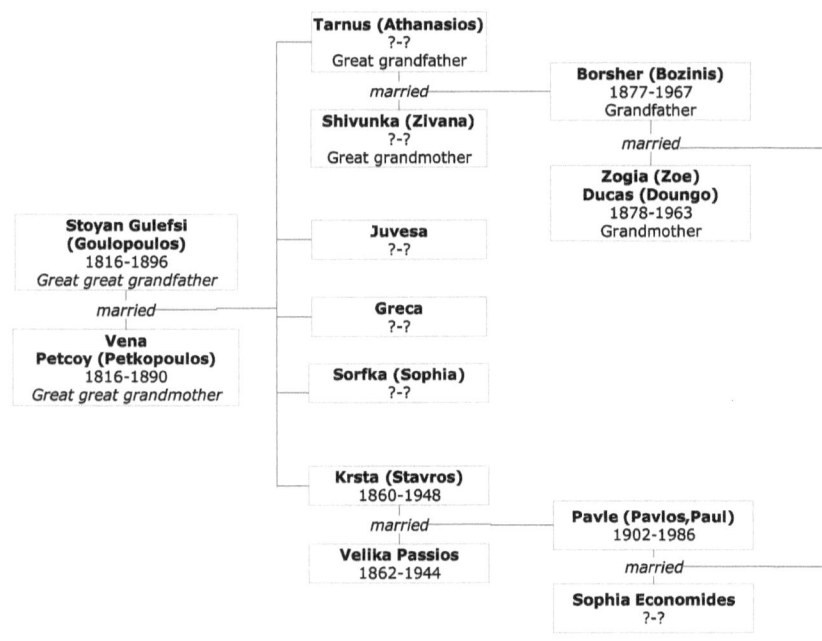

Family Trees

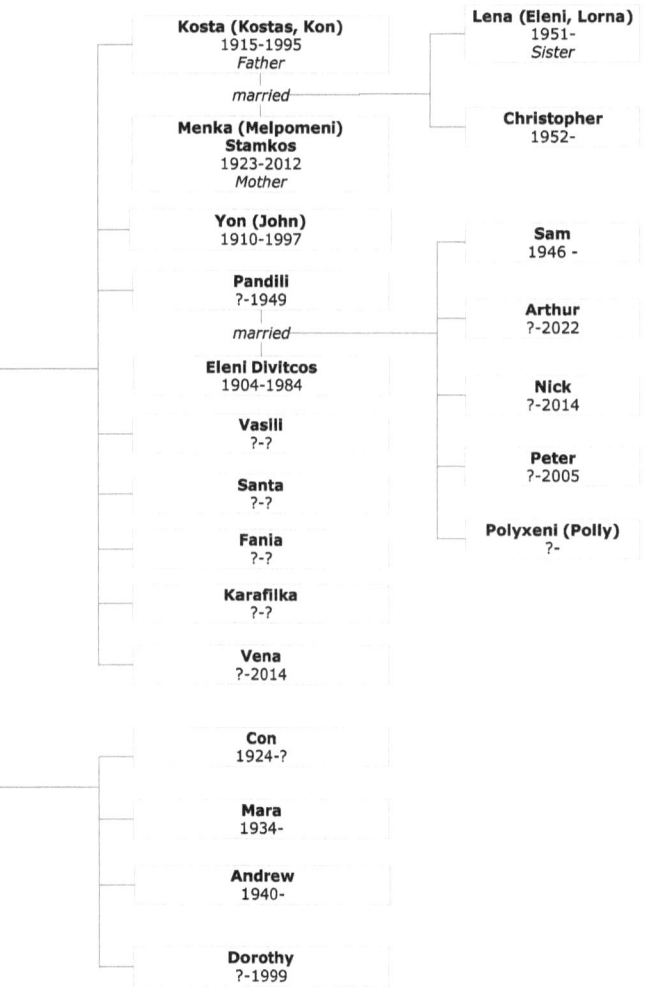

Stamkos family tree

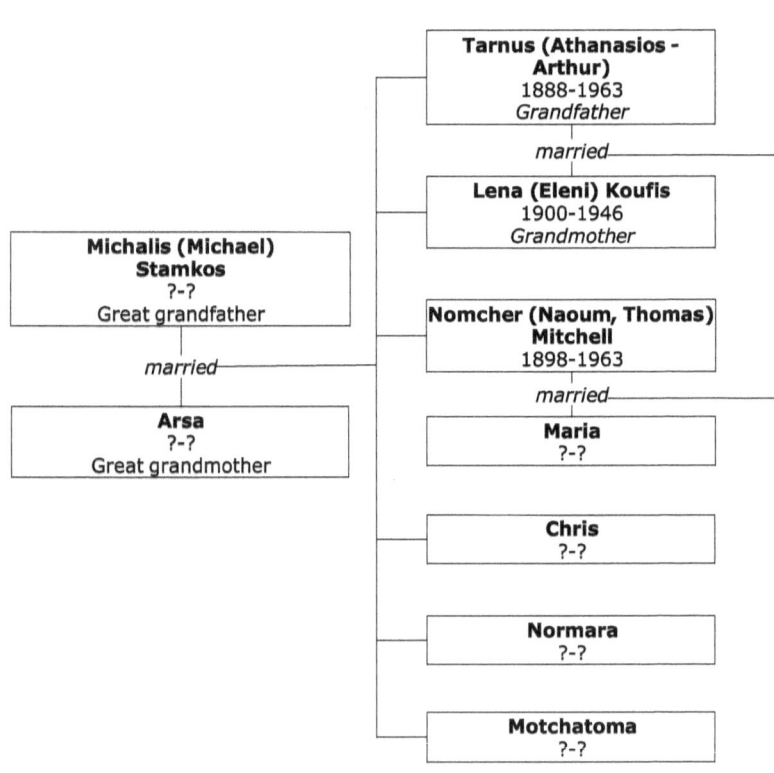

Family trees

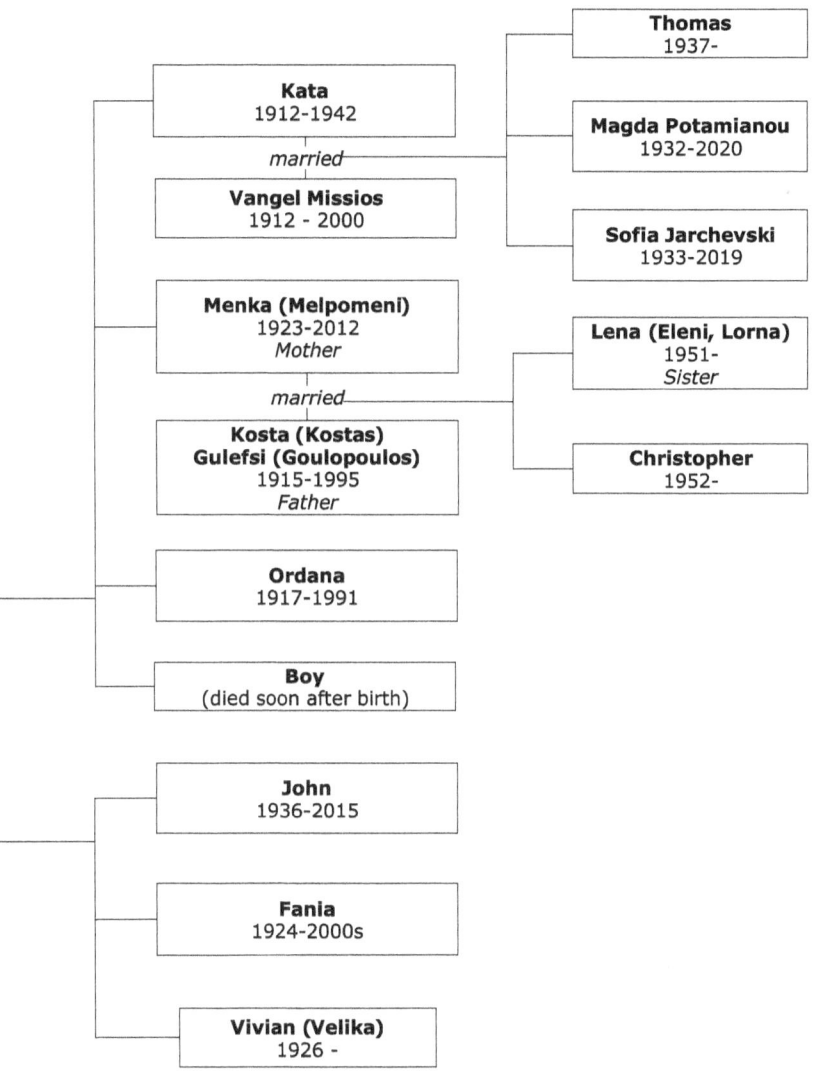

Bibliography

Texts

Achia, V., and Eraclides, G. *Stupendous! The Rise and Rise of NMIT: The History of NMIT 1912–2012*, Northern Melbourne Institute of TAFE, 2014.

Allimonis, C. 'Greek Macedonians' – *The Australian People – An Encyclopedia of the Nation, Its People and Their Origins*, edited by James Jupp, Cambridge University Press, Australia, 2001.

Aspinall, H. 'From Regent Fitzroy to HSV-7 Teletheatre', *Cinema Record*, 2007.

Cutton History Committee of the Fitzroy Historical Society, *Fitzroy Melbourne's First Suburb*, Hyland House Publishing Pty Ltd, Australia, 1991.

Dick, W. *A Bunch of Ratbags*, Collins Clear-Type Press, London and Glasgow, 1965.

Fitzrovians, *Reflections of Fitzroy*, School of Historical Studies, University of Melbourne. Melbourne, 2008.

Hanson, I., 'The Regent Fitzroy From Nitrate to Television to Rocky Horror Show', *Cinema Record* 2004.

Hill, P. 'Macedonians', *The Australian People – An Encyclopedia of the Nation, Its People and Their Origins*, edited by James Jupp, Cambridge University Press, Australia, 2001.

Morwell, S., *Heart of the Valley Toolamba 1840–1983*, Toolamba History Book Committee, 1983.

Schofield, P., *An essay on A history of Collingwood Technical School 1912–1987*.

Scott, D.I., 'The Fifties and Sixties', *Coltech: Technical Education in Collingwood – 1870–1987*, 1988.

Tamis, A.M., *The Immigration and Settlement of Macedonian Greeks in Australia*, Latrobe University Press, Melbourne, 1994.

Bibliography

Online

Alcock, J.B, and The Editors of Encyclopaedia Britannica, Britannica, *The third Yugoslavia*. www.britannica.com/place/Yugoslavia-former-federated-nation-1929-2003/The-third-Yugoslavia

Australian War Memorial. www.awm.gov.au

Australian War Memorial, *22nd Australian Infantry Battalion*. www.awm.gov.au/collection/U56103

Ballantyne, A. Realcommercial.com.au, *$20m-plus asking price for Fitzroy's Tankerville Arms Hotel,* 6 September 2017. www.realcommercial.com.au/news/20m-plus-asking-price-for-fitzroys-tankerville-arms-hotel

Blake, Thom., Thom Blake Historian. www.thomblake.com.au/secondary/hisdata/calculate.php

Browniecam, *Brownie Box Cameras.* www.browniecam.com

City of Melbourne, *The three historical fountains of Carlton Gardens.* tomelbourne.com.au/historical-fountains-carlton-gardens

City of Yarra. *25 years on – Fitzroy Save Our Pool Campaign. Monday 16 December 2019.* www.yarracity.vic.gov.au/news/2020/01/13/save-fitzroy-pool-25-years-on

Coinworks. *The 1930 Penny.* coinworks.com.au/1930-penny

Collingwood Technical College. collingwoodtechnicalcollege.weebly.com

Collingwood Technical College, *Turawan School Magazine, Brass Band.* collingwoodtechnicalcollege.weebly.com/turawan-1965

Collingwood Technical College, *Turawan School Magazine 1965, Choir Notes.* collingwoodtechnicalcollege.weebly.com/turawan-1965

Danforth, L. Britannica, *North Macedonia.* www.britannica.com/place/North-Macedonia

The Editors of Encyclopaedia Britannica, Britannica, *Charles Atlas – American bodybuilder.* www.britannica.com/biography/Charles-Atlas

The Editors of Encyclopaedia Britannica, Britannica, *Greek Civil War – Greek history.* www.britannica.com/event/Greek-Civil-War

The Editors of Encyclopaedia Britannica. Britannica *– Guy Fawkes – English Conspirator.* www.britannica.com/biography/Guy-Fawkes

eMelbourne, *Fireworks*. www.emelbourne.net.au/biogs/EM00569b

Find and Connect, Turana (1955-1993).
www.findandconnect.gov.au/guide/vic/E000626

Fitzroy Football Club, *History*. www.fitzroyfc.com.au

The Fitzroy History Society. fitzroyhistorysociety.org.au

Fitzroy Primary School, *School History*.
www.fitzroyprimaryschool.vic.edu.au

The Franklin Institute, *Kodak Brownie Camera*.
www.fi.edu/history-resources/kodak-brownie-camera

The Greek City Times, *October 12 – German Forces withdraw from Athens*. greekcitytimes.com/2016/10/12/german-forces

Gojszyk, M. The Corner Flag – *Generations Unite as Heidelberg Launch Season*, 19 February 2016.
www.cornerflag.com.au/generations-unite-as-heidelberg-launch-season

Hall, R.C.,1914-1918 Online International Encyclopedia of the First World War, *Balkan Wars 1912-1913*. encyclopedia.1914-1918-online.net/article/balkan_wars_1912-1913/2014-10-08

Hellenic American Project Department of Sociology, Queens College, CUNY, USA, *First Wave of Mass Immigraton ((1900-1924)*.
hapsoc.org/greeks-in-america

Melbourne Museum, *Phar Lap*. museumsvictoria.com.au/melbournemuseum/whats-on/phar-lap

McMahin, N. The Age, *'The 6 o'clock swill: we'd not have a bar of it now*, January 12, 2014. www.theage.com.au/national/victoria/the-6-oclock-swill-wed-not-have-a-bar-of-it-now-20140111-30ns3

Museums Victoria. origins.museumsvictoria.com.au/countries/greece

Museum Victorian Collections, *Traffic Control Signal – Marshalite*, 1940-1960. collections.museumsvictoria.com.au/items/408344

Nachmani, A,.*Origins Current Events in Historical Perspective, The Greek Civil War, 1946-1949*.
origins.osu.edu/milestones/march-2016-greek-civil-war-1946-1949

National Archives of Australia. www.naa.gov.au

National Geographic, *Macedonia*.
education.nationalgeographic.org/resource/macedonia

Bibliography

New World Encyclopedia. *Greek War of Independence.* www.newworldencyclopedia.org/entry/Greek_War_of_Independence

New World Encyclopedia. *Battle of Greece.* www.newworldencyclopedia.org/entry/Battle_of_Greece

NSW Government States Archives & Records, '13 Apr 1962 – standard gauge Sydney-Melbourne'. www.records.nsw.gov.au/archives/magazine/13-apr-1962-standard-gauge-sydney-melbourne

Parliament of Australia, *No.2 – The Opening of Parliament,* updated July 2019. www.aph.gov.au/About_Parliament/Senate/Powers_practice_n_procedures/Senate_Briefs/Brief02

Royal Commission into Institutional response to Child Sexual Abuse, *Report into Victorian state run youth training and reception centres released,* 14 September 2016 www.childabuseroyalcommission.gov.au/media-releases/report-victorian-state-run-youth-training-and-reception-centres-released

Reserve Bank Museum. *Dollar Bill Turns 50 Years Old.* museum.rba.gov.au/exhibitions/the-decimal-revolution/dollar-bill

Shields, S,. MERP (Middle Eastern Research and Information Project: Critical Coverage ODF the Middle East Since 1971), *The Greek-Turkish Population Exhange – Internationally Administered Ethnic Cleansing,* In: 267 Summer 2013. merip.org/2013/06/the-greek-turkish-population-exchange

Taylor, B,. National Film and Sound Archive of Australia, *Decimal Currency in Australia – Making Sense of Dollar and Cents … Fifty Years On.* www.nfsa.gov.au/latest/making-sense-dollars-and-cents-50-years

To Melbourne.com.au, *The three historiacl fountains of Carlton Gardens.* tomelbourne.com.au/historical-fountains-carlton-gardens

Trove. National Library of Australia. trove.nla.gov.au

Tully, H. National Film and Sound Archive of Australia, *Celebrating the Vision and Voices of Melbourne's ATV Channel O.* www.nfsa.gov.au/latest/fourth-channel-vision-and-voices-created-melbournes-atv-channel-o

Victorian Certificate of Education (VCE), Australian History, *Immigrants.* vceausthistory.weebly.com/life-during-the-great-depression

Wikipedia. *Graham Kennedy* en.wikipedia.org/wiki/Graham_Kennedy

Wikipedia. *Penny (Australia Coin).*
   en.wikipedia.org/wiki/Penny_(Australian_coin)

Wikipedia, *Television in Australia.*
   en.wikipedia.org/wiki/Television_in_Australia

Wikipedia. *World of Sport (Australian TV Program).*
   en.wikipedia.org/wiki/World_of_Sport_(Australian_TV_program)

Wikipedia. *Zig and Zag (Australian Performers).*
   en.wikipedia.org/wiki/Zig_and_Zag_(Australian_performers)

Documents

Department of Human Services Victoria, Freedom of Information, 9-5-1960 to 14-11-1962, 34 pages (31 full release, 3-part release).

www.ingramcontent.com/pod-product-compliance
Lightning Source LLC
Chambersburg PA
CBHW020314010526
44107CB00054B/1831